CRIME AND CRIMINALS OF VICTORIAN ENGLAND

CRIME AND CRIMINALS
OF
VICTORIAN ENGLAND

ADRIAN GRAY

The
History
Press

For Andy White and Kevin Rumens – good neighbours

Cover illustration used with permission of the British Newspaper
Library, Colindale.

First published 2011

The History Press
The Mill, Brimscombe Port
Stroud, Gloucestershire, GL5 2QG
www.thehistorypress.co.uk

British Library Cataloguing in Publication Data.
A catalogue record for this book is available from the British Library.

ISBN 978 0 7524 5280 7

Typesetting and origination by The History Press
Printed in Great Britain
Manufacturing managed by Jellyfish Print Solutions Ltd

Contents

1

The Criminal World of Victorian England

CHANGING IDEAS OF CRIME

In some ways crime has changed little, though attitudes to criminals have changed much. This book attempts to consider what both were like in Victorian times, drawing upon particular examples to illustrate general themes. It covers crimes that have been forgotten for 150 years but also some examples of very well-known major Victorian cases – though it is not necessary to repeat the best known in any detail.[1] The Victorians were especially worried about two particular crimes of theft: burglary and variations of highway robbery. Burglary was a fear because it involved people breaking into houses, and was severely punished. The forms of robbery on the street and highway varied according to the times: the highwayman faded away as trains destroyed his stock in trade, but the dark streets of the Victorian city bred instead the footpad and the garrotter.

Much thought went into crimes of a sexual nature, yet the law was slow to protect women and children from abuse. 'Criminal conversation' meant an adulterous affair, whilst a man (or a woman) could still be sued for breach of promise. Meanwhile, there was a debate as to whether a married woman could, in law, be raped by her husband and there was no criminal law of incest.

Some Victorians were interested in phrenology, the belief that the shape of a person's head or features could indicate their criminal tendencies. As a result, court reports often described the accused's features in detail and the belief was satirised in a famous picture of Charlie Peace. James Clark, an old man arrested in Dover for assisting in the murder of a constable, was described as having 'a low forehead, sunken eyes, and a lower jaw unusually long, the loss of his upper teeth rendering it more particularly prominent'. Press accounts of trials often

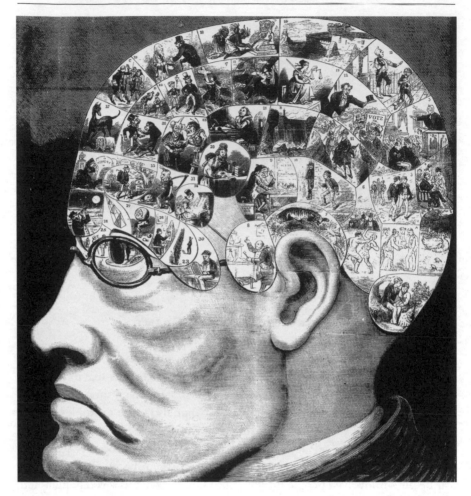

Phrenology was the 'science' of predicting a person's character by their appearance. Charlie Peace was notoriously ugly, but none of it explains this very strange depiction of him!

emphasised convicts' physical characteristics, ugliness and criminality being seen as part of a spectrum.

One of the key themes of the era is the way in which previously accepted behaviour became criminal. This also had an effect on crime statistics, as more crimes were added to the statute book. Areas affected included sexual behaviour, specifically issues surrounding prostitution, and public order offences. Some types of sport were banned because they were seen as cruel or disruptive, or both, although the general disapproval of betting contributed to this. Prize fighting and cockfighting are both examples of this; when thirty-four people were fined for attending a cockfight in 1865, *The Times* commented that by fining them, 'for doing what their fathers did with perfect impunity, [the magistrate] satisfied the feelings of the community no less than the requirement of the law'.[2] Portmanteau legislation, such as the 1892 Burgh Police Act, introduced powers to prosecute on a range of offences, including water, sewage, housing and dairy products. Relatively innocent acts, such as that committed by Giuseppe Baccarini in playing an organ in Clerkenwell, came within regulation and he was fined 2s 6d for being a nuisance in 1861.

Gambling and betting were types of 'moral crime' that attracted ire as the century developed, although as early as 1843 'lotteries in public houses' were condemned by the Inspector of Prisons as 'unmitigated evil, combining the excitement for drink and idle company with the thirst for sudden and inordinate gain'.[3] The 1853 betting legislation[4] closed betting shops and forced bookmakers on to the streets where municipal bye-laws limited them even further; the Metropolitan Traffic Act made it illegal to be 'in a public thoroughfare for the purpose of betting'. From the 1890s, premises had to be licensed for gambling and there were prosecutions if not. When the landlord of the *Northumberland Arms* in Hackney was found to be collecting betting slips and money, he was fined £30 and the bookmaker he worked with £50.

Legislation of 1853 struck at the advertising of betting and made it illegal to bet 'in an office or place'. It was ruled that a stool or umbrella counted as a 'place', yet the police rarely prosecuted betting at Epsom or Goodwood. It was illegal for bookmakers to accept cash bets on the street, so it became common to use children as runners and further legislation was passed in the 1890s to outlaw this.

The criminalisation of betting affected only the lower class; in 1891 Mr Pickersgill told the House of Commons that 'the existence of gambling hells in the West End of London is notorious ... I want to know why the poorer classes are alone interfered with, while the so-called better classes are allowed to go scathless'.[5] The law had produced some ridiculous inconsistencies: six barges on the Thames were sent to prison for playing a betting game with pennies; Christmas goose clubs were shut down as 'lotteries'; and East End and Liverpool working men's clubs were raided. In contrast, the Park Club was ruled to be a gentlemen's club and therefore exempt from prosecution, and despite a ruling that baccarat was illegal in 1889, clubs such as the Brabant Club openly featured it nightly! Pickersgill was especially incensed about Tattersall's, which he argued was just a front for huge amounts of gambling.

While betting was considered a 'moral' crime, poaching was seen as a crime of theft, but also in some ways as a 'moral' crime in that a traditional activity was increasingly regarded as crime. It was defined by a leading legal writer as one of a number of crimes 'which derive their moral significance exclusively from the fact that they are forbidden by the law'.[6]

The criminalisation of previously acceptable behaviour caused a sense of confusion about the law. In *Phineas Redux*, Anthony Trollope mused about the arrest of a former MP, Browborough, for electoral corruption: 'The idea of putting old Browborough into prison for conduct which habit had made second nature to a large proportion of the House was distressing to members of Parliament generally.'[7]

Another theme is the way in which the demands of a modern, industrialised society prompted the acceptance of greater regulation to benefit all. New rules covered social offences, such as the nuisances regulations, which were intended to control disease by declaring what could be burnt, cooked, processed and buried within urban areas. Later legislation added to this, for example by criminalising the disposal of some materials into rivers. There followed the Removal of Nuisances and Prevention of Epidemic Diseases Act 1846, the Smoke Nuisance Prevention Act of 1853 and the Rivers Pollution Act of 1876. Typically, magistrates would serve an abatement of nuisance order and impose fines with costs. The Smoke Nuisance Amendment Act also regulated river transport on the Thames and elsewhere, so six tugboat captains were all fined £5 each in 1861 as their tugs 'did not consume their own smoke'. The Alkali Act was one of a number of efforts to extend the law to industrial pollution.

'Sporting activities' were increasingly suppressed by legal means, usually because they disturbed the peace – or trade. This also included other forms of celebratory disorder, with behaviour around 5 November a priority – the rolling of tar barrels, setting off of fireworks and even firing of guns being still common in the 1840s. The Explosives Act 1875, section 80, prohibited 'throwing or setting off fireworks on any highway, street, thoroughfare or public place'.

Alcohol was increasingly regulated. Undoubtedly much crime was linked to alcohol, and the arrests made by some police forces involved a suspiciously high proportion of drunks. The Beer Act of 1830 had made beer available almost without limit or tax in order to wean people off gin, but by the 1860s attitudes had changed: new beer houses had to be licensed from 1869 and after 1872 the Licensing Act gave the justices control of the whole lot. It has been estimated that alcohol was a factor in 40 per cent of the 'lesser crimes' committed in 1876. The informal selling of alcohol was almost eradicated, though people in isolated places still tried to profit from it if they could: in April 1891 John Tyrell, a 'hut keeper' on the Manchester Ship Canal, was fined £50 for selling drink without a licence – presumably to the passing trade.

In health, legislation was intended to control threats to public health, and a series of Vaccination Acts made vaccination against smallpox compulsory for children under three months from 1853. Laws of 1867 and 1871 introduced fines of up to 25s or even prison for parents who refused to comply. It took at least four separate acts to clarify the position, but by linking the new requirements to the Poor Law it created a stigma for public health. Due to weaknesses in the 1861 Act, by 1863 only 14 per cent of Poor Law unions had acted[8] and it was not until vaccination officers were brought in under the 1871 Act that prosecutions became common. Between 1870 and 1874 there were 5,490 prosecutions and 2,650 convictions, including two people convicted sixteen times and two nineteen times.[9] One man had been summonsed forty-four times. By 1884–85, prosecutions were 2,806 a year. In 1876 the Poor Law guardians of Keighley were imprisoned in York Castle for contempt as they refused to implement the law. Leicester was notorious for its opposition: in 1884–85 there were 11,010 prosecutions and 922 convictions in the town,[10] but of 6,300 births a year, only 80 were being vaccinated in 1898. This was despite men (usually) being sent to gaol, often for fourteen days, and others having their property seized to meet unpaid fines. Here was a whole new addition to the court statistics, to which can be added, from 1881, prosecution for non-attendance at school, which also affected parents.

Laws such as the Common Lodging Houses Act of 1851 (see Chapter 5) attempted to regulate areas deemed as health risks. Laws also regulated the sale of milk in order to reduce the risk of tuberculosis. The Contagious Diseases (Animals) Act of 1869 meant that a farmer's animals now came within the compass of the law if they succumbed to such problems as Foot and Mouth disease.

In religion, the law controlled how you could worship, most notably through the Church Discipline Act of 1840 and the Public Worship Regulation Act of 1874, intended to stamp out ritualistic worship in the Church of England. More than a dozen clergymen were prosecuted under the latter and several sent to prison, often for contempt: Father Enraght of Bordesley was arrested at his vicarage and put in Warwick gaol for forty-nine days;[11] Arthur Tooth spent a few weeks in Horsemonger Lane. Though a minor addition to the judicial statistics, these offences occupied vast areas of newsprint.

The law also reached out into commercial areas with, for example, the Master and Servant Act. This governed relations between the two protagonists of its title, and indeed could work either way. As an example, a Lambeth boilermaker was summonsed under this act in 1867 for non-payment of wages; the 'Master' claimed his 'Servant' had done poor work, but the court took this as merely an excuse and he was ordered to pay £1 1s 9d.

HOW MUCH CRIME WAS THERE?

It is impossible to trace the extent of crime with any certainty throughout the Victorian era because other factors changed so much. In 1837 there was no national approach to policing, but by 1901 the police were everywhere, so even if the law had stayed the same, the chances of falling foul of the legal system were considerably increased. But the law did not stay the same; new offences were

Reverend Shore was arrested for preaching without a licence and also prosecuted for officiating at a service in unlicensed premises in 1846.

introduced with great regularity. One might argue that an offence that barely changed – such as wilful murder – might offer a secure guide, but the chances of detection for crimes such as poisoning were enhanced by scientific discovery and more efficient legal enforcement, compared to the days of the Norfolk poisoners when wholesale poisoning took place with impunity for many years. When the Parliamentary Committee on the Game Laws questioned Colonel Robertson about the apparent high level of poaching in Hertfordshire in 1874, they received an answer that might have appeared opaque:

Q: Is there a great deal of poaching in Hertfordshire?
A: There is a great deal of detection of poaching in Hertfordshire.

Robertson's point was that the seemingly high level of crime in the county was due to their success in catching the poachers.

Perception was as influential as reality. In March 1847 Mr Justice Coleridge told the grand jury gathered at Salisbury that 'the increase of crime in late years is fearful and appalling'[12] – clearly hoping the jury would do its bit in convicting as many miscreants as possible. Yet the Parliamentary Blue Books covering 1841–50 showed that the population had increased by 12.5 per cent whilst crime had only increased by 11.3 per cent; convictions showed an actual decline in most respects.[13] In 1863 Sir Richard Mayne, Commissioner of the Metropolitan

Police, reported that 10,000 fewer people had been taken into custody in 1862 compared to 1857 – which did him little good at a time of 'moral panic' over street robbery.[14]

Some Victorians were optimistic. The release of the annual crime figures by Manchester police in September 1875 were celebrated for their emphasis on a five-year decline: burglary and housebreaking were down 40 per cent and robberies from the person with violence down 74 per cent. Some offences showed small increases, such as embezzlement by servants, and offences against the person such as manslaughter showed little change, but overall crime was down 30 per cent. One opinion expressed was that the introduction of flogging for robbery with violence had led to a decrease.[15]

Some very young people became habitual criminals and made frequent court appearances. There were a number of extreme cases, such as that of a girl from Truro named Bennett. Aged 19, she was sentenced at Bodmin to nine months in prison in 1867 for stealing 4s 6d from her own mother, but her list of previous offences was impressive: wilful damage (twenty-one days), stealing apples (fourteen days), stealing money (twenty-one days), disobedience in the workhouse (fourteen days), wilful damage (one month), lodging in an outhouse (twenty-one days), lodging in a wagon (twenty-one days), lodging in a stable (three months), prostitution (three months), lodging in a hayloft (twenty-one days), stealing jewellery (six months). All these offences were committed in a six-year period since she was 13, her life literally measured out in prison sentences.

PRISON & PUNISHMENT

The reform of criminal law had begun before the Victorian era, with the number of capital offences being reduced to only eleven by 1841. The last death sentence for a crime of property – burglary – was abolished in 1837, although burglary with attempted murder or wounding remained capital until 1861. A few other capital offences remained on the statute book after the Criminal Law Consolidation Act of 1861, including arson in royal dockyards, high treason and piracy, but were not used.

Public executions were a celebrated form of entertainment at the start of the era, but their popularity dwindled. The execution of Samuel Seager at Maidstone, in March 1839, was made worse by the presence of the murdered woman's jeering husband in the front row and a large number of women, many of whom had brought their children to watch. Thackeray wrote an essay on *Going to see a man hanged* after the execution of Courvoisier in 1840 and argued for the abolition of capital punishment. The execution of the Mannings in 1849 was witnessed by about 30,000, following which Dickens wrote to *The Times* that 'the conduct of the people was so indescribably frightful that I felt for some time afterwards almost as if I were living in a city of devils'. He was appalled by the crowd:

> I believe that a sight so inconceivably awful as the wickedness and levity of the immense crowd collected at the execution this morning could be imagined by no man, and could be presented in no heathen land under the sun ... When the sun rose brightly ... it gilded thousands upon thousands of upturned faces so inexpressibly odious in their brutal mirth or callousness that man had cause to feel ashamed of the shape he wore, and to shrink from himself as fashioned in the image of the Devil.

The public hanging at Bury St Edmunds in 1847 of Catherine Foster, a young woman of barely 18 who had poisoned her husband after only three weeks of marriage, was said to have been especially 'heart-rending' and led to questions in the House of Lords.[16]

The case for hanging was not helped by bungled executions, such as that in 1856 of William Bousfield for killing his wife and three children in Soho, London. Bousfield displayed eccentric behaviour after his trial, refusing to speak for long periods or insisting that everything was a dream. He threw himself face first into the fire in his cell and was horribly burnt. After that he spoke not a word and his hideously marked face was covered with a linen cloth. He appeared to be dying, and a surgeon was brought in to check he was still alive. He was carried up to the scaffold on a chair: 'It is almost impossible to imagine a more hideous and revolting spectacle than the death like and swollen appearance of the face, and the utter helplessness of the limbs as they hung downwards, and nothing can be compared to it than a bloated and swollen mummy.'[17]

Hangman Calcraft fixed the motionless man to a short rope while positioned on the chair; then the drop fell, at which point the apparently almost dead man burst into life and fought to get his legs back on to the platform. Three times he got a footing on the edge, and three times the turnkeys pushed him off again, the hangman having slipped from the scene, terrified after threats that he would be shot.

After the execution of Franz Muller in 1864, a bill for reform of the capital punishment system in 1866 attempted to introduce 'degrees of murder'. This failed and little further progress was made on reform in this area during the Victorian era, although public execution ceased.

Transportation had already become established as an alternative to execution, but by 1860 only about 60 per cent of those sentenced to transportation actually were transported. Transportation to New South Wales stopped in 1840 and it ceased to Van Diemen's Land in 1853, though some continued to Western Australia until 1867 and also to Bermuda and Gibraltar. By 1860 the government

Dartmoor was one of the prisons that took over from transportation; in this scene a convict makes an ill-fated bid for freedom, 1884.

was spending £640,000 a year on 'penal discipline', of which £200,000 was being spent abroad (however, there were only 3,200 prisoners in the colonies and only 269 had been sent there during 1860). The total number in prison in England and Wales fell from 25,000 to 18,000 between 1858 and 1860.[18]

Transportation was then only used for sentences of fourteen years or more, and was replaced by Penal Servitude from 1853. Other criminals were sent to new 'public works' prisons such as Portland (1847–49) and Chatham (1856), which replaced the 'hulks'. The 'silent' and 'separate' systems were introduced: in 1869 Sir Edward du Cane emphasised 'hard bed, hard board and hard labour', though the demeaning crank was stopped in 1898.

In the 1889 House of Commons debate on the penal system and punishment, Mr Pickersgill highlighted a number of relatively minor offences that had received severe punishments:

At the Liverpool Summer Assizes last year, four lads, aged about 17, were found guilty of robbery from a poor woman of the sum of 3s., the robbery being accompanied by personal violence. It was a most dastardly offence and richly deserved a severe punishment. But what was the punishment actually inflicted? Penal servitude for 14 years, on lads of 17! I am not surprised that the Report of the proceedings says the severity of the sentence caused great surprise. With the permission of the House I will quote a few words from the language used by the learned Judge in pronouncing sentence. He said:– It is truly intolerable that a set of rascals like you, just between boyhood and manhood, should be allowed to become the terror of all decent people.

Pickersgill compared punishments for similar offences:

I mean the well-known case of the boy Osborne, 17 years old, convicted at the Central Criminal Court,[19] of an attempt to blackmail a gentleman by threatening to accuse him of an odious crime. Of course the crime committed by Osborne was a crime of the most serious character, a crime which requires to be treated with heavy punishment. But what was the sentence pronounced by the learned Judge on this lad of 17? No less a sentence than penal servitude for life! A few months afterwards, at the same Court, but before another Judge, a man was convicted of a similar crime, a crime which the Judge who pronounced sentence said was one of the worst possible description of its class, and he concluded by passing a sentence of ten years' penal servitude.

There was growing realisation that sending people to prison for minor offences was ineffective – and expensive. A perceptive clergyman questioned the approach in Dorset in the early 1840s by identifying particular cases: he referred to a man who stole 4d worth of lime, was held in custody for forty-two days before trial and then given a week in gaol, costing the ratepayers £12 8s 4d. A person who stole seven eggs spent eighty-eight days in custody, costing twice as much. A girl of 11 who stole a bucket cost the ratepayers £10 11s 8d. Cheaper solutions had to be found.

THE NEW POLICE

All parishes were meant to have their own constables, a system that was already discredited in 1837, although it was not until 1872 that the law was changed so that parishes were not obliged to have one. Permissive legislation, such as the County Police Acts of 1839 and 1840, allowed local authorities to set up their own forces similar to that already created in London. Some did, but others disliked the cost. Often it took a shocking event to galvanise the ratepayers into sacrificing their personal funds: in one area, 'Mr Hollest's murder obtained the county police for Surrey'.[20] The County and Borough Police Act of 1856 made a force compulsory in every area.

Nonetheless, authorities still tried to keep costs to a minimum. After riots in 1855, the Home Secretary wrote to the Mayor of Wolverhampton about the inadequacy of his force, which was then increased from thirty-nine to fifty-four.[21]

One factor behind the eventual acceptance of the police was public disorder. Reluctant authorities avoided the cost of the police until unrest persuaded them that it was a price worth paying – in the case of Staffordshire, it was miners' riots in 1842 that convinced them.[22] Authorities preferred to maintain a slender police force and use the powers of the Riot Act to call in the military when there was risk of serious disorder. At least the Chartist troubles provided a marvellous incentive to make better use of the railways and the new electric telegraph, both of which began to be used from as early as 1839, and General Napier made efficient use of railway lines to control the northern districts as described in Chapter 9. As one historian has written: 'The British railway network raised markedly the efficiency of the military force which was maintained on home service, by making the troops stationed in the southern part of England more readily available for the restoration of order in the manufacturing districts of the North.'[23]

Metropolitan officers were often sent to help in areas where there was no similar force, getting cheap fares. However, by the 1850s most areas had reasonable police forces of their own and the use of railways and the military was much reduced.

The cost of the police was estimated at £3 million a year in January 1869, whereas the loss from crime was put at £7 million a year.[24]

The electric telegraph was soon put to use to capture fugitives, one early and famous example being after a murder at Salt Hill near Slough in 1845. John Tawell put some cyanide into a woman's drink before escaping by train to Paddington, but a telegraph message was sent ahead of him: 'A murder has just been committed at Salt Hill and the suspect has been seen to take a 1st class ticket to Paddington on the 7.42pm. He is dressed as a Quaker with a long overcoat down to his ankles. He is sitting in the second 1st class carriage.' Tawell was tracked to a coffee house and arrested.

The telegraph was also used to summon extra support during rioting, such as in 1851 when the fishermen and trawler owners at Great Yarmouth were at loggerheads. A huge crowd gathered outside the police station to demand the freeing of some incarcerated fishermen, but the 11th Hussars were summoned from Norwich by telegraph; attempts to stop their arrival by pulling up the tracks at the railway station were thwarted when the soldiers got out of the train before it reached the platforms.

The spread of the police reduced the frequency of 'freedom riots', where crowds attempted to release people from custody – or the opposite problem where mobs exacted retribution on witnesses. An example of the latter was at Windsor in 1844, when a mob of over 200 stripped three men and ducked them in the Thames for giving evidence against a beer shop keeper who had permitted gambling on his premises. In 1875 a man was arrested at a Birmingham public house for burglary, but the two constables taking him into custody were themselves attacked by a mob intent on freeing him. Extra police arrived, but the mob also increased in number, with stones flying and weapons being brandished. Sergeant Fletcher was stabbed and PC Lines stabbed in the head, from which he died. Jeremiah Corkery was executed for this murder and four others sent to prison for riot and assault.

A 'CLASSIC' VICTORIAN CRIMINAL: CHARLIE PEACE

Charlie Peace came from the backstreets of Victorian Yorkshire but became so famous – or infamous – that a comic book hero of the 1960s was based around him. After enjoying the veneer of bourgeois respectability in London, he was hanged at Leeds on 25 February 1879 for the squalid murder of a lover's husband. His trial and execution attracted great publicity.

Perhaps one of the reasons for his cult success was that the legend was more glamorous than the reality. Supposedly an artist, poet and musician, he wrote only doggerel, played music on a violin with one string and his artistic endeavours at Millbank Prison consisted of 'cutting out of a rough kind of cardboard a variety of objects – birds, beasts, fishes, horses and the like'. Neither was he handsome; one journalist described him as 'short and meagre but wiry, and his face one of the ugliest ever set on human shoulders ... and his mind was a sort of sewer'.

Peace was born in Sheffield in 1832. As a boy he suffered a leg injury and struggled with walking thereafter. He was first arrested for burglary in 1851, getting a one-month sentence. He served two prison sentences for burglary in Yorkshire and Lancashire, on the latter occasion showing a violent side that eventually led him to the gallows. Peace was back in prison at the end of 1866, again for burglary near Sheffield, and this time received a six-year sentence.

At Whalley Range in 1876, prowling around at night, he was challenged by PC Nicholas Cock who he shot in the chest and left to die. Two brothers were arrested and tried for the murder in Manchester; Peace attended the trial in November 1876 and watched as William Habron was sentenced to death, although the youth's sentence was commuted to life imprisonment. Later, Peace confessed to this crime and the young man was freed. 'Some people will say,' Peace mused afterwards, 'that I was a hardened wretch for allowing an innocent man to suffer for my crime, but what man would have done otherwise?'

Meanwhile, in Sheffield, Peace had developed an obsession with a neighbour's wife, Mrs Dyson. Eventually Mr Dyson moved his family away from Darnall, where Peace lived, to Banner Cross. Almost as soon as they had arrived, Peace

A POLICEMAN SHOT BY A BURGLAR.

When this picture of a desperate burglar being captured was published, it was not known that the villain was Charlie Peace, wanted for murder in Yorkshire.

turned up and made a show of his revolver to Dyson. Only a couple of days after the Manchester trial, he waylaid Mrs Dyson at the back of her house and when Dyson came out to intercede he fired at him twice. The second shot struck Dyson in the head and he died soon afterwards.

Peace escaped to a house in Hull where his wife lived. Chased by detectives, he escaped arrest by climbing out and hiding behind a chimney. In Nottingham he took a mistress called Susan Gray and on one occasion police arrived to find him in bed with her, but even then he managed to slip away from their clutches.

After moving to London he passed himself off as a musical instrument dealer, but continued with burglary. He took two houses in Billingsgate Street – one for his wife and one for his mistress. In May 1877 he moved to Peckham and continued his interest in scientific gadgets, developing a design for raising sunken vessels.

In October 1878 Constable Robinson saw a light appear mysteriously in a window of a house at St John's Park, Blackheath, at two o'clock in the morning. Joined by two other officers, Robinson had not reckoned on the thief having a gun. Despite firing five shots, Peace was eventually brought to the ground, although Robinson was severely wounded. At this time the police had no idea that they had captured an infamous murderer from Sheffield.

Peace's wife and mistress both fled, but they were eventually traced by the police and stolen property with them was identified. Peace was tried for robbery

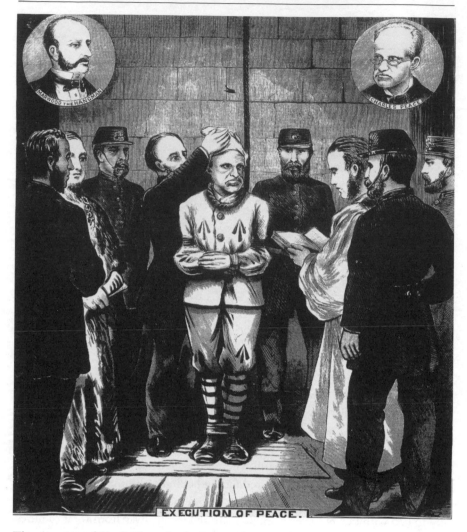

The execution of Charlie Peace for the Banner Cross murder at Leeds, 1879.

and attempted murder at the Old Bailey in November 1878; despite putting up
the appearance of being senile, he was found guilty and sentenced to penal servitude for life. He was then put on a train to Sheffield, but Peace made a daring
attempt to escape by leaping through the window. One warder caught hold of
his leg and Peace dangled out of the speeding train for 2 miles, before eventually
falling to the ground at Kiveton Park. He was too insensible to run off and was
soon picked up again.

Peace was tried for murder in Leeds in February 1879, by which time the tales
of his crimes and burglaries had been repeatedly told – and somewhat exag-
gerated – in the popular press. It took the jury only ten minutes to agree on

a verdict of guilty. Once convicted, Peace confessed to the murder at Whalley Range, giving evidence about the scene that convinced the prison governor. He was hung at Armley on 25 February 1879.

Notes

1 Jack the Ripper features only in passing; there is already a whole library of books about this one series of crimes and little point in adding further to it.

2 *The Times*, 24 April 1865.

3 *Report of the Inspector of Prisons*, Parliamentary Papers, 1843, p. vi.

4 There was a Betting Act, Betting Houses Act and a Lottery Act in that year.

5 *Hansard*, House of Commons, 17 March 1891.

6 J. Fitzjames Stephen, *Criminal Law*, London, 1863, p. 100.

7 Anthony Trollope, *Phineas Redux*, first published 1869.

8 S. Williamson, *The Vaccination Controversy*, Liverpool, 2007, p. 202.

9 *Hansard*, 3 July 1877.

10 Judicial statistics, 1884–85.

11 Enraght also spent time at St George's in the east, where there were notable riots, described in a later chapter.

12 *The Times*, 7 March 1847.

13 *The Times*, 4 January 1856.

14 James Winter, *London's Teeming Streets*, London, 1993, p. 62.

15 *Manchester Guardian*, 28 September 1875.

16 *Hansard*, 23 April 1847.

17 *The Observer*, 6 May 1856.

18 Evidence from Parliamentary Debate of 1 March 1981, recorded in *Hansard* and *The Times*.

19 In 1886.

20 *The Times*, 30 October 1851; Hollest, a curate, is considered in Chapter 4.

21 D. Philips, *Crime & Authority in Victorian England*, p. 58.

22 Ibid.

23 F.C. Mather, *Public Order in the Age of the Chartists*, Manchester, 1959, p. 161.

24 *The Times*, 15 January 1869.

2

Murder

Wilful murder was the worst capital offence in Victorian England, but juries hesitated to convict a man or woman if there was the slightest doubt. Towns such as Maidstone were notorious for not convicting for a capital offence: 'now, so strong is the feeling against punishment by death, that it is extremely difficult to get a jury to convict … at one time at Maidstone it was difficult to get a jury to find a man guilty, even upon the clearest evidence, if they knew that an execution would follow.'[1]

Juries were reluctant to hang on the basis of circumstantial evidence. Perhaps the most famous man to be hung for murder on circumstantial evidence was Palmer, the Rugeley poisoner. In *Phineas Finn* one of the characters observed: 'We were delighted to hang Palmer, – but we don't know that he killed Cook' – the latter his most noted supposed victim.[2] Later in the same novel, Madame Goesler tries to convince herself that her hero, Phineas Finn, is safe: 'Juries are always unwilling to hang … and are apt to think that simply circumstantial evidence cannot be suffered to demand so disagreeable a duty. They are peculiarly averse to hanging a gentleman, and will hardly be induced to hang a member of Parliament.'[3]

An example of this is the murder of 14-year-old Sarah Watts at West Woodlands near Frome in 1851. Watts was alone at a dairy farm which was invaded by burglars who raped and then killed her. Three men, including William Maggs and William Sparrow, were reported as having been seen in the area before and after the murder, and Sparrow was supposed to have described what happened to a woman he met. Saying little about the rape, he described how the girl had been beaten about the head, drowned by being placed head down in the whey tub, and then her body dumped on the floor. A handkerchief found on the kitchen table was linked to Sparrow.

Despite forty-three witnesses for the prosecution, others came forward to say the men had been in Frome at the time and all three were acquitted of the murder. Witnesses for the prosecution reported having been terrorised, with windows broken at night and threatening behaviour in court. In the minds of the jury, nothing could prove what had happened and all evidence was circumstantial. However, all three were tried and convicted of other felonies and Maggs was later transported for fifteen years.

Were people hung by mistake? One suspects Trollope of being ironic when he has the elderly Duke of St Bungay say: 'I do not think that in my time any innocent man has ever lost his life upon the scaffold.'[4] But there is clear evidence that Priscilla Biggadyke[5] went to the gallows in error, and a number of others died protesting their innocence to the last.

Of course, the most famous Victorian murderer, Jack the Ripper, was never caught. All the authorities received much criticism for this and Sir William Harcourt, the Home Secretary, was blamed in 1888 for his failure to offer a reward; he replied that large rewards often produced inaccurate information.[6] Sometimes referred to as the first serial killer, Jack's crimes were unusual in their method and subject, but he was far from being the leading killer of the era. The killings continued sporadically until 1891, after which they appear to have stopped.

What types of murder attracted the most press attention? The press betrayed a definite class bias: when the victim was middle or upper class, or especially if the perpetrator was, then the story would run and run. The murder of Lord Russell, described below, is a good example, as is the murder of Rev. Hollest, Vicar of Frimley, by a burglar (see Chapter 4). James Bloomfield Rush, a tenant farmer in Norfolk, shot his landlord Isaac Jermy and his son in 1848 at Stanfield Hall; a mixture of well-to-do rural life, mad vengeance and an illicit affair or two added to Rush's mystique, and his decision to represent himself at the trial added still more.

It is difficult to identify what made Charlie Peace such a celebrated criminal. One author has suggested that the act of confession robbed a murder of its greatest interest – hence Palmer lives on but William Dove faded away.[7] Dove murdered his wife with strychnine in Leeds in 1856 and was hung at York, attracting a crowd of over 10,000, but a full and detailed confession was circulated before his demise.

POISONINGS

If there was a classic early Victorian murder weapon, it was arsenic. It was the method of choice for many of the murderesses of the era, though its 'golden age' was essentially the 1840s. From 1859–80, fewer than 5 per cent of executed murderers had used poison.[8]

On 11 March 1838, in the Norfolk village of Hempnell, neighbours of the Daynes family found Mrs Daynes, two of her children and a neighbour, Mrs Mills, 'lying on the floor in a state of the greatest sickness and agony, complaining of burning heat in the stomach and throat, and the severest pain in the body'. Mrs Mills and one of the children died of poisoning, arsenic and nux vomica or 'fig powder' being found in the kettle.

Charles Daynes, a labourer, was charged with two murders and the attempted murder of his wife. He was tried in Norwich in April 1839, firstly on the count of murdering the child; he was acquitted, largely because a wife could not legally give evidence against her own husband as a 'competent witness' and there was no clear motive. However, she could give evidence where she was the victim of the crime and so Daynes was tried again the next day for attempting to murder his wife. On this occasion there was an additional witness – a widow named Ann Lloyd – who told the court that Daynes had wanted to marry her and had told her his wife would soon die. He was hung at Norwich, perhaps more for the crimes he was not convicted of than the one he was brought to justice over.

Jonathan Balls died at Happisburgh on 20 April 1845, aged 77, of suicide by arsenic poisoning. His death came only five days after that of his granddaughter Elizabeth Pestle, who also showed arsenic symptoms; she was buried on the same day as Balls' wife. The trigger for Balls' suicide appeared to be the determination of his daughter, Mrs Ann Pestle, to go to the coroner with material from the poisoned infant.

On 18 May 1845 there was an inquest at the Balls family home, Hill House, on the bodies of Balls, his wife, aged 83, and four grandchildren. The bodies of the old lady and the young girl were 'remarkably preserved' – a sign of arsenic poisoning. The Norwich surgeon, Frith, said the bodies contained enough arsenic to have killed the whole parish. Phoebe Neave told the jury that both Balls and Mrs Pestle had asked her to get arsenic for them in previous years. Balls' suicide led to the unravelling of a history of indiscriminate murder stretching over twenty years that shocked the nation. The Home Secretary, Sir James Graham, was so concerned that he sent an officer to investigate.

In early June 1846 the bodies of Balls' grandchildren, Martha, William and Maria Green, were exhumed at East Ruston. Maria had died in 1836, taken ill while staying with her grandparents at Happisburgh; no post-mortem had been conducted, the doctor assuming her death to be from 'spotted fever'. In succession, William and then Martha also died while staying with their grandparents. In 1845 Mrs Green, their mother, and the servant girl Sarah Kerrison were both taken seriously ill after eating herrings given to them at Balls' house, but they recovered.

The exhumations found arsenic in the body of Maria. The coroner went to Ingham to exhume the child of another of Balls' daughters, Mrs Peggs.

Neighbours recalled that Balls had had yet another daughter, Mrs Lacey, who had died suddenly in 1833, which Balls had said was due to being kicked by her husband.

The number of people killed by Balls is difficult to prove. Sir James Graham told the House of Commons on 12 June 1846 that it could have been twenty or more. In a period of ten years Mrs Green had lost eight children, Mrs Pestle four and a husband, and Mrs Peggs one, Hannah. But, going back further, Balls' own parents had died in 1822 soon after coming to live with him, and several 'labouring friends' who had been visitors to his house had also died suddenly. Two of his sons had died in the 1830s, and there was the daughter Maria Lacey. He had also been twice charged with arson and what was referred to as a 'disgusting offence'. It was supposed that Balls planned it mostly so that he could be well supported by his daughters – getting rid of their children as a risk to the family finances.

Finally, a curiosity about the case was how Balls was found in his coffin – with a walking stick on each side, a poker, handkerchiefs and a piece of plum cake in each hand; one of his daughters said this was in accordance with his wishes.

In April 1845 Sarah Freeman was hung at Wilton gaol, Taunton, for the murder of her brother by arsenic, but she was accused of more: 'infanticide, fratricide and matricide'.[9] Freeman, from Shapwick near Bridgewater, was described as 'an abandoned woman' and 'a loose character before her marriage' who had several illegitimate children. Her first illegitimate child was by a Church of England clergyman, who later more or less bribed a man to marry her.[10] Two of her victims – her daughter and her husband, who died in December 1843 – were probably poisoned so she could claim £20 from the burial club. Her daughter died with violent stomach cramps and vomiting in March 1844, after which she went off to London, probably with a lover. Then she poisoned her mother and brother in December 1844. In January 1845 the body of her son James, aged 7, was exhumed; he had died in 1843 and the coroner's inquest had recorded a verdict of natural causes on the advice of a surgeon. However, when the corpse was examined it was found to contain arsenic. Sarah was accused of four murder counts and found guilty of the murder of her brother; her death was watched by thousands.

These cases caused a furore about two things in particular: firstly, the way in which the parish authorities tried to save money by not having a proper inquest;[11] and secondly, about the dangers of arsenic being so easily available. Sir James Graham, the Home Secretary, was scathing about penny-pinching local authorities. *The Times* campaigned on the question of easy access to arsenic, complaining in September 1847 about the 'alarming increase of deaths through the criminal or accidental administering of arsenic'. One of the things it drew attention to was the impossibility of knowing how many had died; in the case of Mary May it was thought there was 'scarcely any limit to the crimes'.

Mary May, 'a repulsive looking woman' in the view of at least one journalist, was arrested for the murder of her half-brother and lodger at Wix, Essex, in June 1848, whose life she had insured in a burial club. May was quickly found guilty of murder at Chelmsford and hung amidst rumours that her first husband and some of her fourteen children might also have been poisoned. The rumours entrapped her sister, Hannah Southgate, who had only recently buried one husband and married another. So in August 1848 the body of Thomas Haw was exhumed from Tendring churchyard, where it had rested since April 1847, and was found to contain arsenic. Hannah, who was clearly a younger and much more attractive proposition than her sister, was reported by her maid to have had a troubled marriage to Haw; the maid knew this since Hannah preferred to sleep with her rather than the husband she 'couldn't bear'. In fact, she often slept at farmer Southgate's house. The maid saw her scraping arsenic on to a piece of bread and butter 'to feed the rats' but it was her husband who died. Two months later, she married Southgate. Despite the clear evidence, the jury were not convinced by the maid, Phoebe Reid, and Hannah Southgate was acquitted. This family tragedy claimed a final victim when Mary May's last husband hung himself in their cottage at Wix in June 1851; she had told him that if he ever married again, she would come back to haunt him.

Sarah Chesham turned the pretty Essex village of Clavering into a scene of destruction. She was arrested for poisoning a baby, Solomon Taylor, and then, in September 1846, on suspicion of murdering two of her children about eighteen months earlier. It was suspected that both had been killed by two pence worth of arsenic, which Mrs Chesham had tried to acquire through the local post woman and also a rat catcher. The Cheshams lived upstairs in a cottage, much to the distress of Thomas Deards who lived downstairs; when the boys were poisoned in January 1845 he complained that 'the vomit came through the cracks of the boards on to my table and floor'. Joseph and James died three days apart and other sons, Philip and John, were also ill for a while. The union surgeon certified them as having died of cholera, for which he later received a sound rebuke from the Lord Chief Justice.

The coroner's inquest implicated farmer Thomas Newport, who had employed one of the boys but was alleged by Sarah Chesham to have beaten them; he also owned a box containing arsenic. It was claimed that John Chesham, a surviving son who was called as a witness, and Wisbey, one of the jurors, had been 'tampered with' by Newport's men – most of the jurors were from the local community. There was a furious row among the jurors, most of whom condemned Wisbey. There was a suspicion that the relationship between Newport and Chesham had been close but she consistently tried to blame him.

The coroner recorded a verdict of wilful murder against Sarah on her two sons and then arranged an inquest into Solomon Taylor, who was the illegitimate son of Newport. Sarah Chesham had visited the Taylors at Manuden several times and John Clare gave evidence that he had heard Chesham say to the Taylor child: 'Damn you, you want putting to sleep for half an hour, like the other two.' The coroner was annoyed because the two witnesses he needed to prove a relationship between Chesham and Newport 'kept out of the way'. Nevertheless, a verdict of wilful murder was recorded.

In March 1847 Chesham, 'a good looking woman' (who four years later was instead described as 'a masculine-looking woman'), was tried at Chelmsford for the murders of Joseph and James Chesham. Though both had clearly died from arsenic, there was no proof of Sarah having possessed any and she was found not guilty. *The Times* was unimpressed, and noted later that 'the evidence was most cogent, and left very little doubt of her guilt'.[12] Chesham was also charged with the murder of Solomon Taylor, and Newport with aiding and abetting the murder. However, Professor Taylor said there was no evidence of poisoning so both were acquitted.

Chesham's escape was extraordinary, but not as extraordinary as her re-arrest in September 1850 for the poisoning of her husband Richard. The unfortunate – if not bizarrely unwise – Richard Chesham had become ill during winter 1849 but supposedly refused to be fed by anyone other than his loving wife. He died in May 1850. Unsurprisingly, Professor Taylor found arsenic, suggesting he had taken a continuous but small amount. Only after the case had been discussed by the Home Secretary and the Solicitor General was Sarah arrested, with the charge of administering poison with intent. On this occasion, arsenic was found in rice in the house. This time also a witness was found, Hannah Phillips, who reported how Sarah Chesham had told her where she hid arsenic. Sarah had told Hannah how to 'season' a pie in order to dispose of unwanted persons – not for nothing was she known locally as 'Sally Arsenic'. Phillips made clear that she had suffered some intimidation over her evidence, which was why she had changed her story. Chesham was found guilty, following which she confessed to murdering her two children. She was hung at Chelmsford alongside Thomas Drory and 'died hard', being a light person – her struggles took over six minutes. Unlike Drory, she was taken away to be buried in a churchyard as she had not been convicted for murder. In the view of *The Times*, her victims might have numbered a dozen or more. Like all the other serial killers on the loose with arsenic, the paper concluded that 'if they were left at large they would depopulate the neighbourhood'.

In 1849 Mary Geering, 'a woman of masculine and forbidding appearance', was sentenced to death at Lewes for three counts of wilful murder and one of attempted murder. Between December 1848 and March 1849 she had disposed of her husband and two of her sons, who were both in their twenties, while one son survived.

The problem of arsenic was tackled through the Arsenic Regulation Act, passed in June 1851. This made it much more difficult to buy arsenic, although the law was criticised for not extending to other poisons. A register had to be kept and it could only be sold to adult men.

Priscilla Biggadyke's story achieved great notoriety in later years when one of her lodgers confessed to having administered the poison. Her story was used as an example of the risks of capital punishment by campaigners such as William Tallack and, later, Violet van der Elst.[13] The case was mentioned in Parliament in 1929 when an MP stated that Priscilla was 'completely exonerated by the confession of another person'.

Biggadyke lived in the fenland village of Stickney with her husband Richard and two lodgers, George Ironmonger and Thomas Proctor, the local rat catcher, described in the Lincolnshire press as 'the most uncouth looking individual in the whole parish, his countenance is very repugnant. He has a high back and his legs appear to have a serious malformation.' Married couple, three children and two lodgers, they all lived in one or two rooms.[14] When her husband challenged her as to whether her third baby was his, Priscilla's unconvincing reply was: 'Well, it is mine at any rates.'

On 1 October 1868 Richard Biggadyke died in agony. Both his wife and Thomas Proctor were arrested, Priscilla's case not being helped by her first suggesting it was suicide (her reports of a suicide note being implausible as the dead man had been illiterate) and then that Proctor had poisoned him with a white powder – arsenic. The jury was convinced that it was the wife who had mixed the poison with the food, based entirely on circumstantial evidence, and sent her to the gallows; she refused to admit guilt to the very end. The executioner fumbled the drop and she died slowly. In early 1882 Thomas Proctor became ill and, fearing divine retribution, confessed that he had put the poison in Biggadyke's tea.

The symptoms of arsenic poisoning became well known, so the clever murderer started to seek alternatives. William Palmer was a doctor from Rugeley; he got married in 1847 and five children were born in quick succession, but four of them died. People linked to Palmer had a habit of dying, including his mother-in-law and people he owed money to. His wife died in 1854, netting Palmer £8,000 in life insurance (it would have been £13,000 except one company refused to pay up); a few months later his housemaid gave birth to a child widely believed to be Palmer's. When his brother Walter died, the life insurance company refused to pay out to Palmer and sent a detective to investigate. An attempt to insure the life of a farmhand for £10,000 failed when the insurance company found out he was not an 'esquire' at all.

The key case, though, was that of John Cook; Cook was a friend of Palmer's who had a very good day at the races, but then died mysteriously. Palmer attempted to disrupt the post-mortem by offering the post boy £10 to upset the stomach contents on their way to the station for delivery to London. Such was Palmer's local notoriety that he had to be tried in London to allow the possibility of a fair trial – which necessitated the passing of the Central Criminal Court Act of 1856. The main evidence centred on claims that Palmer had bought strychnine, and circumstantial evidence around Cook's death. He was found guilty and executed on 14 June 1856 before an enormous crowd at Stafford. In the popular press, he was reckoned to be responsible for sixteen deaths.[15]

The range of poisons known to the courts was further extended in 1882 by the trial of 'Dr' George Lamson for the murder of his wife's 18-year-old brother, Percy John. Lamson had married Kate John in 1878, one of five orphaned siblings from a moderately well-off family under the guardianship of a Mr Ormond, who did not like Lamson and took care to ensure the marriage settlement did not place all of Kate's money in his hands. In 1879 one of Kate's brothers, Herbert, came to stay with the Lamsons at Rotherfield – and died. Under the terms of the will, his portion of the family's money was shared out amongst the others.

Lamson went to Bournemouth and took up medical practice, but the Bournemouth Medical Society discovered that his qualifications were false and he was ejected from its membership. In August 1881 he was at Ventnor when Percy John came to stay and Lamson tried to poison him with 'aconitia'. In December 1881 Lamson visited Percy at Blenheim House School in Wimbledon and left him with some pills; he then died.

At his trial in March 1882 Lamson was painted in a dark light. He was known to be a drug addict, taking atropia. By stating his name and giving false medical qualifications he was able to get enough poison to kill twenty people. He stood to gain £1,500 from Percy's death. Doctors Stevenson and Dupré tested fluid from the dead boy's stomach on mice, which were dead in fifteen and a half minutes, and Stevenson even tested it on himself, following which he unsurprisingly felt unwell. Lamson was found guilty and sentenced to death, with the jury expressing the view that the government should 'stringently forbid the sale of poisons of any kind'. Lamson's view was clear: 'I protest before God that I am innocent.'

There were protests after the trial for two reasons: Lamson was 'an opium eater' and not fully in control of himself, with a history of insanity in his family and, as The Observer expressed it, the evidence was 'entirely circumstantial and that no man should suffer death upon circumstantial evidence'.[16] However, Lamson is reported to have confessed before his execution, though he denied killing Herbert. He was executed at Wandsworth in April 1882.

Poisons were often easily available around the house. On occasions this led a child to commit murder. William Allnutt, a 12-year-old in Hackney, murdered his grandfather in 1847 by mixing arsenic in sugar. He took the arsenic used for

William Allnutt, a boy from Hackney, who poisoned his grandfather possibly under the inspiration of reading about murders in the newspapers.

rats and put it in the sugar that was added to gruel or baked apples, nearly killing his mother too. A defence of insanity was undermined by evidence of the boy's precocity and bad behaviour, and it was argued that he had got the idea from the newspapers which he read avidly. A sentence of death was recorded but the judge recommended mercy and he was taken away for life.

SOMETHING NASTY UNDERFOOT

The murder committed by the husband-and-wife team of the Mannings was certainly a crime in which sex played a part. Maria Manning had been a maid to the Duchess of Sutherland, but strung along two men, marrying one, Frederick Manning. However, she continued to see Patrick O'Connor, a man 'with an extraordinarily prominent chin',[17] and he would often visit their house in Bermondsey during which Maria's husband would go into the garden, leaving the two of them alone. Manning also liked quizzing the medical student, who lodged upstairs, on topics such as 'Which part of the skull is most vulnerable to a blow?' and 'Do you think a murderer has any chance of getting to heaven?' After O'Connor came for dinner in August 1849 he was never seen again.

Under suspicion, the Mannings bolted in different directions: she went to Scotland to try and sell O'Connor's share certificates, while he went to the

Channel Isles. Meanwhile, a flagstone in their kitchen was prised up to reveal a corpse covered in quicklime. Both were arrested and started to blame each other, though Frederick Manning eventually told police: 'I never liked him so I battered his head with a ripping chisel.' After the verdict had been read out, Maria Manning shouted at the judge, arguing forcefully that if she had been going to murder anyone, it would have been her husband. Their execution on 13 November was a defining moment for Charles Dickens, who witnessed the behaviour of the huge crowd with horror. The combination of a couple, with Maria's glamour and Swiss origins, plus the sexual element, made Maria Manning in particular a 'celebrity murderer'.

Henry Wainwright was a famous murderer because he killed his mistress and yet came from a middle-class background. In the early 1870s he ran a business making mats and brushes, kept a wife and four children, and paid a mistress named Harriet Lane £5 a week – and soon had two extra children. This was too much for Wainwright's finances, so he shot Miss Lane at his warehouse and buried her body under the floor. Wainwright's explanation to her friends that she had gone off with an auctioneer caused problems when the auctioneer was contacted and denied it.

Wainwright decided to burn down the warehouse and claim the insurance money, but the insurers refused to pay. Now he feared the body might be discovered, so with his brother's help he dug it up and took it in pieces to the brother's cellar in Borough High Street. Wainwright even got an innocent man, Stokes, to help carry some of the pieces but, worried by the smell, he opened the package and discovered a hand! Unable to find a policeman, Stokes followed Wainwright's cab to Borough where police later found other parts of the body. Wainwright was hung on 21 December 1874.

Another famous murderer who buried the bodies 'at home' was Frederick Deeming. On 3 March 1892 the new tenants of a house in Melbourne, Australia, complained about a bad smell; buried in cement by the fireplace they found the mangled corpse of a woman. She was identified as Mrs Emily 'Williams' née Mather who, it transpired, had been murdered by her husband.

Mr 'Williams' was hunted across Australia and captured hundreds of miles away, where he had got a job as a mining engineer. By this time he had met a Miss Rounsefell via a matrimonial agency and was in the act of persuading her to marry him – she was one of two women in the story who had a lucky escape. Williams had already given her rings taken from the fingers of his murdered wife.

The dead woman was the daughter of a widow who kept a tobacconist's shop in Rainhill, near Liverpool. Enquiries there soon elicited some interesting facts; notably that Williams had married his new wife at Rainhill parish church only in September 1891. The couple had enjoyed a honeymoon and had then left rather suddenly.

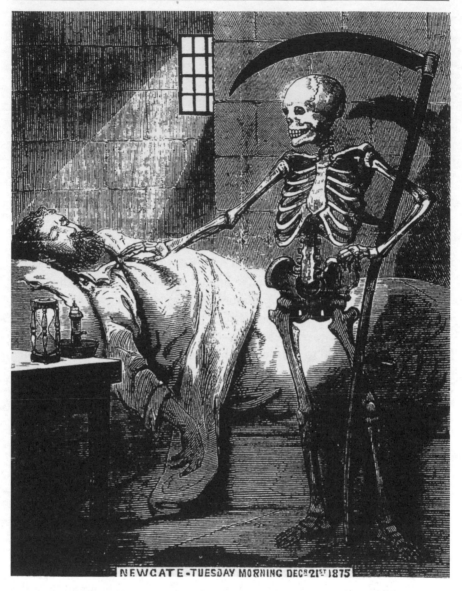

NEWGATE-TUESDAY MORNING DEC° 21ˢᵗ 1875

Death comes calling for Henry Wainwright on the day of his execution for the murder of Harriet Lane, his mistress.

Whilst at Rainhill, Williams had lived sometimes at a hotel where he had been visited by a mysterious veiled woman dressed in black; he had then rented Dinham Villas on the condition that it was not to be let for at least six months after he had gone. Two weeks after the discovery at Melbourne, the house in Rainhill was dug up and, similarly buried in cement, were found the bodies of a woman and four children aged between 2 and 9. The woman was identified as a Mrs Deeming of Birkenhead, who some people thought to be Williams' sister. Enquiries in Birkenhead revealed that Williams had visited her briefly there, following which she had sold all her furniture and moved with the family to Rainhill. The family were probably killed around 1 August 1891.

It transpired that 'Williams' was actually Frederick Deeming and the Birkenhead family was that of his wife Marie, whom he had married in 1881. The Deemings had married in Tranmere in February 1881. They left for South Africa soon after and were in Sydney in 1882, where Deeming was given six weeks in prison for theft. He was back in South Africa in 1883 using various names, including Doeming, and was suspected of many swindles and the murders of 'a white man Graham, a Hottentot and a Kaffir' at Johannesburg.

In January 1888 he was supposed to have been in Adelaide but left for South Africa with his wife and children in order to escape a fraud charge. A brief career in South Africa, posing as a mining engineer, netted a substantial amount of money and also some Masonic regalia, which he had himself photographed wearing. The whole family seems to have returned to Birkenhead in August 1888, but Deeming was soon off to South Africa again where he was involved in more swindles. He reappeared in Birkenhead in September 1889 but a private detective, Ellis, was watching Mrs Deeming there and was soon on his trail to Camberwell, Stockton and other places. To shake him off, Deeming left the country but went only to Egypt before returning.

He arrived in Hull in November 1889. At the same time he was courting a Miss Matheson of Beverley, with whom he enjoyed a short honeymoon as 'Mr and Mrs Lawson' in February 1890, before disappearing – still a wanted man; she was another who had a narrow escape.

Deeming left England yet again but was arrested in Montevideo and brought back by a Hull detective. He was given nine months in prison in October 1890, where he was known to the governor of Hull gaol as 'Harry Lawson'. Following his release from Hull gaol, in July 1891, he visited Birkenhead and set up at the hotel in Rainhill – it was most likely his wife who had visited him as the 'veiled lady'. He then married Miss Emily Mather, a local shopkeeper's daughter, and rather suddenly sold all the furniture at Dinham Villas and left for Australia. Among the items he sold to a brother was a spade on which cement and blood were later found.

Deeming and his new wife reached Melbourne on 16 December 1891, where he rented a house and immediately bought cement. By early March he was already seeking a new wife in Sydney.

He was convicted of the Emily Mather murder on 2 May 1892 and was executed on 23 May, a petition on the grounds of insanity having been rejected. Claims that he 'spoke' with his dead mother every day, and that she ordered him to kill the women in his life, were dismissed.

BURIAL CLUB MONEY

It remains the case in Britain today that a parent cannot take out life insurance on their children. This is because of the scandal of the Victorian burial clubs, which ostensibly offered a means of paying for a person's funeral but actually became a meal ticket for some heartless parents, as we have seen in some of the poisonings above.

Some writers of the era alleged that the use of burial clubs was so great as to account for the high death rate amongst children in towns such as Preston and Manchester, who were rarely considered worth the expense of a doctor.[18] In Preston, children under 5 formed 59 per cent of the deaths but only 13 per cent of the doctors' businesses.[19] The Marquis of Normanby told Parliament in 1845 that many children were entered on the books of several burial clubs as soon as they were born, and then only cared for by an opium-based medicine, Godfrey's Cordial; Chadwick's report on the health of towns mentioned one child insured in ten clubs – the child died. Although the Friendly Society Act of 1847 had placed a restriction on insuring under 6s, it only applied to new clubs so did not resolve the problem. Reform of the law occurred in 1850, when a new act set out that only the cost of a funeral could be paid out for a child and that all deaths had to be certified by a surgeon or coroner.

The number of children who died because of the burial club money can never be identified. In April 1846 James and Richard Pimlet, both young children, died at Runcorn at the hands of their mother, and at York Assizes John Rodda was tried in 1846 for murdering a child aged 1 with a mouthful of sulphuric acid or 'oil of vitriol' at Skipton; this was done for 50s from the burial club. Thomas Moore, who had previously been arrested for failing to support his wife and stepchildren, returned to collect the two boys in September 1853 and then was alleged to have drowned both in the canal near Reddish in order to claim £19 12s in burial club money. He was acquitted at Liverpool Assizes because no one had seen him drown the boys. Despite this verdict, the grand jury at Liverpool Assizes chose to record its views about the evils of burial clubs.

Mary Ann Cotton, perhaps the most infamous murderess executed at Durham, may have been motivated by insurance money in some of her murders: she is alleged to have killed possibly three husbands, a lover, ten of her children, her mother, a sister-in-law and five stepchildren. In 1873 she went to the gallows for poisoning Charles Cotton, a stepson who was insured for £4 10s.

Laws to protect children were strengthened by further legislation such as the Infant Life Protection Act of 1872 and the Infant Life Preservation Act of 1897.

A famous double execution at Liverpool in February 1880 followed the murder of Patrick Tracey at Widnes in October 1879. At first it was thought that Tracey had been shot in his bed by burglars, who had come in through a down-stairs window and stolen £15, but basic police work showed that the dirt and cobwebs at the window had not been disturbed. Tracey's wife, Mary, had taken out a number of policies on her husband's life in the previous few weeks and one of their lodgers, Burns, had bought a pistol from a Widnes pawnbroker only two days before.

Burns, another lodger named Kearns and Mrs Tracey were tried for murder. During the trial it was claimed by the prosecution that 'perhaps the prisoner Kearns and Mrs Tracey were on terms of greater intimacy than they ought to have been'.[20] Kearns at first said that it was Burns who had shot Tracey, but after all three were found guilty of murder and sentenced to death he retracted this, denied that he had fired the shot himself, and refused to say who had. This left only one possibility – but Mrs Tracey was pregnant and her death sentence was commuted to life; the two men went to the gallows.

MURDERS BY SERVANTS

Respectable Victorian society depended on servants being available all day and night, and many of them lived in the homes of their employers. The spectre of murder by your servants sent fear through the dreams of the genteel.

The most famous murder by a servant was the brutal killing of Lord William Russell in his bed in London's West End by his Swiss butler in 1840. First thoughts were that he had been killed by burglars and no one immediately sus-pected Francois Courvoisier, the butler who had been with him for five weeks. However, some enterprising detective work identified that a chisel in the valet's possession matched marks on furniture, and marks on the back door matched the pantry poker. Eventually the skirting board in the pantry was prised off and money was found hidden behind it.

The fashionable world was horrified that a lord could have his throat cut in his own bedroom, supposedly by a man who did the deed naked. Charles Greville recorded the scare in his diary: 'Visionary servants and airdrawn razors or carving

In the Euston Square mystery, the servant killed the mistress and hid her body under coal in the cellar.

knives dance before everybody's imagination, and half the world go to sleep expecting to have their throats cut before the morning.'

Courvoisier was tried in June 1840; he was doomed as soon as a French hotel proprietor testified that he had asked her to look after a box of silverware stamped with the Russell crest. The murder had been witnessed by a gentleman, who was in the room of a lady opposite and saw it happen through the windows; he gave evidence in a protected manner in order to save the lady embarrassment. Courvoisier was executed on 6 July 1840 before a crowd of thousands, the situation made worse by prejudice against a foreigner. An incidental victim was the novelist Harrison Ainsworth, whose novel *Jack Sheppard* was blamed for inciting Courvoisier to robbery and murder.

A more humdrum servant murder took place in Lincoln in 1838. Samuel Kirkby, 15, worked for a respectable butcher called John Bruce who used to beat him. The boy decided on revenge and put arsenic in the tea kettle. He killed Bruce, but also made two women dangerously ill. The boy, full of bravado, told the arresting constable: 'I suppose you will go to all the druggists in the town, but if you do you'll not find anything out.' In fact, he had got 'white mercury', or arsenic, off another boy, who ran errands for a chemist that sold it as rat poison. Kirkby was sentenced to death, but this was commuted to life transportation; he went to Australia laughing: 'he laughed and grimaced … and said that now his head was out of the hemp he did not care for what might come.'

Sarah Thomas, aged only 18, went to the gallows at Bristol for the murder of her elderly employer, Elizabeth Jefferies. Jefferies was a recluse of 'very infirm and violent character' who sacked servants almost as rapidly as they could leave of their own accord. Many former servants of hers – and the agencies that supplied them – came forward to describe her tyrannical and oppressive behaviour. Sarah Thomas coped with this for barely a couple of days, including a night where the old woman locked her in the pantry. In her confession, Thomas described how she reached a point of wanting to do away with the old woman, and so fetched a stone to batter in her head as she lay in her bedroom. She then threw the equally annoying dog down the privy, took the valuables, locked up and went home to her parents.

Thomas was soon arrested, with almost all the stolen goods at her home; she said the murder had been committed by a former servant who wanted revenge for being refused a 'character' (reference). The judge listened to the jury's verdict of guilty and the recommendation for mercy, and noted, 'she was a good look-ing woman with nothing in her face to indicate the criminal tendencies which she had exhibited'. But mercy was refused, despite a petition from 3,500 Bristol women, and the girl – for she was little more – broke down on the final morn-ing, it needing seven gaolers to get her out of the condemned cell.

In 1879 Kate Webster was given her notice by her Richmond employer, Mrs Thomas. One night after Mrs Thomas returned from church, Webster disem-bowelled her and cut her up. She then boiled the pieces on the cooker. Other parts were sent off on a journey down the Thames, creating a mystery at Barnes. Meanwhile, Webster liquidated what she could from the house and went to Ireland – from where she was brought back and executed.

In 1877 Hannah Dobbs was a servant for Mrs Bastendorff, who rented rooms to genteel ladies at Euston Square. That October, Mrs Bastendorff returned home to be told by Hannah that one of the ladies, an elderly spinster named Miss Matilda Hacker, had moved out. All that was left was a stain on the carpet. Eighteen months later the remains of a body were found under rubbish in the coal cellar, with a rope around the neck. The stain on the carpet was now found to be blood, and a woman from next door came forward to say she recalled hear-ing a scream from Miss Hacker's rooms.

Dobbs was arrested; she had in her possession an old money box belonging to Miss Hacker and the spinster's 'dream book'. However, further evidence was problematic – the state of the corpse was so bad that doctors said they could not prove she had been murdered, despite the rope. If it was the rope, there was no proof who had put it there. Dobbs was acquitted and the police offered a reward for further evidence, which was claimed by the woman to whom Dobbs had sold all Miss Hacker's clothes. Dobbs thus escaped the hangman because she had already been acquitted of murder.

MURDERS OF POLICEMEN

Some members of the police were killed whilst trying to bring drunken riots under control. An example of this occurred on a Sunday afternoon in Dover in September 1844, when a constable was killed by being struck across the face with a piece of iron whilst trying to bring a battle between gangs of chimney sweeps and prize fighters under control. Thomas Clark was the perpetrator but he escaped, despite a £50 reward.

The killing of police most commonly took place when they discovered criminals in the act of perpetrating a crime. After the shootings of PC Shorter and Inspector Drewett near Hungerford in December 1876, William Day and three brothers by the name of Tidbury were all arrested. After the coroner's hearing, a large crowd followed the four arrested men and their police escort to Hungerford station, hissing at them and shouting 'Hang the villains'. Boot prints led directly from the murder scene in the road to the Tidburys' cottage. Guns were traced to Henry Tidbury's possession and found hidden near his cottage. Henry and Francis Tidbury were found guilty of murder, their brother William an accessory and Day was acquitted; the two murderers were hung in March 1877.

Moses Shrimpton, a habitual thief who mixed poaching and poultry stealing, was surprised by PC David when returning from some fowl business in February 1885, and killed the policeman. He was hung in May 1885: 'A long drop was given to the culprit, whose head was partially severed from the body.'[21] Three of the Netherby burglars were executed at Carlisle in February 1886 for the killing of PC Byrnes at Plumpton (see Chapter 4), with associates linked to the murder of Inspector Simmons at Romford in January 1885, for which one other man had been hung. Also in 1886, PC Austwick's attempts to deal with poachers led to a row with James Murphy at Dodworth, near Barnsley; Murphy went and got his gun and shot the policeman in cold blood. After being arrested, he escaped from police custody but was recaptured after a desperate struggle at his sister's house in Barnsley; he was hung in November 1886.

In April 1892 John Gurd was an attendant at the Wiltshire County Asylum in Devizes where he had formed a relationship with a colleague, Florence Adams. There was a row between them and Adams went off to her family in Melksham, to where Gurd followed. He calmly shot dead her uncle, Henry Richards, and then disappeared for two days until found by Sergeant Moulden near Warminster. He shot the policeman dead too but was actually executed for the first of the two murders.

In September 1895 Detective Sergeant Kidd was stabbed nine times with a penknife at Kay's Siding, Wigan. Three men were arrested but at the first hearing Elijah Winstanley shrieked, 'Kill me, kill me. Go on, it's murder, I did it.' He was executed at Walton Gaol.

MURDERS OF WOMEN & CRIMES OF PASSION

Crimes of passion and especially the murder of women attracted the greatest interest when they involved the middle classes and 'respectable' people. However, the reality was that many women were killed by those closest to them, often a husband, and often drink was involved. There has been much discussion of changed attitudes towards the killing of 'bad' wives – the killing of 'good' wives having always been condemned.[22] The prosecution of 'good wife' cases increased markedly over the period, from five in the 1850s to thirty-four in the 1870s. Wife murder was also a class crime – only 12 of 141 wife murder cases in the 1870s involved middle-class men. Between 1841 and 1900 there were forty-three trials of married persons for murdering their adulterous partner, of whom forty-two were men; the only exception was Elizabeth Gibbons, who shot her husband at Hayes, Middlesex, in 1884. Men occasionally killed another man who they thought to be having an affair with their wife; this seems to have been treated more leniently than the murder of the actual wife.[23]

Rather unusually, Mrs Hannah Giles was shot dead whilst going to babysit for some friends on a snowy day at Otterden in Kent in January 1839. Her body was found by the little boy she was meant to be looking after, and footsteps could be traced in the snow back to a house inhabited by Samuel Seager, one of her lovers. When Seager was arrested at Birmingham he tried to strangle himself with his boot laces, but was executed at Maidstone in March 1839. The scenes in which the dead woman's husband gloated over the body caused considerable repulsion and contributed to the opposition over public executions.

Many murders of women were grubby, desperate affairs. In 1850 Elizabeth Forbes was murdered by her husband Patrick at Cloggers Entry, Newcastle. He was a 'violent, drunken character' and attention was drawn when cries of 'Murder!' were heard from an upstairs room. Both had spent the day drinking and neighbours had had to help Elizabeth upstairs as she was so drunk. Police arrived to find Forbes sitting on a chair by the fireside with specks of blood on his clothing; he 'professed total ignorance of the manner in which his wife had come to her end'. Knives were found in his pocket. He was executed in August 1850, but the hanging was badly bungled and Forbes had to be 'dropped' twice.

A more traditional 'crime of passion' was the murder of Jael Denny by Thomas Drory at Doddinghurst in Essex in 1850. Drory, a respectable young farmer, killed a girl whose stepfather worked on his farm; she was eight months pregnant, living at his farm while her mother was his housekeeper. She seems to have had a colourful reputation, including performing 'dances' in the back rooms of public houses. A note written by the girl to say he was not the father of her child was allegedly inspired by a gift of £10 as Drory wanted to marry someone else. Drory met the girl out in the fields and happened to have a strong rope in his

The murder of Jael Denny by Thomas Drory attracted great public attention and was used in many broadsheets; in typical fashion, the illustration was then reused to publicise other, quite different murders.

pocket; he pinned her to the ground and strangled her with it, with bite marks that matched his teeth being found on her hand. He confessed before his execution and went to the gallows with the poisoner Sarah Chesham.

The 'Lambeth poisoner', Thomas Neill Cream, was obsessed with women. He was a Scottish-Canadian doctor who was sexually motivated and, apart from being a poisoner, was unusually interested in abortion, conducting one on his own girlfriend; he was later forced into a marriage with her by an irate father. In Canada and America he seems to have earned a living from abortion, although at least two women died; he was also sent to prison after a mistress' husband died from strychnine poisoning – he was released early due to ill health.

Cream came to London in 1891 where he frequented the music halls and bars of Lambeth and Brighton, earning money from abortions, talking to young women and showing off his collection of pornographic pictures. He carried around with him his own 'medical' supplies: capsules containing strychnine. In October 1891 a 19-year-old girl was found dying in agony in her rooms; strychnine poisoning was evident, but she could speak only of cross-eyed 'Fred' before she died. Although another man was questioned, Cream pretended to be a detective who could help find the murderer and wrote a string of letters blaming

Dr Cream, the 'Lambeth Poisoner', preyed on women and killed them with strychnine in 1892.

the son of W.H. Smith, the bookseller. A week later another woman, Matilda Clover, died in agony in Lambeth, but as she was an alcoholic prostitute her death attracted little interest.

Cream again wrote 'poison pen letters', accusing both Lord Russell and a leading doctor. These letters included unpublished details about Miss Clover dying from strychnine and later proved to be crucial evidence. Another woman, Louisa Harvey, survived a night with Cream only because she did not like the look of his pills and just pretended to take them. In April 1892 two young prostitutes died in Stamford Street. Cream foolishly wrote to the father of a medical student who lived in the same house as himself saying the student had killed the women and demanding money. He also boasted of his activities to a local photographer, who wrote everything down and then told the police. Cream was arrested in June 1892 and it took the jury only ten minutes to decide on his guilt.

Most 'crimes of passion' were motivated by casual cruelty or spiteful vengeance. Wife murders remained very common throughout the era and in the 1890s just under a third of all executions were of men who had killed their wives, with several others for murder of girlfriends. Of the fifteen executions in 1899, only one was for the murder of a man.

SOME OTHER FAMOUS MURDERS

The cases involving Thomas Bacon are a curious mixture of Victorian gothic: dead children, madness, inheritance and legal bungling. On 30 December 1856, Bacon's wife Martha was found in a mentally deranged state at her home in Walworth and her two young children were found with their throats cut so savagely that their heads had almost been severed. Mrs Bacon, who was known to be prone to hysteria and even violence, told a tale of a man breaking into their house and stealing banknotes. Thomas Bacon was away, but when he returned the police gradually began to shift away from their initial view that Martha Bacon had killed the children. Banknotes reportedly stolen had actually been used a few days before, whilst a stolen watch was found nearby, and Bacon had a cut on his hand that he seemed confused about.

Mrs Bacon had not spoken a word since the deaths, but at Lambeth magistrates she wrote a note saying her husband had killed the children. Bacon was arrested on a murder charge and news about the case dredged up some memories from his home town of Stamford, Lincolnshire. People began to say that Bacon had killed his mother there before going to London. Bizarrely, the murder trial in London in May 1857 found Martha guilty of the murders, though insane, whilst Thomas was immediately arrested for the murder of his mother in Lincolnshire in 1855.

Bacon's mother had died after suffering stomach pains and vomiting, leaving her property to Bacon; an exhumation of her body from Great Casterton churchyard was ordered. Professor Taylor found arsenic. However, Bacon could only be found guilty of the lesser charge of administering arsenic with intent to commit murder. Extraordinarily, he had escaped the hangman twice.

Exactly who killed Thomas Bacon's children was disputed, but in the view of the contemporary print sellers it was the father rather than the mother.

One of the best-attended executions was that of John Gleeson Wilson at Kirkdale, Liverpool, in September 1849. Wilson, a 'respectable seaman', took lodgings with Mrs Henrichson at Leveson Street, Liverpool. Her husband was on a voyage to Calcutta, but she shared the house with her young boys of 3 and 5 and a servant girl, Mary Parr. The morning after his arrival at Leveson Street, Wilson hit Mary Parr around the head with the fire tongs as she cleaned the grate, killed one of the children in the same room, 'horribly butchered' Mrs Henrichson in the passageway and then seemingly chased the other boy into the kitchen where he cut his throat.

The murders were discovered when a young girl arrived at the house for a music lesson: the dying servant girl and the dead child could be seen on the floor of the lounge. Wilson, it was discovered, had taken other rooms in the city on the same day as with Mrs Henrichson, and had patrolled around the house there as if seeing what to rob, but he had gone to Leveson Street for the night. Captain Henrichson discovered what had happened when he read a newspaper whilst stopping at St Helena on the way home. Mary Parr was able to give a statement before she died and Wilson was caught in possession of a stolen watch, so his trial was almost a formality except being noted for the riotous behaviour of those present; when the judge left for a few moments, those in court started shouting and hissing at Wilson, who shouted back. His execution was a huge event, to which people were ferried by excursion train.

Constance Kent was a murderess who escaped the courts for several years but eventually caused a major religious controversy. In June 1860, while living in Wiltshire, Constance's 4-year-old brother had been found stabbed and with his throat cut. The family nursemaid, Elizabeth Gough, was suspected and twice arrested amidst suggestions she was having an affair with Mr Kent.[24] Suspicion later pointed to Constance but there was little evidence; however rumour pursued her everywhere. The crime became one of the great sensations of the year, partly because of the way its middle-class subjects were treated by the police.[25]

Constance became interested in nursing and then, through a recommendation, came to Brighton to help at St Mary's Home, where the wealthy Anglo-Catholic priest Rev. Arthur Wagner provided for the 'fallen women' of the town. She began to treat Wagner as a confessor and in 1865 admitted that she had murdered her half-brother. Using his political connections, Wagner went to speak to the Home Secretary; Constance confessed to the police and was arrested, causing an outcry of condemnation against Wagner on the subject of religious confession in general. The case gave rise to much anti-Catholic feeling. Constance pleaded guilty and was sentenced to life imprisonment, though she was released in 1885.

John Jones was the son of a tailor from Byfield near Daventry, who married a widow and set up running a beer house, but he lost his licence for running a 'disorderly house' in 1855. He left his wife and became an itinerant blacksmith and thief, during the course of which he did some work for a blacksmith at Denham, near Uxbridge, Emmanuel Marshall. The two men fell out when Jones' poor work caused a row with a local farmer, and they had a fight – Jones punched Marshall in the eye, and Marshall refused to pay him.

Jones left but had several sojourns in gaol, being released on 20 May 1869 after serving eighteen months for stealing a lamb and ewe at Abingdon. Full of hatred for Marshall, he went straight to Uxbridge and surprised the blacksmith at his forge early the next morning. Jones killed Marshall with a hammer, then picked up an axe and went into the house where the women and children were still in their nightgowns. In an act of frenzied evil, Jones killed everyone there – Marshall's wife, sister, mother and his three children. Two children were found huddled in one corner and two of the women in another room; Marshall's sister was due to be married two days after she was murdered. The third child, aged 4, was found near its grandmother's body. Jones then changed into the dead man's clothes, leaving his own clothes behind in the bedroom. He was soon arrested and hung, his case being used as a powerful argument against abolishing the death penalty. To the last he showed no remorse, criticising his family for 'snivelling' on a visit, pretending to be a Catholic so that a priest had to be fetched from miles away but who he then refused to speak to, and asking to spend his last two nights alive sleeping in his own coffin.

Notes

1   The Observer, 20 September 1863.

2   Trollope, Phineas Redux, op. cit., Oxford edition 1983, p. 178 (2).

3   Ibid., p. 149 (2).

4   Ibid., p. 124 (2).

5   Biggadyke was hung in Lincoln, but years later the Lincolnshire Chronicle was able to report the confession of her former lodger to the murder of her husband.

6   The Times, 13 November 1888.

7   Owen Davies, Murder, Magic and Madness, the Victorian Trials of Dove and the Wizard, p. 208.

8   K. Watson, Poisoned Lives, London, 2003, p. 202.

9   The Times, 20 January 1845.

10   The Observer, 20 January 1845.

11   They did not inform the coroner officially, but concerned locals wrote in to complain and raise their fears.

12   The Times, 7 March 1851.

13   Van der Elst published On the Gallows in 1937. Tallack was secretary of the Society for the Abolition of Capital Punishment and the Howard Association.

14   Evidence to the Agriculture Commission, Parliamentary Papers 1867, p. 457. Some other sources say two rooms.

15   R.D.Altick, *Victorian Studies in Scarlet*, London, 1970, p. 154.

16   *The Observer*, 19 March 1882.

17   H.M.Walbrook, *Murders and Murder Trials*, London, 1932, p. 89.

18   L. Playfair, *Report on the Sanitary Conditions of Towns in Lancashire*, as well as the more famous *Health of Towns Commission* who reported in 1844.

19   *The Times*, 13 December 1847.

20   *Manchester Guardian*, 13 February 1880.

21   *The Times*, 26 May 1885.

22   Martin Wiener, *Men of Blood: Violence, Manliness and Criminal Justice in Victorian England*, Cambridge, p. 170.

23   Ibid., p. 203.

24   Altick, p. 130.

25   Jane Sturrock in A. Maunder & G. Moore (eds), *Victorian Crime, Murder and Sensation*, Aldershot, 2004, p. 73.

3

Manslaughter, Madness & Other Violent Assaults

Greater understanding of the connection between criminal behaviour and mental illness developed in mid-Victorian Britain. The Criminal Lunatics Act of 1800 instructed that any person charged with murder or a felony could be placed in an asylum, although the first state institute did not open until 1815. As there were virtually no public asylums, many mentally ill people ended up in prison – the authorities at a Middlesex gaol in 1841 complained that they had had to send nine prisoners to the Bethlem hospital within a nine-month period;[1] most of these were awaiting transportation and one was referred to as 'a very strange character from the first'. Another eleven were of 'unsound mind' but did not need to be sent to Bethlem. Sending such people to prison did little good; a man from Abingdon named Willoughby exhibited frequent violent behaviour towards his wife, and after one 'murderous assault' he was sentenced to five years penal servitude. However, he was then released, returned to live with her, and in 1885 killed her after a row by hitting her on the head with a coal hammer; then he cut his own throat. There are many examples of such crimes.

Broadmoor opened for women in 1863 and men in 1864. In 1863 there were only 877 criminal lunatics in custody, although it was estimated in 1869 that one in nine prisoners were 'more or less insane'. An analysis in 1867 showed that there were then 1,244 criminal lunatics in custody, of which 64 per cent had apparently become insane after their trial; 30 per cent of them were committed for murder and 23 per cent for attempted murder, suggesting that earlier diagnoses might have led to different results. From 1889 magistrates were instructed that they could send lunatics straight to an asylum, not to prison first, though there was no law to this effect until the 1913 Mental Deficiency Act. Nevertheless, there was some criticism of the policy of keeping for life people who might otherwise have been executed, especially after two murderers escaped from Broadmoor in 1873.

Broadmoor asylum was built in a healthy position on the crest of a hill and became one of the famous institutions of Victorian England.

In autumn 1843 the body of a man was found at Cobham, Kent. Charles Dadd had been a chemist in Rochester but had moved to London, where he had had some success after inventing an improved form of oil for artists' paint. More shocking, then, that he had been murdered by his own artist son.

The Dadd murder is well known for two reasons: firstly, the artistic fame of its perpetrator; and secondly, because the murder had a profound impact on Dickens, who knew the area well. Richard Dadd, the murderer, had shown great promise as a young artist and in 1842/3 went on an artistic tour to the Middle East from which he returned 'labouring under aberration of intellect'. In August 1843 his father decided to take him to Chatham to watch the army manoeuvres. It seems that the younger Dadd used this as a chance to kill his father, for he bought an 8-inch knife and a cut-throat razor in Covent Garden before they left. At Cobham, they checked in at the Ship Inn, then Richard Dadd suggested an evening walk – from which neither returned.

Charles Dadd's body was found the next morning. The first assumption was suicide, as the man still had money in his pockets and a gold watch; however, the victim's coat had clearly been pulled over his head after his throat had been cut. The razor was found beneath the body and a knife a few yards away. The body was taken back to the Ship Inn and a search began for the strange young man who had been there the night before.

Richard Dadd had gone to Rochester, where he washed the blood off and stole the towel on which he had left blood marks. At Dover he hired a boat to take him to France for £10. In France he launched an attack on a passenger in a carriage and he was placed in a lunatic asylum, where he was seen to spend hours in conversation with an imaginary person. The Kent authorities brought him back to England in March 1844. The press showed some sympathy for his condition, though reports in the Kent papers that he had lost his ability to paint proved unfounded. An appearance in the magistrates' court showed the degree of his problems: the *Maidstone Journal* reported Dadd as saying, 'I tell you I didn't do it; no gammon about it; no, I shan't do it; I dare say; I can say; I shan't do that; I never did it, I tell you; oh gammon, I know sir.' He also mimicked the magistrates skilfully.

At the Kent Assizes in autumn 1844 Richard Dadd was certified insane. Later, through medical supervision, it emerged that he had not really understood it was his father he was killing, but had felt motivated by the need to make a sacrifice. He was sent to Bethlem hospital – popularly known as 'bedlam' – where he remained until transferred to Broadmoor in 1864. Later in life he was well looked after and, his artistic interests encouraged, he produced many fine – if obsessive – works. He died in 1886.

Edward Oxford attempted to shoot Queen Victoria in 1840. He was sent to Bethlem hospital and then moved to Broadmoor in 1864. Records at Broadmoor from his arrival state: 'That he did it under the impression that he should thereby become a noted person and that he had not the smallest intention of injuring Her Majesty.' By 1865 he was 'a fat, elderly man … has now perfectly recovered his sanity, and is the most orderly, most useful, and most trusted of all the inmates of Broadmoor'.[2] In 1867 he was released on condition that he went overseas and stayed there; he went to Australia.

On 20 January 1843 the Prime Minister's private secretary, Edward Drummond, was shot from behind between the Admiralty and Horse Guards by a stranger. The man was drawing another loaded pistol when he was grabbed by a police officer. Drummond was wounded, but 'No fatal results are at present expected to accrue from the wound', declared *The Times*, after the shot had been removed from beneath Drummond's stomach. He died a few days later, showing the ineffectiveness of early Victorian medicine.

The killer was an eccentric Scotsman, Daniel McNaughton.[3] He had grown up in Glasgow, where he had developed a suspicion of Jesuits and Tories equally, before falling out with his father and leaving for London. There he was successful as a wood turner and amassed £1,000 in savings before developing very eccentric habits and losing interest in his business. He became obsessed with Tories, later telling officials: 'They have accused me of crimes of which I am not guilty; they do everything in their power to harass and persecute me. In fact they wish to murder me.'[4] McNaughton therefore conceived a plan to kill Sir Robert Peel, but killed his private secretary instead. First impressions, however, were not that he was insane, *The Times* noting: 'So far as we can judge, the assassin McNaughton seems to have been a tolerably sane person except upon the subject of Toryism.'

The criminal lunatic asylum at Broadmoor provided an alternative to the Bethlem hospital or prison for those judged insane.

The coroner's jury reached a verdict of wilful murder, though not without some comedy as they challenged the identity of the body in front of surgeon Guthrie. 'I knew Mr Drummond,' Guthrie replied, 'and there is no other dead body at 19 Grosvenor Street, except the body of Mr Drummond.'

At his trial, there was overwhelming evidence of insanity presented by a number of experts, such as Dr Edward Munro. McNaughton was taken to Bethlem hospital for life and later to Broadmoor. But there was public criticism of what was seen as lenient treatment and the Lord Chancellor was forced to make a statement in the House of Lords on 19 June 1843; this set out what became known as the 'McNaughton Rules', though they were never statutory. In summary, these rules state that a person cannot be held responsible for a crime if they were 'labouring under such a deficit of reason from disease of the mind to not know the nature and quality of the act; or that if he did know it, that he did not know that what he was doing was wrong'.

Others were not as fortunate as Oxford. The Brighton police chief was murdered by a wandering labourer in 1844, after which his widow was awarded £500.[5] The crime occurred when John Lawrence, a former seller of 'soft water' at Tunbridge Wells, was brought into the police station having been arrested by

PC Banden for stealing a piece of carpet. Lawrence struck the police chief on the head with a poker; 'I hope I have killed him and then I shall be hung for it,' he said. The police chief, Mr Solomon,[6] died the following day.

Lawrence was found to be a young man from a 'respectable family' who had 'contracted habits of dissipation'. His desire to be hung seems to have weakened by the time of his trial, which he started 'in an almost fainting state' and finished 'carried from the dock in an almost insensible condition by the turnkey'. He was executed at Horsham on 6 April, pleas of insanity having borne no fruit. In contrast, in 1873, PC Israel May was battered to death with his own truncheon at Snodland by Thomas Atkins. Atkins was proved to have had a history of mental illness and his father had murdered his mother, so he was given fifteen years penal servitude.

Stephen Forwood also behaved erratically. At his trial, he blamed the Bishop of London, Lord Palmerston and the Earl of Dudley for contributing to the murders he had committed, but an appeal to the Secretary of State to spare him for reasons of insanity failed because Dr Kirkman of the Kent lunatic asylum could not support it. After a youthful dalliance with a religious sect called the 'Faulknerites', Forwood married and began a bakery business in Ramsgate, but this failed and he slid into vice – it is possible his mental aberrations were the result of syphilis. After more business failures, and abandoning his family, Forwood discovered a talent for billiards, which eventually took him to Brighton. There he met a suicidal woman named Mrs White, and life took a turn for the better when he won a bet worth £1,172 from the younger brother of the Earl of Dudley.

Sometimes using the name Southey, Forwood became obsessed with this money which the earl refused to pay. Though Mrs White was at times involved, and at other times intent on escaping his influence, Forwood eventually hired rooms in Holborn in August 1865 where he murdered three of Mrs White's children with a spoonful of prussic acid each. Why he did this was never clear, but he may have feared the loss of White (who was talking of Australia), was concerned about not having money to support them, and even considered that the Earl of Dudley would be held responsible. Then he left for Ramsgate, where he shot both his wife and their daughter dead. Magistrates were stunned when, hauling him up for the double murder, he announced that he had left three other children dead in London – and that Gladstone, Disraeli and the Earl of Dudley were to blame!

Forwood was tried at Maidstone, although things got off to a confusing start when he insisted on being called 'Southey'. His defence that his wife was already dead when he shot her proved unsuccessful and he was executed early in 1866.

In contrast, Rebecca Law was clearly a disturbed woman but there was little help for her husband and young family. Aged 24, she had already had four children, although two had died, and as her husband was in prison, she spent

Christmas 1861 in Saffron Walden workhouse. When her husband was released in January 1862, he took the family back to a cottage at Starlings Green where, after four days, she killed her husband with a bill hook and her baby with a hammer. A neighbour arrived to find blood trickling through the ceiling from upstairs. When the constable arrived, Mrs Law said: 'Poor Sam is gone. I did it. I chopped him with the chopper. Oh dear, I am lost for ever.'

Over the next few days she explained how she had seen a vision, three months earlier, of a murder in the house and a surgeon reported her as having 'weak intellect'. At Essex Assizes, a verdict of not guilty due to insanity was recorded and she was detained indefinitely.

Such cases of parents who killed their own children occurred regularly. In 1864 Catherine Dawson of Chorley cut the throat of her third child in Toxteth Park, Liverpool, having also tried to kill her other children and to commit suicide. She was found to be insane and held at Rainhill asylum for about two years, after which she managed to escape. She was found living with her husband, but was then taken to Broadmoor where she gave birth to another child.

In Somers Town, London, in 1866, a man walking past a house saw a water butt move; looking inside, he was surprised to see a woman and hauled her out. Inside Mary Butcher's house her two children were found, laid out on their beds as if ready for burial, with 'their jaws tied up'. Mrs Butcher's husband, a baker, had been out at work all night and she was known to have been 'ill and melancholy' for several weeks. Having killed her children by drowning them, she had then tried to drown herself in the butt. However, very few such cases ended up on the scaffold. The 1867 'Kennington tragedy' involved a woman who killed her two children and then herself.

A woman who undoubtedly suffered from mental illness and who was understood to be thus – rather than paying the penalty of the gallows – was Christiana Edmunds of Brighton. Edmunds became emotionally entangled in 1869 with a married doctor, Dr Arthur Beard, who later claimed it was simply a 'flirtation'. The result was, nonetheless, that in September 1870 Christiana tried to poison Mrs Beard with a gift of chocolates laced with strychnine bought from a dentist. Although she failed to kill the doctor's wife, who disliked the chocolate and spat it out, Miss Edmunds became obsessed with poisoning chocolates and started to buy them from shops, lace them with poison and return them to the shelves. In June 1871 a small boy on holiday in the town died after eating the chocolates, but the reason for his death was not fully understood at the time. Instead, the shop owner, John Maynard, experienced great stress when it was found that chocolates he had sold contained strychnine.

Christiana next began sending parcels of sweets to well-known local personalities, also sending some to herself to deflect suspicion; her intention was that Maynard[7] would be blamed.

Roderick McLean was found 'not guilty, but insane' after his attempt to shoot Queen
Victoria at Windsor in 1882.

She was arrested and found guilty of murder, but Sir William Gull and Dr William Orange visited her on behalf of the Home Office and concluded that she was insane. She was sent to Broadmoor instead, although the surgeon at Lewes gaol thought this was the wrong decision. At Broadmoor she was obsessed with her appearance, was always trying to have false hair smuggled in, and continued to show predatory sexual interests.

People in this situation were habitually found 'not guilty by reason of insanity'. This changed after Roderick McLean shot at Queen Victoria at Windsor in March 1882. Queen Victoria was walking across the station yard when a man, 'wretchedly clad who was standing at the gateway of the yard, deliberately raised a pistol and fired it at Her Majesty's carriage, which was about thirty yards distant'.[8] McLean, aged 32, had walked from Portsmouth to Windsor with no food and was in no fit state to defend himself as he was 'belaboured over the head and shoulders with an umbrella by an Eton boy'. Tried for treason, he was found to be not guilty, but insane. 'Insane he may have been, but not guilty he most certainly was not, as I saw him fire the pistol myself,' the Queen is reputed to have said. The law was then changed so that a person might be found 'guilty, but insane'.[9]

THE DECLINE OF THE DUEL

Various attempts had been made to change the law on duelling in the early 1700s, but the last known execution of someone for participating in a duel was the case of Colonel Campbell in 1808. During a Parliamentary debate on Edmund Turner's Anti-Duelling Bill in March 1844, duelling was condemned as 'immoral in its tendency' and 'contrary to divine command', and it was claimed that there had been four duels in 1838 and 1839 apiece.

A fatal duel was fought on Wimbledon Common on 22 August 1838 between 'Captain' Elliott[10] and a former silk draper, Charles Mirfin, which was the result of a collision between their respective conveyances on Derby Day. The argument took root in a 'sink of vice', the Saloon in Piccadilly, a resort of prostitutes. Both men missed with their first shots, but Elliott's second hit Mirfin in the heart. Murder charges were laid against Elliott and three others, but only two attended court, were found guilty, and a sentence of death was recorded against them; after twelve months in prison they were given a free pardon.[11] Elliott escaped to Dieppe and Boulogne, where he continued to get into trouble.

James Brudenell, Earl of Cardigan, was upset when he read reports about himself in the *Morning Chronicle* which he traced to a member of his own regiment: Lt Harvey Tuckett. Brudenell challenged Tuckett to a duel, which was fought on Wimbledon Common on 12 September 1840; both men missed with their first shots, but Tuckett was wounded at the second. Lord Cardigan must have made a colourful sight when he had to appear before Wandsworth magistrates and was eventually charged with 'shooting with intent to murder'. Cardigan then became an easy target for the press, who seized on examples of his prejudiced rule as lieutenant-colonel of the 11th Light Dragoons. For a time he became the most hated man in England and *The Times* actually felt that hanging would be too good for him; what he needed was 'the terror of cropped heads, oatmeal diet and the treadmill'.[12]

It was discovered that Tuckett had used 'normal' pistols while Cardigan had used French 'rifled' ones with a hair trigger that gave a distinct advantage – ungentlemanly conduct. Cardigan was tried by the House of Lords, which was usual for a member of that house. A total of 120 peers pronounced on the case, declaring that he was not guilty on account of the full name of Captain Tuckett not being proved; only the Duke of Cleveland showed the morality to dissent, however marginally, from this feeble charade by declaring 'Not guilty legally, on my honour'. Many considered the technical error to be deliberate, since the evidence against Cardigan was otherwise overwhelming. Cardigan must have been worried, nevertheless, as he spent £10,000 transferring all his estates to his nephew in case they were forfeited.

A famous duel in 1840 was fought between Prince Louis Napoleon – the future Emperor Napoleon III – and le Comte Leon on Wimbledon Common; both were charged with committing a breach of the peace and bound over in the sum of £100.

On 1 July 1843 a dying Colonel Fawcett was carried to the Camden Arms public house. Fawcett and his conqueror, Lieutenant Munro, 'a stout gentleman', were married to two sisters but had had a furious row about the sale of a property in Brighton. Fawcett had made a comment which Munro had taken as suggesting he had mishandled his brother-in-law's property. After the duel, Fawcett was carried on a board first to the Brecknock Arms, where a waiter refused admittance, and then to the Camden Arms, where he told a PC that he had been shot by accident, although this was unlikely with a chest wound. He died on 3 July at 5.50 a.m.

In the aftermath, Mrs Fawcett was said to be 'much upset' about comments made about her husband and the 'odium' attaching to herself. Mr Gulliver, the surgeon of The Blues, was ordered to attend the coroner's court but did not do so, and *The Times* wanted all involved charged with wilful murder, including the seconds, Lieutenant Grant and Lieutenant Cuddy. Gulliver and Cuddy were tried for aiding and abetting but were found not guilty due to a lack of proof; Grant and Munro had disappeared. Grant surrendered on 12 February 1844 and was also found not guilty, but by this stage the headlines were being stolen by Parliamentary debates about Mrs Fawcett being refused an army pension.

Alexander Munro eventually returned to England; he was found guilty of murder in August 1847 and, although a sentence of death was recorded, he eventually was sentenced to twelve months in prison.[13]

The final fatal duel occurred on 20 May 1845 at Titchfield, near Gosport. Lieutenant Henry Hawkey had become annoyed at the persistent attentions paid by James Seton to Mrs Hawkey, culminating when he repeatedly asked Mrs Hawkey to dance. A row took place in the card room. In the duel, a ball passed through Seton from the right hip to the left groin. Internal infection developed and not even the great surgeon Robert Liston could save him from death on 2 June. Hawkey's second, Charles Pym, surrendered first but was acquitted at Winchester in March 1846. Hawkey was perhaps encouraged by this verdict and also surrendered, standing trial in July 1846 – he was also acquitted, the jury taking 'less than a minute' to decide the verdict. Hawkey was then able to resume his career in the marines and was soon appointed captain.

OTHER CRIMES OF MANSLAUGHTER

The boundary between wilful murder and manslaughter was hugely important in Victorian England, largely because the first invariably carried a death sentence. This could be a problem in itself, because it was known to deter juries from convicting when there was even the faintest doubt. As a result, people were sometimes charged with lesser offences such as intent to murder or manslaughter.

Generally, some indication of premeditation had to be proven. If it were not, punishments were sometimes surprisingly light, such as when one of a group of drunken tramps died at Dartford in February 1838. Michael Larkin fell to the ground with a 4-inch knife wound in his stomach following a row with Eliza Wright, with whom he lived, about another woman. With no evidence of premeditated murder, Wright got away with only a year in prison. In 1889 Samuel Suddaby of Newark had a row with his mother, who was 89, and kicked her so hard that she crashed into the wall and broke her thigh; she died ten days later. Suddaby was found guilty of manslaughter and sentenced to five years penal servitude. In 1890 Emmeline Young of Derby, 22, was sentenced to twelve months in prison for the manslaughter by neglect of her baby stepsister, who she had deliberately allowed to starve despite her father paying her to look after the child.

One of the most unusual 'manslaughter' cases involved the death by drowning of Sarah Cartwright, which occurred at Monks Copenhall near Crewe in 1843. Two members of the 'Mormonite' sect – both blacksmiths, and one her husband – were arrested after she died during a baptism ceremony in a flood-swollen brook. One of the few witnesses who turned up said that the spot where Mrs Cartwright died was 'very beautiful, and likely to dispose the mind to serious and proper feelings'.

Mrs Cartwright had agreed to be baptised after her husband had pleaded with her, but the chosen spot where water was normally a foot or two deep was actually more than 6ft deep and in flood. The woman drowned, and her body was later found under a hedge dressed only in a singlet to her waist – a circumstance that caused almost as much shock as her death. However, the trial at Chester Assizes was undermined by the non-appearance of most of the witnesses, almost all of whom were Mormons. The two blacksmiths were acquitted due to lack of evidence in January 1844.

Another unusual manslaughter case occurred on the night of 3 August 1863 at Sible Hedingham. A poor old man known as 'Dummy', who lived in a hovel in the woods and was a mute, was accused of having bewitched Emma Smith. She helped drag him off to a brook and pushed him in, following which Samuel Stammers and a number of others pushed him in repeatedly in a mockery of the old 'swimming' of a witch. After the assault, one of the workhouse guardians and the rector both went to the old man's aid and arranged for a cart to take him to the workhouse infirmary. Nevertheless, he died a month later and medical opinion connected his death with the 'swimming'; Smith and Stammers were subsequently accused of manslaughter. Smith implicated most of the people in the village, including Stammers, who she said had grabbed Dummy by the heels and thrown him into the water; both were given six months. The rector wrote to *The Times*, anxious to dispel the 'stigma' that would be attached to his village after such a case.

The assumption that if a man was defending himself then it could not be murder was a common one. In December 1867 some keepers stopped a pair of poachers near Wavendon Hall, Buckinghamshire, but they were not on their own land. In a tussle, a gun went off and one of the keepers died. Although it was also argued that the gun went off by accident, the salient point was that this could not be murder, so James Inwood received twenty years for manslaughter instead.

Deaths resulting from drunken rows also fell into the manslaughter category. There were many of these, of course, including the incident at South Shields in 1885. Patrick Welsh and his wife were both quite elderly; they had had an evening of drunken rows when he finally beat her round the head, 'stupefying' her. She then went out and fell down the stairs, though it was apparently the head injuries that caused her death. He received five years hard labour.

Manslaughter was also used where individuals were considered to have caused death through carelessness or ignorance. Such cases involving railway workers and abortionists are covered in other chapters. In 1867 a Newcastle herbalist was tried for manslaughter after a pregnant young woman died. The herbalist had treated her with raspberry leaf tea and cayenne pepper, which was considered 'as good as nothing'. She had a rare condition, however, known as *placenta previa*, which killed her. The herbalist was found not guilty as evidence showed he had sent for an experienced midwife when he realised the problem and the chance of death had been very high at any rate.

A BATTERY OF ASSAULT & BEATINGS

Victorian towns and cities were places where violence was endemic, but it was often associated with alcohol, just as it is today. There were some interesting if perhaps difficult to explain variations, nonetheless, between places. When the *Essex Standard* conducted its own analysis of the crime figures for 1864–65, it found that prosecutions for being drunk and disorderly varied from town to town in East Anglia: the worst was Cambridge, at 3.95 per 1,000, followed by Colchester on 2.82 and Norwich on only 1.07.

The public house was a venue for many a battle. On 20 December 1838 there was an incident in the tap room of the Rodney at Little Baddow. Mr and Mrs Perkins were enjoying a drink when three male members of the Lucking family came in and demanded a share of Mrs Perkins' beer. When she refused they trod on her toes, then assaulted her husband and 'srip't and paid him', as they put it. The defence argued that Mrs Perkins was such a powerful woman that she was capable of holding them all off on her own, and had started the trouble by throwing the Luckings out and had knocked down her own husband. The magistrate Rev. Brooksby listened to all this, fined the oldest Lucking 2s 6d, and then 'advised Perkins in future to send for his beer and drink it by his cottage fire-side'.

One week in Rochdale produced several typical cases. In the first, John Nicholson was drinking at the Freemasons' Arms in the town when the landlord told him to be quiet and pushed him – Nicholson fell over. When the land-lord's back was turned, Nicholson struck him over the head with a poker. This was adjudged to be wounding without felonious intent, and punished with six months. Two other cases resulted in fourteen years transportation for Larky Farrell, who also used a poker, and for James Brennan, a tailor; Brennan had spent a day drinking with a friend, who he fell out with over a trade issue. He pulled an iron bar out of his coat and struck his erstwhile friend on the head. It is per-haps difficult to see, at this distance, why Nicholson escaped so lightly.

Random attacks were often associated with drink or untreated mental illness. For example, in November 1847 passengers on a train to Ely were attacked by a man with whom they were trapped in the compartment: he suddenly leapt up

Fights in public houses were commonplace. This one in Birmingham in 1867 ended in one death and several injuries.

and attacked, 'making the blood flow in all directions'. He had to be locked up in a cage overnight. A 'respectable man', he was said to suffer from 'determination of blood to the head' after drinking a glass of brandy and was fined only £5.

Another type of assault occurred when people simply fell out, often over injudicious words. At Dukinfield in 1874 a collier named Henry Winstanley was passing up the street when he saw Mary Lee at an upstairs window. He abused her and called her 'a foul name'. She happened to be holding a poker which she – apparently – accidentally dropped so it nearly hit him. Winstanley then burst into the house, ran upstairs and assaulted her, kicking her with his clogs until she passed out. The jury found him guilty and recommended mercy, though the judge could not see why and gave Winstanley five years.

'Words' also caused a dispute between two workmen in 1884. At Haigh, Lancashire, Peter Finn was annoyed when his colleague John Duffy made a comment about his wife, so he hit him with a hammer; in this case the judge did consider the man to have been provoked and, since he had already spent two months in gaol, let him out as 'bound over'.

Attacks on the police were treated very seriously; one committed by Andrew Goulding in December 1883 in Liverpool was especially grave. Goulding was a friend of Michael McLean, wanted for murder, and helped his friend to resist arrest by stabbing PC Carson several times – thrice in the chest and once in the arm so badly that it shattered his bone. Goulding got fifteen years for stabbing and wounding.

Women were often the victims of assault, so the 1853 Act for the Better Prevention of Aggravated Assaults upon Women and Children was an attempt to confer greater protection with up to six months in prison. The Summary Jurisdiction (Married Women) Act of 1878 allowed women to go to court to get separation or maintenance from an abusive husband.

Assaults on women made up a high proportion of all assaults, though social factors influenced the pattern considerably; a study found that they constituted almost half the assaults in Lambeth from 1850–53, but only about a fifth in Westminster.[14] However, convictions for aggravated assaults on women and children declined between 1861 and 1891.

In 1853 John Mason was cohabiting with Elizabeth Ekins at Kimbolton, Bedfordshire, when they fell out over who owned a shawl. The couple decided to split up, and Ekins wanted to take the shawl: 'If it's yours take it, but I'll mark you for this,' he said. He went to a chemist, bought some 'oil of vitriol' and threw it in her face three days later, burning and scarring her. He received twelve months hard labour for this casual act of violence.

In March 1865 Richard Lockyer, who had 'not been known to do a twelve month of work', was brought to court for assaulting his wife. He had stabbed her in the hand, beaten her and thrown a kettle of boiling water at her. The police gave evidence that this was typical behaviour for the couple and that once Mrs Lockyer had leapt out of the window to escape her husband's violence. It was reported that 'he had sent her out in the streets for prostitution, and he frequently knocked her down in the street, but she refused to charge him'.[15] Lockyer was given five years penal servitude, but the woman had already endured ten years of misery and enforced prostitution.

In another domestic incident, Robert Morris hit out at his wife with a brush at their home in Manchester in July 1867. Unfortunately she was holding their baby at the time, and Morris hit the baby's head and killed it. He was given a four-month sentence for manslaughter, it being considered that he had suffered 'much provocation'.

It was not always the woman who was the victim. At Stockport on 21 January 1883 Sarah Hadfield had been having a drinking session with her father and another man; they had consumed fourteen pints when her husband returned home and complained that there were only potatoes for dinner. She threw the poker, point first, straight at him, penetrating his brain 'which oozed out of the hole when the poker was withdrawn'.[16] Not being aware that he was dead, she then threatened to cut his throat with the carving knife. For this she was given a twelve-month sentence.

Notes

1   *Sixth Report of Inspector of Prisons*, Parliamentary Papers vol. 4, 1842, p. 228.

2   *The Times*, 13 January 1865.

3   His name was variously reported as M'Naughten and MacNaughten.

4   *Indian Journal of Psychiatry*, 2007, pp. 223–4.

5   *Brighton Gazette*, 14 March 1844. By 10 April, *The Times* reported subscriptions to the family of a substantial £1,200.

6   Solomon was, in the context of the times, rather surprisingly Jewish; he had eleven or twelve children and had been police chief in Brighton for twelve years.

7   Maynard's firm became famous for its wine gums.

8   *The Times*, 3 March 1882.

9   Berkshire Record Office, *Broadmoor Revealed: Edward Oxford*, 2009.

10 Although Elliott was the son of a major-general, his own rank was considered of doubtful provenance.

11 At least one book cites Mirfin as being convicted of murder, but repeated articles in *The Times* indicate that he was the victim and the inquest was held on his body.

12 *The Times*, 2 October 1840.

13 Edward Walford, *Old and New London vol. 5*, London, 1878, p. 378.

14 G.K. Behlmer, *Child Abuse and Moral Reform in England 1870–1908*, Stanford, 1982, p. 13.

15 *The Observer*, 12 March 1875.

16 *Manchester Guardian*, 4 February 1883.

4

Burglars & Other Robbers

It is commonly said – though nonetheless true – that Victorian society regarded crimes against property more seriously than crimes against the person. It is certainly the case that some property crimes, such as burglary, were treated as amongst the most serious offences of the era. Various forms of theft were capital offences until the immediate pre-Victorian era, including housebreaking until 1833 and stealing Post Office letters until 1835. These offences continued to carry heavy punishment, yet street robberies were punished less severely despite the occasional fear of 'garrotters'. Even minor crimes against property seem, to modern eyes, to have been punished disproportionately compared to crimes of violence; for example, in 1842 a man was sent to Bodmin gaol for nine months for stealing potatoes worth only 9*d*.

We can take one specific type of theft to illustrate this point. Theft from the Royal Mail was considered very serious, almost an offence against the state. The prevalence of robbery from the Royal Mail meant that it developed an effective detective system of its own from an early date, although sometimes this only worked after a whole series of losses. This happened at Rugby in 1845, when the postman William Garratt was arrested after a series of letters containing money had gone missing. Letters containing marked coins were posted to Rugby and their contents found in Garratt's possession. However, the administration of the post in the town was found to be a complete mess – some of the sorting was done by the sister of one employee, whilst the town carrier often opened the sacks on the way from the station so he could sort the newspapers. Garratt, who earned 7*s* a week, was known to spend over 3*s* a day in public houses!

Punishment was severe. In 1847 a sorter at Plymouth was given seven years transportation after being found with two half crowns removed from a letter and sentences remained heavy throughout the mid-Victorian period: George

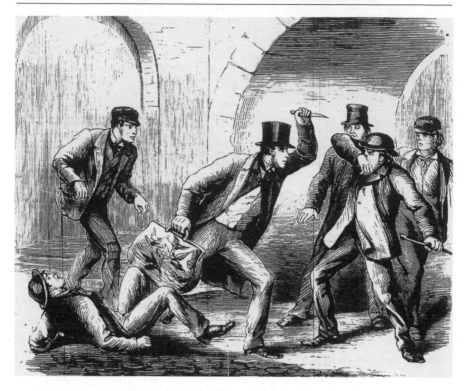

During the garrotting panic, gentlemen started to arm themselves before going out – but this man must have been foolish to venture out with such an interesting bag!

Dawe of Bristol got four years penal servitude in 1856 for stealing two letters. He had been suspected, so a lookout was posted who could see into the sorting office toilet, which was where Dawe would go to remove the contents of letters. By 1900 sentences were lighter: the postman at Cerne Abbas and Sydling St Nicholas in Dorset was only given a year's hard labour despite having 300 stolen letters in his house.

BURGLARY: THE PROPERTIED CLASSES' NIGHTMARE

Burglary, because it involved breaking into a person's house, attracted long sentences. Although theft statistics show some decline in the second half of the nineteenth century, the figures for housebreaking and burglary did not and were thus 'at a proportionately greater level'.[1] Since burglary was heavily punished, organised gangs often resisted arrest with violence, especially the 'professional' gangs who had much at stake. A burglar was therefore more likely to be 'desperate' and several famous murders of the period were committed during burglaries.

The ultimate nightmare was perhaps a gang of desperate criminals breaking into your house in the dead of night. This happened at South Wraxall Manor, Wiltshire, in 1841. Miss Awdry was awoken by noises and terrified by a knock at her bedroom door. Three men burst in with clubs and threatened her: 'If you keep quiet we will not hurt you, but if you make a noise we will beat your brains out!' They took money, gold chains and ornaments, and then threatened to murder her if she did not find them more valuables. They scared her elderly mother, put a pistol to her head, and were angry when she proffered two £5 notes which could be easily traced. They consumed the family's wine stock straight from the bottle, before leaving through the window. Miss Awdry thought there had been at least five in the gang – far too many for the family or their female servants to handle.

This was no professional gang, but a starving group motivated by desperation who repeatedly made their economic needs clear to Miss Awdry. After the crime they fled, but one was arrested at Southampton, another near Wellington and a third in Smithfield with Mr Awdry's watch still in his possession. Nine were arrested for robbery and four for receiving stolen goods. Six were tried at the assizes and one pleaded guilty. All except one were found guilty and transported for life.

The 'Frimley Gang' became notorious after one of their burglaries led to a murder. They hit the headlines in 1850 when four of them broke into the parsonage of Rev. Hollest, the curate at Frimley Green in Surrey. Hollest had left his door ajar in case his sons woke, and two of the masked burglars were able to surprise him in bed. At first the clergyman thought it was his sons playing a trick. While one held back his wife, another shot him in the stomach, and then they ransacked the house. Hollest died two days later.

Three of them were soon arrested in Guildford, having been seen in the village at the dead of night by a maid in another house. Magistrates were told that Hiram Smith was the leader, and this was not a case of balanced reporting: 'His face, which wears a sallow unhealthy hue, is extremely forbidding in its expression, the features having that sharp prominent character which marks the rogue, while the doubtful and hesitating glance of the eye indicates a disposition at once cunning and irresolute.'[2]

Surprising then that Smith was never found guilty of the murder, no evidence being offered at his trial. Three were tried for murder at Kingston where the judge explained they had been acting together for a felonious purpose and therefore were all guilty of a capital offence; the jury found Levi Harwood and James Jones guilty and they were sentenced to death, though the jury agreed with the prisoners that they had not fired the shots. Before their execution, Jones confessed that he had helped in the burglary and had watched Levi Harwood fire the shot.

The gang was known to have been large and prolific. It had included seventeen members, who had all been arrested by April. One of them, James Hamilton, confessed and gave a detailed account of their criminal lifestyle – sleeping in tents on common land while looking for suitable houses to rob under the leadership of John Isaacs. They robbed a house at Kirdford, then met up at Holmwood Common before robbing an old farmer near Horsham. They robbed the Misses Kennard near Haywards Heath, a shop at Hambledon in Surrey, the Old Pie public house near Groombridge, and Miss Farncombe's house near Uckfield – a wide area. Isaacs was caught at Frome with a ring from the Farncombe house still in his possession. It was thought that the gang had stolen £1,500 in a two-year period, shifting their goods through Guildford and then to London to be sold.

Some of these gangs used the new railways to plot burglaries out of their geographical area and to escape rapidly afterwards. In October 1885 one such gang used trains to raid Netherby Hall near Carlisle, using a ladder to get in upstairs. They stole valuable items from Lady Graham's bedroom. A hue and cry was set up but the gang hid out in railway wagons until, being spotted, they opened fire and escaped towards Carlisle. They now had a problem, for in such an area opportunities to catch a train back to their homes would be difficult, so the gang split up and headed for different stations. PC Byrnes was shot dead by one of the gang near Plumpton station. Others climbed on to a goods train, terrifying the guard who wrote messages on pieces of paper and threw them out at stations. The train was halted at Tebay, where railway staff captured two of the men, with a third being picked up at Lancaster; a valuable diamond star was found under a railway bridge in the River Lune near Tebay station. Another gang member was arrested in London.

At the trial it was explained how the killer, Martin, had shot dead Inspector Simmons at Romford in January 1885, in a similar burglary using the railways. Three of the gang were hung for murder at Carlisle in February 1886. The hanging was conducted by Berry, with a well-spoken assistant identified as Charles Maldon. This person was 'uncovered' as actually Sir Claude de Crespigny of Champion Hall, Essex, leading to substantial press and parliamentary interest in the acceptability of 'amateur hangmen'.

Some country house jobs were literally 'inside'. In 1874 at Friskney, Emma Tutty, a 16-year-old servant, waited for her employers to go out before signalling with a lamp. An 18-year-old lad then faked a burglary by prising a window with a knife, then the girl handed out wine, cakes and cigars through the window – all witnessed by the police. Both got six months in prison.

In 1879 the rectory at Edlingham in Northumberland had some unwelcome visitors in the middle of the night. Rev. Buckle was roused by his daughter and attacked the two burglars with his sword, but they shot him in the shoulder. Two local poachers, Michael Brannigan and Peter Murphy, were arrested and

A gang of burglars, who had been robbing a church, are captured by police in Woolwich, 1867.

sentenced to penal servitude for life. The combination of poaching and burglary in a rural area was an unusual one, but these men knew how to cross gravel silently with sacking strapped round their feet. They had served nearly ten years when Charles Richardson and George Edgell confessed that they were actually the guilty men. Brannigan and Murphy were released on licence and subsequently given £800 compensation, whilst the two newly confessed thieves said the gun had gone off accidentally in the scramble and received five-year sentences. The police inspector and two of his assistants who had gathered evidence on Brannigan and Murphy were then themselves arrested and put on trial for conspiring to obstruct and prevent the course of justice. In a sensational case, they were acquitted and Justice Denman made very clear that he thought Brannigan and Murphy were actually guilty. It was implied that all four knew each other as habitual poachers and, following an incident in which Sergeant Grey had been shot, possibly by Richardson, some clever bargaining had taken place.

The houses of the gentry in London were also favoured targets. In March 1875 burglars broke through the roof of a house in Piccadilly and stole a number of items while the servants were at supper. Servants commonly followed very set routines which made burglary easy, especially when 'the family' was away. Breaking through the roof was also quite a common tactic.

Another example was the raid on Alderman Wilson's house in Brighton in 1844; the gang gained access to the roof through the empty house next door and then pretended to be workmen come to repair the roof. The maid let them into a bedroom so they could melt lead and, as the robbery was discovered, they were able to escape out of the door of the neighbouring house – from which 'they were allowed to pass without hindrance or question by the stupid crowd'.[3]

Some burglars were surprisingly inept. Clement Fletcher broke into William White's house at Stansted Mountfichet in 1863 but it was too dark to find anything, so he got a pie from the pantry and settled down to wait for dawn. At 7 a.m. the next morning White came downstairs, saw the cellar door open and fired his pistol, causing Fletcher to leap from the sofa and run out into the back garden. This was surrounded by a high wall, so he could not escape; he was captured at gunpoint. He was accused of burglary and attempting to murder a servant girl by firing a shot.

Two other amateurish burglars attacked Miss Whitwell's house in Spalding in 1868; she was woken by a heavy blow to the body and as she leapt out of bed a burglar grabbed her by the throat. She was still able to scream: 'Hear me, blessed heavenly Father.' The men ran off, but a passing policeman was astonished to see anyone running at 2.15 a.m. and they were arrested. They were given a year's hard labour each.

Commercial premises were also likely to be raided. Two men, freshly released from Bodmin gaol in January 1843, decided to rob Wallis' carpentry shop in the town. They stole an iron bar and a pickaxe from a nearby quarry, then broke in through the roof tiles to steal £30 and a 'Bank of Elegance' £50 note. They then walked to Liskeard, hired a gig to drive to Devonport and tried to buy clothes. The tailor refused to accept the 'flash' £50 note but at this point the law caught up with them and one was captured. The other walked back into Cornwall and pleaded for food and money at the house of another man he had been in prison with; however, while he slept in until 10 a.m. the next day, the man's wife went out and got the police.

In February 1880 thieves stole £2,000 of jewellery from a shop in Nottingham, which they broke into by removing the tiles from the roof, and in September 1883 a gang stole the entire meat stock from a butcher's shop at Hockley Heath near Birmingham. This was an organised gang including William Biddle, styled the 'King of the Poachers', who had only just returned from seven years in Australia, and Samuel Longthorne, a cab proprietor who provided the transport. The butcher, Satchwell, traced the goods to Longthorne's depot, and when the gang attempted to drive off with all the meat he clung to the back of the cart. They tried to get rid of him by stabbing at his hands and head, but were arrested by the police who were also on the trail.

CRIMINAL GANGS & CRIMINAL WOMEN

Small gangs commonly worked crowded places in Victorian towns and cities, such as marketplaces and railway stations, with the big stations in London and Manchester being especially notorious. In the former, Ludgate Hill was described as being 'infested with thieves'.[4] The range of results was vast, from the 1s 10d stolen by two men at Ardwick station, Manchester, in 1845, which cost them their liberty, to the Countess of Dudley's loss of jewels said to be worth £50,000, which disappeared whilst she was catching a train at Paddington in December 1874.[5] The Prince of Wales had been passing through the station and had caused such a commotion that the Countess' jewel case was momentarily left on the pavement by one of her maids, and the diamonds were lost forever. During one of the trials of 'Madame Rachel'[6] in 1878, this notorious fraudster claimed to have some of the Dudley jewels, but the Countess' maid did not identify them.[7]

The theft of Lady Ellesmere's diamonds by a gang of habitual street thieves, Attwell, Saint and Witty, was also famous. On 22 January 1856 Lady Ellesmere caught a cab to the railway station through the streets of London with her dressing case strapped to the cab roof. Witty and Attwell followed the cab through the streets and Witty managed to cut the straps so the case fell off into the street with a bump, causing the horse to rear. They were able to make off with the case and caught a cab themselves to the shop of Edward and Anne Jackson. There were suspicions at the time that cab drivers were often in league with thieves and took side streets to make robbery easier.

The thieves did not at first realise what they had got – the case had been so carelessly stowed on the cab that they assumed the jewels to be paste – and, by his own account, it was only Attwell that queried their true status. Some diamonds were sold off for as little as 5s before the advertising of a large reward made the gang realise what they had stolen.[8] By this stage the diamonds were 'hot', but they managed to offload an emerald and diamond necklace 'to a Jew in Bishopsgate Street' for £300.

Attwell was already in prison for a different crime at Springfield, Chelmsford, by December 1857, when he made a full confession. As a result, he was given only an additional six months. Edward Jackson was charged with possession of stolen goods and, with a previous felony against his name, was sentenced to ten years transportation.

What was the value of Lady Ellesmere's loss? The Jacksons were charged with possession of stolen clothes worth £15,000 and at the trial the diamonds were said to have been worth £16,000, but it is unclear whether this covered all of the jewels.

This case shows clearly that networks existed for handling stolen goods. One was run by a qualified barrister, James Saward, later immortalised in a stage play

An apparently relaxed scene in a Victorian pub, but it includes a woman with a black eye, giving her baby a 'drop', and small children trying the beer they have been sent to get for their parents.

as 'Jim the Penman'.[9] Saward's speciality was handling stolen blank cheques. From his base in Walworth, Saward ran a sophisticated operation. For example, he received two blank cheques stolen in 1855 from an ironmonger in Spitalfields; he then visited the premises to assess a 'safe' amount to claim off them, deciding on £150. When cheques were stolen off a solicitor, he went through an elaborate process to get the signature to copy. They often used entirely innocent young men to take the cheques to the bank. Eventually, two of the gang, Henry Atwell[10] and a man named Hardwicke,[11] were caught after attempting to pass cheques in Norfolk and sentenced to life transportation, whilst Saward went into hiding in central London. On 17 November 1856 he was named in court by Edward Agar, the train robber, as having passed on gold worth £1,600, causing some amusement when it was reported that he was a barrister. In March 1857 he was sentenced to life transportation for forgery. The financial cost of Saward's crimes cannot easily be computed, although contemporaries guessed: 'The bankers of London have been saved £10,000 a year since he was convicted,' wrote Mary Carpenter, the social reformer.[12]

Another trick was to use a pretty young girl to get the unwary into situations where they could not easily be rescued. A young photographer at Weston-super-Mare in 1897 should have been suspicious when 14-year-old Leah Tregonning asked him to go for a walk with her, and he should not have been surprised when he was accosted by Edward Jennings, a young man of 20, who claimed that Leah was his wife and that he had been insulted. The two young people then demanded money from the photographer, beat him and took a number of small objects. They were soon arrested for a similar offence in Bristol and Leah was sent to a reformatory for five years; Jennings, who had previous convictions, was given six months hard labour and twice sentenced to be flogged with the cat o' nine tails – twenty-five times on each occasion.

Women featured often for minor thefts. Of thirty-one women in Liverpool gaol in 1843, twenty were there for minor thefts, one for a major theft and seven of the rest for vagrancy. What they had stolen tells its own story: clothes, a bonnet, bedding, boots, shoes, sheets and flour. Often such crimes were committed by domestic servants – in 1867 10 per cent of larcenies committed by women were by servants.[13] At the Central Criminal Court in 1851, the recorder complained that the punishment of servants for larceny was often disproportionate and came close to excusing their crimes on the basis that their very low wages subjected them to excessive temptation.[14] Women who stole more could pay as heavy a penalty as men: in Wymondham, Norfolk, a 69-year-old woman received four months for stealing three bushels of turnips and a 25-year-old got ten years transportation for housebreaking. There were far fewer convictions of women than men, but there were still some habitual female criminals; Mary Ann King, convicted for larceny in 1859 in London, had had fifty-two committals in the previous three years and over 200 since 1847, including offences connected to drink, disorderly conduct and prostitution.

CHILDREN

Early in the era children could often be found in gaol, either because their mothers had been sent there or because they had been sent there themselves. Children were most often in trouble for minor thefts, though sometimes they committed felonies. Three examples from Preston in 1842 illustrate this. In the first case, two boys – recently released from gaol – returned to the court house during the sessions and stole from the people there; one of them had had a factory job, but his father had taken him away as the pay of 3s a week was considered too low. In the second case, a 7-year-old illegally pawned a shirt he had stolen, his mother having taught him about pawnshops. In the third case, two boys, aged 10 and 12, stole a watch from a barge and sold it to buy fruit, cakes, clogs and a cap.

In 1846 an 11-year-old girl in Dorset stole a bucket; for this she spent thirty-eight days in custody and was then given a week in gaol, costing the county £10 11s 8d. Gradually sense prevailed, and it was understood that this sort of punishment for petty offences was both inefficient and ineffective.

The greatest attention was paid to families of 'criminal children'. In 1843 it was reported that one family of six children, aged between 10½ and 18, had all been in prison; of them, the youngest had twice served a sixty-day sentence, the 13-year-old had been sentenced to seven years transportation after the sixth offence, and their mother 'has all the appearance of being a worthless character'.[15] Coming from a bad family or a bad neighbourhood was seen as influential; staff at Liverpool gaol in 1842 analysed child prisoners' backgrounds and found that eighty-six had bad companions or were from a 'low neighbourhood', eighteen were destitute, fourteen suffered 'ill-usage' at home and the remaining thirty-five had no apparent cause for having 'gone wrong'.[16]

Children especially populated the local lock-ups and cells. On the night of 11 August 1843, the Sheffield lock-up had ten children in custody, including one of 9 and four of 13–14 years. Most were there because of vagrancy or 'garden-robbing', the inspector noting that 'juvenile delinquency is much on the increase from the number of unemployed children in Sheffield'.[17] A few miles up the road, Wakefield gaol had fifteen between the ages of 12 and 16. Nearly half the males imprisoned for theft in Brighton in 1859 were boys;[18] the local campaign for industrial schools was an attempt to tackle this problem.

Attempts were made to separate juveniles from adults in the criminal system; the Juvenile Offenders Act of 1847 provided that children under 14 should be tried in separate courts. Mary Carpenter, a social reformer, proposed reformatories

A street boy, typically without shoes. Children such as this were easily tempted into criminal activity.

Driver's reformatory aimed to turn out smartly dressed boys with an improved attitude to work.

and opened her own at Kingswood near Bristol in 1852.[19] She wrote a book on juvenile delinquency in 1853 and opened a girls' reformatory in 1854. The Reformatory Schools (Youthful Offenders) Act of 1854 and the Industrial Schools Act of 1857 placed the reformatories and industrial schools on a legal footing, though they were at first funded with only 7s a week per child. This two-tier system aimed to separate actual offenders from those at risk of offending. Magistrates could now send children of 7–14 years to industrial schools which were, in effect, a type of secure boarding school, often just on the grounds of vagrancy, while offenders could be sent straight to reformatories which began to receive state funding. By 1858 there were forty-seven certified reformatories in Great Britain, with 1,184 inmates.[20]

In 1861 legislation was amended so that children could be sent to the schools for begging or wandering, if they committed an imprisonable offence but were under 12, or if their parents declared them to be out of control.

Reformatories provided for children who had committed several offences. Hundreds of children were sent away to them, though it was not automatic: in 1868–69 Liverpool magistrates sent 403 to industrial schools and 139 to reformatories.[21] Some reformatories were afloat, such as the training ship *Cornwall* in the Thames; two men, both known to be drunkards, were ordered to pay 1s 6d a week for the upkeep of their sons on the ship in 1871. The Redhill Farm School was run by the Royal Philanthropic Society and opened in 1849; it reported that 40 per cent of its pupils subsequently emigrated and only 1.2 per cent re-offended in England.[22]

The reformatory and industrial schools system gradually removed children from the criminal justice system, replacing institutions such as Parkhurst, which became a prison for boys in 1838 and was used mostly for those awaiting transportation. In 1854 there were 536 boys there, but in 1863 it became a prison for women.

STREET CRIME & 'GARROTTERS'

The Victorian era was not the heyday of the highwayman and crimes of the road were usually more prosaic. Although the 'garrotter' was a figure of urban fear, the dark country lanes were just as dangerous, if not more so.

The most common street criminal was the pickpocket or the 'footpad', later the 'garrotter'. The latter depended on disabling the victim, and picking on a drunk was a good start to this process. In 1841 Mr Coupe of Haigh, near Wigan, spent the evening in a pub at Scholes and then walked 2 miles home at 1 a.m. Near his house he was 'rushed' and knocked down by a thief who then fell on him, kicked him in the head and rifled his pockets. He was carried into the

The Home Secretary, Sir George Grey, was satirised by *Punch* for his lack of a response to the garrotting crisis.

nearby Von Blucher pub – still open – and propped up to recover. One man went out to find his hat for him, at which point another man came in, wearing his hat, and sat by the fire. Despite his injuries, Coupe was so angry that he attacked his attacker, James Bilton.

Baron Watson, speaking at Worcester Assizes in 1842, suggested that crimes of robbery in the Black Country followed a set pattern: 'Nearly all the cases … happened in this way. The lower class of people resorted to public houses and beer-houses, and on coming out at night, they were followed, knocked down and robbed.'[23]

The term 'garrotter' came to be used for robbers who disabled their victim, most commonly by attacking from behind.[24] It referred to a Spanish method of execution which was actually suggested as an alternative to hanging by the Marquis of Westmeath in 1847. The term came into common use in the early 1850s, there being a series of such attacks in Birmingham in 1851, in which the garrotte was used as a noose around the neck or a trap for the feet. In early 1853 the term was used to describe an attack on the road between Brigg and Wrawby in north Lincolnshire, in which a man was robbed of £2 – two men were given fifteen years transportation for this.

Over the next few months there were reports of 'garrotte robberies' in Liverpool, Leeds and Hull; in the latter case a man died, but those arrested were acquitted. In Liverpool, an Irish cattle dealer was garrotted and lost £145 in gold; the two who were tried said they had found the man drunk at a lamp post, but were transported for fifteen years.

Garrotters attacked William Nichols of Nottingham at Newmarket in 1860, netting £1,800. There was a particular reaction to the attack of James Pilkington, the MP for Blackburn, in Pall Mall at about 1 a.m. on 17 July 1862. He was knocked to the ground and robbed by 'garrotters' and the attack was debated in the Commons. Trollope used the incident in *Phineas Finn*. The Security from Violence Act of 1863 authorised flogging, with those over 16 getting up to fifty strokes and up to twenty-five for those of more tender years.

The popularity of the term 'garrotte' declined after the 1860s and it is rarely mentioned from then onwards. The severe punishment and the use of flogging were considered to have been effective deterrents against the garrotters.[25]

Popular events such as race meetings attracted pickpockets and the two brothers arrested at the Hertford Agricultural Show in 1875 would not have been unusual. The older brother already had six previous convictions and a sentence of seven years penal servitude, so this time he was given ten years; his brother only got fifteen months hard labour. The Harwich Naval Review of 1863 persuaded London criminals to try their luck on the trains and two conspired to rob a man of his watch at Witham station; they were captured, however, after one had been chased into the toilet – he received three months hard labour. Markets were also

Crowded events like race meetings offered rich pickings for the pickpocket and casual thief, but the police knew this and could be vigilant. In this scene from 1875, a thief is being arrested on the way to Doncaster Races.

a dangerous place for losing your money and at Grimsby market in 1868 a young woman lost her purse; Sergeant Allbones was watching the crowd and arrested Henry Fielding and John Watson. They both had long coats with the bottoms cut out of the pockets, so they could pick others' pockets while appearing to have their hands in their own.

Serious difficulties were encountered from gangs of London criminals who flocked into Brighton for the holiday season and the annual races, especially once the railway had opened. In 1842 *Brighton Gazette* readers received worrying news: 'We are credibly informed that many of the "swell mob" have arrived in Brighton during the past few days. We warn our readers, therefore, to be on their guard as to their pockets and their houses.'[26] In January 1845 it was reported that a gang of 'London pickpockets' were in town.

London had a problem with youths robbing and intimidating, following bands of marching men as they came into the West End in 1867–68.[27] Some northern towns became notorious for similar intimidation by young men known as 'corner men' or 'scuttlers'. They gathered at street corners, making demands on pedestrians; 'they make it their regular business to assault and plunder all such unfortunate stragglers as may happen to come within their reach'. The problem was worst in Liverpool. In 1874 Richard Morgan was kicked to death by three young men after refusing to give them 6*d* for liquor; John McCrave, 20, and Michael Mullen, 17, were hung for this, and a third man was reprieved from the gallows at the last minute. Liverpool police were criticised for conniving with the ruffians, and only a couple of days after the executions, a seaman who had refused to hand over money 'for a drink' – because he had none – was beaten and stabbed in the arm by a gang. The recorder, J.B. Aspinall, blamed the police for tolerating behaviour in the 'lower' parts of the town that would not be permitted in the better areas.

In 1898 a gang of four, all 20 or under, were arrested for beating a man who refused to give them 'something to smoke' in Portland Road, Liverpool. He was knocked about, robbed and stabbed in the back. Sentences were up to seven years penal servitude. As Elizabeth Stanko has demonstrated, the 'corner men' were particularly reviled in the press for their cowardly behaviour and un-English use of boots or clogs as weapons.[28]

OTHER CRIMES OF THEFT

Shoplifting was certainly common in Victorian times, though perhaps more difficult. It was necessary to distract a shop assistant and to be able to organise a rapid escape, passing the goods quickly to someone who had not been into the shop. Those who did not manage this could be punished heavily in the early part of the period, even if young. William Kitchen, a 'hardened urchin' who stole a loaf of bread from a shop in Coggeshall, Essex, in 1839 was given ten years transportation.

In March 1870 Catherine and John Mullen were part of a gang who stole linen from shops by pretending to want babies' hoods. Both were caught in Hulme, Manchester, but the other members of the gang got away. John Mullen received one month in prison and five years at a reformatory; the woman got two months. Another trick was to distract the shopkeeper with other purchases and then steal something else. In 1854 Robert Sewards bought half a pound of butter from a shop in Corby Glen, but also stole a pound of mixed coffee; the shopkeeper had his suspicions and Sewards was sent to gaol for a month after the coffee was found at his house.

New national systems for delivering items and goods were open to abuse through pilfering. Theft from the Royal Mail was severely punished but railway companies also carried goods and parcels so were open to abuse, especially by their own staff. For example, in 1848–49 the Lancashire & Yorkshire and London & North Western Railways were victims of organised theft involving a group of goods guards who changed parcel labels to redirect them to a receiver named Wood, based in Manchester. Two of the LYR guards were arrested in Huddersfield in September 1849, by which time the company had already paid out £500 in compensation for losing parcels sent from that town. William Stones, a former Lincolnshire PC, joined the railways as a watchman at Sheffield Victoria station in 1867; he was arrested only three months later and his house was found to hold blankets, rugs, boots, slippers, shawls, lard, cheese, cutlery, crockery, pipes, a hare, a duck and a revolver – all pilfered. Even worse were the eight LYR employees who stole a cask of brandy at Miles Platting; they spent the evening drinking until two passed out and one died of alcohol poisoning.

Notes

1   Clive Emsley, *Crime and Society in England 1700–1900*, p. 32.
2   *The Times*, 19 October 1850.
3   *The Times*, 25 February 1844.
4   *The Railway Press*, 23 August 1889.
5   The maid, Isabella Scott, later reported at the trial of Madame Rachel that they were worth about £9,000. The reward offered was £1,000.
6   See Chapter 11.
7   *Manchester Guardian*, 12 April 1878.
8   *The Observer*, 6 December 1857.
9   He is also mentioned in *Finnegan's Wake*.
10   Note this is a different person to the Attwell of the Ellesmere case.
11   Hardwicke, at least, was a convict returned from Australia.
12   Mary Carpenter, *Our Convicts*, London, 1877, vol. 1, p. 13.
13   England and Wales crime statistics for 1867.
14   *The Times*, 7 January 1851.
15   *Report of the Inspector of Prisons*, Parliamentary Papers, 1843, p. 26.
16   Ibid., p. 27.
17   *Report of the Inspector of Prisons*, 1843, p. 166.
18   Graduate of London University, p. 105.
19   This remarkable woman was also vice-president of the Ladies' National Association for the Repeal of the Contagious Diseases Act (see Chapter 10).
20   *Journal of the Royal Statistical Society*, vol. 22, p. 536.
21   *The Times*, 18 September 1869.
22   *The Times*, 13 September 1883.
23   D. Phillips, *Crime and Authority in Victorian England: the Black Country*, p. 250.
24   For an account of the issue, see P. King, 'Moral Panics and Violent Street Crime', in Godfrey, Emsley, et al., *Comparative Histories of Crime*, Cullompton, 2003, p. 53.
25   The recorder's charge to the grand jury in February 1881 made this connection.
26   *Brighton Gazette*, 10 February 1842.
27   J.H. Winter, *London's Teeming Streets*, London, 1993, p. 63.
28   Elizabeth Stanko, *The Meanings of Violence*, London, 2003, p. 27.

5

Crimes of Poverty & Desperation

WORKHOUSE PROTESTS

The introduction of the workhouse system following the passing of the Poor Law Amendment Act in 1834 prompted many riots, some of them spectacular.

In rural areas, the seasonal nature of farm work made the 'indoor system' particularly inappropriate, but the Poor Law was introduced in rural southern and midland counties first. At Shepshed, a number of rioters were arrested and convicted, but others then burnt down the wheat and oat stacks belonging to the father of one of the witnesses. As the structure was introduced in the north, the trouble moved there too: in northern towns such as Bradford and Halifax, military support was required.

Commissioners visited each area in turn, so trouble could be predicted and the authorities learnt to prepare. Rioting started in 1835, but continued sporadically throughout the rest of the decade, including in Cornwall in 1837. There was a notable riot at Kingsbridge in Devon, where a pauper attempted to assault the workhouse governor and 150 people forced entry into the workhouse. At Wakefield and Huddersfield, street fights connected to the election were linked to anti-Poor Law campaigning by Richard Oastler. At Oldham the commissioners billeted three or four soldiers at each of the public houses in advance of the commissioners' visit in December 1837.

In May 1838 the meeting of the Huddersfield guardians was interrupted by anti-Poor Law guardians and campaigners. They were tried for unlawful assembly and rioting but acquitted on the grounds that, as guardians themselves, they had the right to be there. In November 1838 James Acland decided to hold a lecture in favour of the Poor Law at the Philosophical Hall in Halifax, prompting the anti-Poor Law group to hold one opposite. The result was a predictable riot and substantial damage to the hall.

Meanwhile, in Bradford, several ratepayers were charged with refusing to pay rates and the overseer of the parish of Langfield, near Todmorden, refused to meet obligations on the grounds that the Poor Law Union was illegally constituted. The response to this in November 1838 was to send two constables from Halifax to seize £5 worth of property from his house, but they had barely arrived when a bell was rung and hundreds of mill workers and railway navvies surrounded the house. They forced the constables out, and stripped them down to their stockinged feet, before giving them a beating.

Over the next few days there were repeated riots, including a systematic tour of all the guardians' houses around Todmorden, wrecking and smashing. Particular hatred was visited on Todmorden Hall, the home of a magistrate and guardian, which was set on fire. A few days after this, 150 special constables were sent to the mill of Fielden & Co. at Lumbutts and arrested forty of the workers on charges of rioting. John Fielden, a noted radical, offered to stand bail for all of them. Dragoons were kept at Todmorden for months. Bradford experienced two waves of unrest – five were arrested for conspiracy to procure arms and for riot, and similar numbers at Sheffield.

In December 1838 one of the opposition leaders, Joseph Stephens, was arrested at Ashton under Lyne for 'having used violent and inflammatory language' at a meeting at Leigh, Lancashire, and Hyde, Cheshire. This was the result of calculation in London, with a government agent sent to identify the best action and two officers from Bow Street arriving to support the action of local magistrates. Stephens was tried in a state prosecution at Chester in 1839 and sent to prison for eighteen months.

At Halstead, there was a series of fires on premises belonging to Poor Law guardians with damage worth about £10,000, so a reward of £700 was offered. After eleven fires, Abraham Rayner, who helped on the local fire engine, was transported for life.

One of the most famous riots was at Stockport in August 1842, which coincided with the Chartist troubles across the north. In Stockport 20,000 men were out of work and the 'indoor relief' system was pathetically unable to cope. Rioters, including many from Hyde, attacked the workhouse and stole 672 loaves. This riot was also characterised by hatred of the Tories and the Church of England. Fourteen were arrested and sent for trial. Francis Warhurst was identified as a leader of the riot and charged with stealing £2, 2 tons of bread, 20lb of meal, 20lb of mutton, 20lb of cheese and the governor's dinner! Warhurst was transported for life.

THE KENT 'MESSIAH'

'The last week has been distinguished by one of those strange and calamitous outbreaks of fanaticism which occur in this country about once every century,' wrote the *Oxford Herald* in June 1838. What had happened in Kent was one of the most serious breakdowns of law and order in early Victorian England; although instigated by John Thom's mental disorder, the fear and desperation among his followers was linked to the Poor Law. The worst events took place in a part of Kent where the building of the hated Herne workhouse – which had no external windows – was already attracting condemnation.

John Thom came from Cornwall, but in 1832 stood for election in Canterbury where he gained a credible number of votes. However, by 1833 he was in the county lunatic asylum after being convicted of perjury for claiming to have witnessed events linked to a smuggling incident, and he stayed there for four years. After his release, he took to calling himself grandiose names such as Sir William Courtenay and the King of Jerusalem. Having left the care of his father, he went to live with a farmer named Francis at Boughton in Kent.

His interests turned increasingly to religion and the workhouses. By 1837–38 he was touring Kent, speaking to farm labourers, claiming that he would call down fire from heaven to destroy all the workhouses. He also began claiming to be the Messiah himself, and developed stigmata.

On 27 May 1838, near Ospringe, he gathered supporters who were prepared to march with him around the countryside. According to the *Maidstone Journal*, 'many of them were so miserably and awfully deluded as to believe that he had the power of rendering them incapable of receiving injury from sabres or bullets'. The next day he led his followers on a march around the district of Dunkirk with, at their front, a pole with a loaf atop – a sure sign that this was, at least in part, a 'bread riot'. At the end of the day he took off his shoes and declared, philosophically, 'I now stand on my own bottom'.

Under the Master and Servant Act[1] farm labourers were not free to simply wander off and join a march, so the Boughton constable, Mears, was sent out to make an arrest. He was accompanied by his brother Nicholas to Bossenden Wood, where Thom shot Nicholas Mears and tried to stab the constable. The local gentry then gathered on horseback and sent to Canterbury for help from the 45th Regiment. A hundred soldiers arrived under the command of Major Armstrong, but Thom formed his followers into a defensive square with a female trumpeter and a flag at the centre.

Unwisely, a Lieutenant Bennett decided to try to talk to Thom. There was a skirmish and one of Thom's men shot Bennett dead. Constable George Catt was also killed. Armstrong determined to bring the crisis to an end and launched an assault, clearly calculating that the death of Thom would cause the others to give

The death of 'Sir William Courtenay' portrayed rather differently, suggesting brutality by the authorities.

up. Thom was one of the first to die, but in the fight that followed six were killed outright and another four mortally wounded. There were twenty-nine arrests.[2]

Thom's 'campaign' had caused fourteen deaths but local newspapers reported that many expected the dead to come back to life. The matter was serious enough to be discussed in the House of Commons in June 1838, but the government did not use the treason or sedition laws to execute those arrested; two were transported for life and six received only a year's hard labour. A source of popular interest was how William Coachworth would give evidence as he had had his teeth and tongue shot out. There was greater national interest in how a man with a known mental illness had been released into the ineffective care of his father with such devastating impact. Subsequently, the area of Dunkirk was made into a new parish with its own church and a school to make the inhabitants less prone to fanciful strangers. Poor education was widely seen as a contributory factor.

WORKHOUSE CRIMES: THE INMATES

The workhouse was very much like a prison, but paupers who caused trouble could be sent either to the 'refractory ward' – or to prison. Some preferred the latter and went often. What could happen was summed up in a *Times* editorial in 1866:

The paupers' favourite mode of evincing a mutinous spirit is the destruction of their own clothing, but there is a pleasing variety in their attempts to annoy those who have sheltered them. Some obstinately refuse to get up in the morning, others become violent on being requested to break stones or pick oakum in return for their night's lodging; others, especially the women, assail the superintendents and matrons with the foulest language out of pure malevolence.[3]

When oakum-picking was introduced to Braintree workhouse in March 1839, some of the paupers refused to do any; ten were sent to Springfield gaol for two or three weeks each. The same guardians had years of trouble with Catherine Breed in 1839–41; her offences included disorderly conduct, destruction of a workhouse blanket, refusal to work and suddenly becoming a Roman Catholic and demanding a priest. Tramps who stayed overnight were expected to work for their board and lodging, but often objected; in December 1839 James Melson refused to work and made a speech encouraging others to refuse as well. He was rewarded with fourteen days in prison. In 1847 a tramp at Louth was given a week's prison sentence for refusing to break stones.

In 1842 the paupers at Stockport refused to work more than seven hours a day on stone-breaking, following the Poor Law Union's decision to increase the hours to ten. The magistrates sided with the paupers, telling them that they could stop work at 4 p.m. rather than the 6 p.m. the guardians expected. In February 1846 the workhouse of St Saviour's, Southwark, expected 'casual paupers' who came for the night to do four hours work the next morning in exchange; a group of fifteen refused so were hauled before the magistrates, complaining that the food had been very poor. The magistrates were rather lenient, considering that not all of the paupers understood the rules, sending only three to the house of correction – whereupon the others asked to be sent too, as the food was good![4]

The destruction of clothing was a common protest. In 1844 the magistrates court at Woolwich could not cope with the 'immense' number of paupers sent there for this offence, to the extent that the dock overflowed with them on a daily basis. They were packed off to the gaol at Maidstone for a week at a time, but the magistrates found that the paupers genuinely had a grievance: the clothes were infested with vermin. At the Guildhall in London, the court had to deal with a dozen cases in a week in 1867 from the West London Union workhouse alone.

There were also the occasional bouts of violence. In 1857 Mary Corney, of the Whitechapel workhouse, threw her shoe at the chairman of the guardians and hit him on the head, and then assaulted one of the officers; taken to court, she was fined £5 with £2 costs, though it was a puzzle as to where the money would come from. At Lambeth in 1868, a young woman misbehaved during the chapel service and was ordered to the refractory ward. She refused to go and a struggle developed, soon attracting forty other women who used 'violent and disgusting language'; a riotous situation developed. The police were called in but paupers tried to block the doors. Four young women were taken to court and given fourteen days in gaol with hard labour; they laughed — what was the difference?

WORKHOUSE CRIMES: THE OFFICERS

Workhouses were beset by periodic scandals concerning abuse of their position by officials or cruelty to paupers. Perhaps the most infamous case of the time was that of Mr Drouet's establishment at Surrey Hall, Tooting, which looked after up to 1,400 pauper children on behalf of the various London Poor Law unions. Tooting was meant to be a pleasant rural site and Drouet had over 50 acres at his disposal, but the children were crowded together and fed on a largely liquid diet of gruel, with meat occasionally. Cabbage also featured. Near Surrey Hall was an open sewer which took most of the waste from Tooting: 'several stagnant ditches are reported as being exceedingly dangerous'.[5]

At the new year of 1849, cholera broke out at Surrey Hall. Within a week 52 children were dead and 229 ill. As the scandal broke, the various Poor Law unions began taking their own children away from Tooting, thus actually risking the spread of cholera across London. The Poor Law Board, the main national authority, disagreed with the removal policy but the local Poor Law guardians clearly felt under great pressure as the press started to condemn the practice of 'farming out' children for only 4s 6d a week. It is difficult to say exactly how many died; 156 died at Surrey Hall alone[6] and around 40 at various locations across London. Four died in Park House, Hackney, which was being used after its owner, Mr Nelm, had been poisoned in suspicious circumstances, but another property owner refused to have any relocated children. Press estimates of a total of 200 therefore seem possible.

The deaths were investigated by several different coroners' juries. In late January, the coroner's court at Holborn set the pace by finding a verdict of manslaughter against Bartholomew Peter Drouet, stating that the children had died 'from neglect, and insufficiency of food and clothing'. The coroner was Dr Thomas Wakely, an MP and also editor of *The Lancet*. Drouet was committed for trial on a manslaughter charge, but acquitted on a technicality over the medical evidence, which was widely criticised. Apart from the 156 children who had died at Surrey Hall, no one else in the district had died at all, and popular opinion clearly felt that neglect had contributed to the deaths. The trial was heavily criticised by Dickens, whilst Drouet himself died in 1849. Dickens wrote:

> While it has released the accused from the penalties of the law it has certainly not released him from the guilt of the charge. And every one must rejoice that a trade which derived its profits from the deliberate torture and neglect of a class the most innocent on earth, as well as the most wretched and defenceless, can never on any pretence be resumed.

There was also routine mistreatment of inmates by workhouse staff. James Miles, the master of the Hoo Union workhouse in Kent, developed a sadistic streak. In 1841 Miles was charged with cruelty and indecent assault on four girls and a boy; he habitually flogged them, sometimes whilst naked, one girl telling the court: 'I was flogged by Mr Miles on the bare lower part of my person ... I received about thirty stripes each time on my back.' The Hoo Union guardians refused to sack him, but eventually had to find a replacement after he was given a six-month prison sentence. More sexual allegations were made against the master of St Pancras workhouse, John Eaton, in 1851. He was said to have forced sexual attentions on a 16-year-old girl, Eliza Smith, who was ill, and rewarded her with 2s. The guardians investigated and the case went to the magistrates, but some of the pauper witnesses changed their stories to favour Eaton amidst accusations of 'tampering'. When the case was suddenly dropped by the magistrates, following expectations that Eaton would be committed for trial, there was uproar, but it did little good to Eliza Smith who was dead before the row had subsided.

There was also scandal at Brighton, where the workhouse was a den of passion. The assistant matron, Celia Brown, was charged with concealing a birth after a dead child was found there in January 1858. In June 1859 its governor had to resign as 'familiarities of a very indecent and flagrant character had taken place between the Governor and the Infant School Mistress'. It was found that the governor was already father to two children by workhouse inmates.

Another workhouse master in trouble was Henry Ramsbottom, who ran the workhouse at Knutsford. Word reached the workhouse one night in December 1873 that John Reece of Sale was ill with typhoid. A 'van' was sent to get him to take him to the workhouse infirmary, reaching Sale about 11 p.m. The van driver returned him to Knutsford, in the early hours, called out the porter and nurse, and then went home. No one bothered to get Reece, and next morning he was found dead in the van. The doctor refused to issue a death certificate, considering he had died because of neglect, and Ramsbottom and the porter were charged with manslaughter, although charges against the latter were dropped.

The jury acquitted Ramsbottom saying it was carelessness not a crime, but they criticised the porter and the nurse. Meanwhile, the chaplain at Knutsford gaol had written anonymous letters to the newspapers about how the work-house was run, as a result of which he was sued by the clerk to the guardians, who won a derisory £10. Ramsbottom also sued, it having been reported that he had beaten six boys and sent them to the gaol in 1871 and had often been intoxicated.

The Poor Law was often a victim of the corruption of its own officials due to lax management. The collector for the City of London Union, Charles Manini, and a clerk defrauded it of £22,000 between 1843 and 1856. The master of Liverpool workhouse defrauded it and then escaped to New Zealand in 1884, although the long arm of the law was able to reach him even there and bring him back for a visit to the prisons. At Chorlton in 1858 the master devised a clever scheme for making a profit by declaring the workhouse to have more inmates than it really had, which he tried to cover up by pasting new pages into the account book. However, most often the fraud was small scale, such as at Halstead, where the workhouse governor, Twose, bought peas ostensibly for feeding the paupers but instead sold them for his own profit. He also stole cutlery, glass and furniture from the workhouse and was given two years hard labour.

BEGGARS & VAGRANTS

Vagrancy Acts were passed in 1824 and 1838; the former effectively outlawed sleeping on the streets or in an outhouse, and begging. The offence of vagrancy was also used for people who failed to support their own children so they became chargeable to the parish. To avoid being a vagrant, a wandering person ought to have some visible means of support – the 2,000 vagrants passing through Chelmsford each year were thus said to contain a large proportion of 'match sellers' who were actually nothing of the sort.[7] The Pedlars Acts of 1871 and 1872 meant that any pedlar needed to have a certificate. They could be arrested for sleeping rough, so most towns had 'low lodging houses' where a bed could be found for 3d; these in turn became associated with crime, so they were regulated by the Common Lodging Houses Acts, 1851 and 1853, which allowed for police inspection. In Dunstable, which was plagued by beggars since the nearest tramp ward of a workhouse was 5 miles away, the authorities put up their own hostel and charged 2d a day.

In 1839 there were estimated to be about 18,000 convictions a year for offences of vagrancy.[8] John Hawsley was arrested for sleeping in an outhouse at Great Hale in 1893, telling the court that he was 'homeless and friendless' – but he was still given two weeks hard labour. Huge numbers were arrested: the Lincolnshire police arrested 522 beggars in 1867 and 1,800 tramps in 1893 – half of their arrests.

Outcast women sleeping in sheds in Whitechapel; however, this was an offence under the Vagrancy Act.

Tramps were suspected of being thieves, and indeed some were. In June 1846 George Woods was sentenced to seven years transportation after stealing four umbrellas as he passed through Billinghay; he had a record of similar offences. Evidence submitted to Parliament in 1839 about the rural constabulary contains an astonishing variety of vitriol about tramps; the City of Lincoln gave its explanation of crime: 'The depredations committed by persons residing within the city bears very small proportion to the whole. The crimes and depredations are principally perpetrated by trampers who prefer the licence of the low lodging houses … to the discipline of the workhouse.'

Collecting money under false pretences was a common ruse. Other evidence submitted in 1839 alleged that fake beggars kept their decent clothes at common lodging houses, and went out by day 'almost naked' in special sets of deliberately poor ones in order to earn more from begging; one 'negro man' in Kent was said to earn enough this way, and by 'singing and dancing', to keep two women. In 1841 Charles Morley made a tour of selected West End addresses equipped with a letter saying that he was deaf and dumb, and had lost a hand in a railway accident; Baroness de Rothschild gave him 7s, but he was spotted by an officer from the Mendicity Society and sent to prison for a year. He said, however, that he had tried to work; he had applied for a job with the Mendicity Society! In January 1884 a woman at Ulceby, near Grimsby, answered her door to a man who told her he was the county court bailiff collecting a 'distress rate' to help the poor during the hard winter. Of course he was no such thing and, when discovered, received four months hard labour although he had only managed to collect 2*d*.

Others used various tricks to try to gain admission to a house in order to steal, going from door to door around the countryside. At Gate Burton Hall near Gainsborough, in 1847, a servant girl answered the door to two women; one of the women started having a fit, turning black in the face, falling to the floor and going rigid. This trick might have proved a powerful distraction or a source of free food and drink, except another servant recognised the woman and the trick from when she had worked at a house near Newark.

In January 1855 a woman went round fenland villages, such as Moulton and Weston, with three dishevelled children. As people were going to church, she would fall down in a fit and the children would beg for alms. After playing this trick once too often, she fled as soon as the constable was called.

The Mendicity Society was set up in the 1820s and employed its own inspectors to watch individual beggars and bring cases against them. In 1840 one inspector found William Wakefield, in central London, pretending to be dying from a desperate illness in order to beg money. When the inspector tried to stop him, Wakefield decided to make a fight of it but was subdued and sent to prison for two months. The Mendicity Society also used other tactics to solve the problem and was serving over 40,000 meals a year during the 1860s. The society

The humble reality of Victorian crime: this scene shows those arrested over night being taken from the cells to the police station to face charges – a mixture of old women and boys.

received some negative publicity, however, when its begging letter clerk, who had worked for thirty-two years on a low salary, was dismissed without provision at the age of 70 and himself became a beggar in 1866.

Street musicians, often Italian, could create problems. In 1842 Lord Frankfort was summonsed for having damaged an Italian organ, having previously taken out cases against the musicians. Now it appeared his patience had snapped, and he had damaged the organ with his fist and had to pay damages. Under the Metropolitan Police Act, a householder could request a musician to move on or he would be subject to a 40s fine – but he had to give a reason; there were many complaints that this was rarely enforced, and the result was torment for householders. Other sufferers tripped up because they were not a householder or forgot to explain their reason. Charles Babbage, the mathematics professor credited with developing the idea of the computer, was an ardent campaigner against the musicians who disturbed his studies at Manchester Square in London, and brought many cases. In 1857 an Italian was fined 20s or two weeks in the house of correction, but he was only one of many. After a gunfight in a bar in London's Italian quarter in 1899, the courts were alarmed to hear that rival organ grinders carried revolvers.

POVERTY & FAMILY LIFE

Failure to support your family was criminal under the Vagrancy Act and the Poor Law. Two particular offences included deserting a family, leaving it chargeable to the parish, and refusing to work, thereby also becoming a charge on the parish. The Maintenance of Wives (Desertion) Act of 1886 meant that husbands who left their families destitute could be summoned to pay £2 a week, if they could be found.

In 1841 Robert Kershaw of Blatchinworth, Lancashire, left his wife and children; details about him were circulated around the country, but meanwhile his family cost the Poor Law guardians £40 to maintain. Kershaw was eventually caught near Bury and sent to prison for three months. Irishman Patrick Gill abandoned his wife in Ireland and went to live in Stockport, where he set up with another woman. Three years later, in 1856, his wife found out where he had gone and arrived at his door asking for support. He refused this unless she came to live in a *ménage à trois*, which she declined. She went to the workhouse for funds and Gill was arrested, being released only after he had repaid the Poor Law funds. Punishments varied, but were typically between twenty-one days and six months in prison.

The first specific law to protect children's welfare was the 'children's charter' of 1889. The Prevention of Cruelty to Children Act gave police the powers to enter

A scene from the bread riot in Oxford, 1867.

a house where children were being badly treated. In 1894 the act permitted children to give evidence in court and allowed for mental cruelty as well as refusal to provide medical attention.

The National Society for the Prevention of Cruelty to Children's 'inspectors' brought many prosecutions. The society originated in Liverpool in 1883 and then the London Society for the Prevention of Cruelty to Children was formed in 1884, changing its name to the present one in 1889.[9]

A typical case was that of 3 Rossall Street, Pendleton in Lancashire, which was visited by a NSPCC inspector in 1894. He found the four Williams children in 'a deplorable state ... clothed in rags and covered in vermin'. They lacked both food and attention, and a baby of 11 months weighed only 8lb – the 'normal' weight being given as 22lb. Catherine Williams was given a month hard labour. In the same house the inspector also found another three children belonging to an unmarried couple in an equally poor condition; in this case the woman was given two weeks hard labour.

The price of food was a hugely important topic for the very poor so bread riots were a long-established tradition, although they were in decline by the 1800s. There were occasional outbreaks, such as at Torquay in May 1847 and Wells later the same year, when 'navvies', objecting to bread being 1d for a 4lb loaf when the price of wheat had fallen, paraded the streets with clubs and smashed the windows of bakeries. There were a number of riots in Devon in 1854, sparked off in Exeter, where twenty-eight arrests were made and sentences of about six months were handed out. A Tiverton farmer who tried to exploit the market by selling inferior wheat was attacked by women, who scattered his grain around the marketplace. In Deptford, in 1867, rioters broke open the bakers' shops and took bread. A large crowd, 600 strong, supposedly of the unemployed, marched to a relieving officer's house and demanded bread; when they were refused they paraded the streets and smashed their way into Mager's bakery, whilst other bakers handed out their stock to avoid being assaulted. A local resident complained that it was not a bread riot at all, since they had ignored other types of food shop and were nearly all young people. Mounted police arrived to drive them away.

Another bread riot in Exeter in November 1867 created astonishment: 'a bread riot is so much a thing of the past in our own times that the report of the disturbances at Exeter is calculated to create no little amazement.'[10] In fact, the riot at Exeter was generally seen as a copycat following a genuine bread riot in Teignmouth, events in Exeter being further sparked by bad feelings about firework displays. The same week there were similar problems in Oxford, where several thousand gathered in the streets and smashed bakery windows, demanding lower prices. On 10 December the same year there was a bread riot in Hoxton, but the baker drove the crowd away at knife point.

REGULATING THE POOR & THE DIRTY

During the Victorian era there was a developing understanding of the connection between poverty, dirt and disease, although germ theory was not well understood until the later part of the era.

Common lodging houses, in which scores of the nomadic poor stayed overnight, were disliked because they were believed to harbour disease and crime in equal measure. The 1851 and 1857 Common Lodging Houses Acts provided for them to be registered and subject to police inspection. The act caught a number of unscrupulous entrepreneurs, but few less likely than Mr W. Booth of the Salvation Army, who was fined 20s in 1890 for running an unlicensed lodging house in London's Whitechapel Road which accommodated 100 men. Inspectors were appointed by the commissioners of police in London, and Thames Court handled many cases involving 'Irish houses ... in dirty localities'.[11] In 1852 a man named Sullivan rented a house for 5s a week and charged 6d per week for men and women to sleep there – eleven in one room alone. He was fined 2s, but was told it would be £5 next time.

The labouring poor were meant to be protected by the first Factory Acts and then the Mines Act of 1842. Some of this legislation was very specific, covering only coal mines and textile mills, but was widened later. The 1895 Factory Act provided for the reporting of cases of 'necrosis of the jaw' following publicity over the plight of the women at the Bryant & May match factory in Bow. The subsequent discovery of a number of unreported cases, including six deaths, led to a successful prosecution of the firm and fines of approximately £15 for each offence. Similar legislation, such as the Factory & Workshops Act, limited the hours of work for younger people, backed up by powers for the magistrates to issue fines.

'Nuisances' were considered in prosecuting anything thought to be a risk to health under legislation such as the Nuisances Removal Act. Many people kept pigs in towns, and authorities across the country tried to eradicate this nuisance; a case in Salford in 1849 centred on twelve pigs kept on a midden and led to the formation of a pig-keeping protection society, but the magistrates imposed strict conditions. When a London pub landlord, Edward Keymer, was brought before magistrates in 1873 to explain a foul and offensive cess pool on his property, he said that it had been there 'for a century'; nevertheless, he was served with a court order and charged costs.

The law could be difficult to apply at times. In 1854 attempts to stop barges discharging 'filth' from a 'manure manufactury' near The Adelphi in London were frustrated because no one had authority over nuisances in the river. A new Nuisances Removal Bill was brought forward in 1855. In 1856 the courts of Manchester held a campaign against 'smoke nuisances' from the city's mills; fines of 40s were ineffective because they were cheaper than fixing the boilers – plus the owner of the Oxford Road twist mill simply offered to make a deal with the corporation to pay £104 a year and 'be left alone to make as much smoke as his neighbours'.

Notes

1   This act of 1823 restricted an employee's ability to simply leave his job, though it was also meant to confer certain limits on the employer too.

2   The 'Battle of Bossenden Wood' has been well covered by historians and E.P. Thompson called it the 'last peasants' revolt'. Early accounts focused on John Thom's mental illness, but later versions have rightly emphasised the strength of popular discontent in the area associated with the Swing riots and the hatred of the New Poor Law. See P. Rogers, *The Battle of Bossenden Wood*, Oxford, 1961 and R. Barry, *The Last Rising of the Agricultural Labourers*, Oxford, 1990.

3   *The Times*, 27 January 1866.

4   *The Observer*, 15 February 1846.

5   *The Observer*, 7 January 1849.

6   *The Observer*, 21 January 1849.

7   *The Times*, 26 December 1839.

8   Ibid.

9   A history of the NSPCC can be found at www.nspcc.org.uk.

10   *The Times*, 7 November 1867.

11   *The Times*, 21 August 1852.

6

Crimes of the Countryside

The countryside suffered periodic bouts of hardship caused by weather or economics. Crime was often linked to poverty such as sheep stealing, which 'peaked during years of exceptional hardship for the agricultural labourer'.[1] Arson and the smashing of threshing machines were common during the Swing riots, although crimes against machinery continued sporadically long afterwards: few were as sophisticated as the attack on a 'mowing machine' at Eckington, Sheffield, in 1870, which involved fixing pieces of iron in the ground.

A witness to a Parliamentary Committee said that the main causes of poaching were starvation and the workhouse: 'I might as well be caught under the game laws and get committed for two months hard labour as to go to the union house.'[2] Poaching was almost entirely a male occupation: in 1872 only twelve in over 8,000 poaching convictions were against women. Crime and protest often blended together, so that poaching and the Swing riots rode on the same tide.[3] Conviction rates were low, partly because of the protection afforded by tight rural communities. A letter to *The Times* in December 1849 reckoned that barely a quarter of incendiaries were detected but convictions were worse amongst the many who committed 'fuel stealing, barn robbing, sheep and poultry stealing'. The author thought as few as 1 per cent of sheep-stealing offences were followed by a conviction. For good measure, he included the 'cunning women' who procured rural miscarriages.

ARSON & INCENDIARISM

'Incendiarism' was one of the classic 'rural crimes' of the 1800s. Although George Rudé referred to it as belonging 'to that shadowy realm between crime and

Dorset agricultural labourers and their families; despite this scene, life for such people could be harsh.

protest where it is often no easy matter to tell the two apart',[4] arson plainly was a crime of protest, though its motives were never personal gain. Friedrich Engels wrote of the agricultural labourers that 'their favourite weapon in the social war is incendiarism'.[5] It attacked the property of the rich and exploited their weakness – farmers could never fully protect their crops once harvested or farm buildings. The spread of 'Lucifer matches' from 1830 was blamed for a new outbreak of incendiarism, though arson purely for entertainment seems also to have been common.

Outbursts of incendiarism clearly occurred in line with agricultural depression. T. Makesheff has shown that Herefordshire had 'peaks' in 1843–44 and again in 1849, whilst similar patterns have been identified in East Anglia where there were eighty-five committals in Norfolk and Suffolk in 1844 alone.[6] David Jones has identified 250 fires on the property of farmers, clergymen or Poor Law guardians in Norfolk and Suffolk between October 1843 and December 1844.[7] The Suffolk Assize in July 1844 dealt with twenty-eight people charged with arson, with fifteen convicted. During this time, the Ipswich Journal noted that many labourers 'were openly exulting in the progress of the fires'. In Essex, there were particular outbreaks in 1843–44 and 1848–49.[8] Over 200 fires were reported in Suffolk and nearby counties, which others attributed to the hatred of the workhouses.[9] Sir Edward Bunbury thought 'the fires prevailing in the eastern counties [were] symptoms of a smouldering and dangerous discontent'.[10] Some blamed the spread of incendiarism that year on the campaigns of the Anti-Corn Law League.[11] The eastern counties suffered renewed outbreaks in the early 1860s and 1874 as farm wages came under pressure.

Incendiarism carried the death penalty until 1837, after which it was only a capital offence if committed against an inhabited house. The rate of conviction was very low; for example, of 101 reported attacks in Herefordshire between 1800 and 1860, there were only five convictions.[12]

Incendiaries were often young: of the 245 committals in 1843–44, 40 per cent were aged 15–25 and a further 39.8 per cent aged between 25 and 40. They were almost always men, with only twenty-one women represented, and poorly educated: 28 per cent were illiterate and 58 per cent only able to read and write 'imperfectly'.[13]

There were two types of incendiary: the embittered local or the angry wanderer. The latter included many itinerant labourers who sought work or solace whilst tramping the country lanes, and who were always the first suspect when a haystack went up in flames. An example is John Ranger, who set fire to several barns and stacks around Eastry in Kent during the early autumn of 1839 – the classic time for such an outbreak. Ranger had been a casual labourer on several farms and, with the harvest work drawing to an end, took his opportunity to gain revenge. He was caught and transported for life. In September 1865 casual labourer Margaret Moore was dismissed from her work at Cradley Hall Farm near Bromyard at 3.30 p.m. By 4 p.m. eight stacks and some machines were on fire. In October 1866 three tramps set fire to a stack at Wyke Oliver Farm near Weymouth, possibly because they had been refused work.

Convicting the 'embittered local' type of incendiary was difficult. William May, who caused £150 worth of damage to his employer's farm at Rayleigh in 1839, had worked for the same man for twenty years but was bitter after being convicted of stealing rabbits; he was transported for life. A rare double conviction was of two labourers named Tudor and Trillo, who set fire to 900 faggots of wood in Herefordshire in 1845. They were already suspected of destroying 500 bushels of wheat the previous September, and footmarks back to their cottage indicated some evidence this time. Tudor was known to have a grudge against the farmer and they were both transported for life.

An unusual 'embittered local' was John Grundy, himself a farmer, who destroyed £1,000 worth of stacks belonging to John Moxon at Lullington, Derbyshire, on 29 December 1858. Grundy had spent the whole day drinking, leaving one public house with a bottle of gin at 10.30 p.m. but then turning up at another at 11.30 p.m. When he got home at 2 a.m. he told his servants that he had set fire to Moxon's property as 'he thought to do me an injury'; he then offered the servants £10 each to keep quiet.

Revenge attacks often occurred in spates. For example, in 1853 there was a series of fires around Tiverton in Devon connected with the spread of threshing machines. The most serious was at Culmstock, where fire in the barns and stables spread to the farmhouse. Several threshing machines were destroyed in this out-break which, typically, occurred in the autumn.

In 1863 a series of fires in east Yorkshire were attributed to a group called the 'Wolds Rangers' who were periodically hauled up before Norton magistrates. The day the last one was said to be in court, in October 1864, fresh fires broke out. Within a week there were huge fires in the district at Scawby, Lincolnshire and Minsthorpe, though children were also suspected. A fire at the Warren, near Barton upon Humber, could be seen 50 miles away and caused damage worth £4,000. However, it was often impossible to say for certain that such fires were deliberate.

The farmers' greatest fear was the concerted campaign, often hidden behind a local wall of silence. Around Bradfield, near Sheffield, this was so bad in the early 1880s that insurers refused to cover farm property; two were arrested but there were no convictions, and another twenty fires broke out in 1881.

Sometimes the 'angry wanderer' could be blamed for a series of local fires which, one suspects, were opportunist revenge attacks. In September 1872 there was said to have been 'complete panic' around Stockton after at least seven fires were started in less than two weeks – at the worst time of year. A tramp, John Smith, was caught in the act of lighting a fire at Egglescliffe; he then admitted to at least one other, but was not believed. The government offered £50 reward and even deployed plain-clothes police.

The popularity of the new safety matches from the 1860s meant they were often accessible to children. In the dry autumn of 1865 a series of fires in Northumberland were attributed to carelessness, although the one at Burnopfield was the fault of a 6-year-old boy who had experimented with his father's matches. In the winter of 1883 a haystack at Addington, near Sevenoaks, mysteriously burst into flames and young Percy Okill, the son of the Sevenoaks police superintendent, was seen running away from the fire. When caught, he claimed that he was himself chasing the real culprit – a boy in a red scarf! Family connections could not save him, however, and he was fined.

One of the worst offenders of this type was Timothy Burch, a Norfolk herring hawker aged 24. At a Kenninghall pub on 21 June 1850, Burch questioned a blind man who had returned from being transported to Australia, and was particularly interested in the amount of rations fed to prisoners. He then declared that he would get himself transported for incendiarism and told everyone that he had set fire to stacks at Tebbingham only a few weeks before. Burch bought Lucifer matches from a little shop and began to set fire to the first stacks that he came across. Men had just started putting one fire out when another one broke out at

Bressingham, and then another – until Burch had lit seven fires marking his route home. Convicting him was easy since he had left a clear trail from one stack to another, even breaking through the hedges in between. He was rewarded, as he wished, with life transportation.

POACHING

The crime of poaching has been romanticised, but in reality it was a hard struggle, often to the death. David Jones has calculated that twenty gamekeepers were murdered in 1843 and 1844 alone.[14] Parliament was told that forty-two had died between 1833 and 1843.[15] Poaching divided society: 'Squires and labourers take very different views of the criminality of poaching,' said J. Fitzjames Stephen.[16]

The Game Act of 1671 defined who was allowed to kill game. The Black Act of 1723 made poaching a felony, with the possibility of capital punishment. Between 1760 and 1820 there was an explosion of game legislation with over fifty new game laws.[17] By a law of 1800, gamekeepers and their servants could seize suspected poachers without a warrant, following which they could be forced into the navy; this sort of legislation made it much more likely that violence would be used in the woods at night. Then Ellenborough's Law of 1803 made it a capital offence to resist arrest.

The Game Law Act of 1831 eased the situation regarding day poaching but people could still be transported for night poaching. The concept of a crime being treated as vastly more serious by night than by day was perhaps a relatively novel one, but was due to the Night Poaching Act of 1828 where the House of Lords had amended the level of punishment. However, anyone with a £5 certificate could deal in game, and the inevitable market forces resulted.

The consequence was a huge wave of poaching prosecutions; in 1844–45 forty poachers were transported and it was reckoned that committals under the game laws reached 4,500.[18] Being a gamekeeper was also a risky occupation due to the heavy penalties on poachers. In 1839 keeper W.H. Hornby was left to die from loss of blood at Billington, Lancashire.

On the night of 4 August 1843 there was a furious altercation at Alsager Bank in Staffordshire following 'continued nightly depredations' of the game. Two poachers were surprised by a pair of keepers, but fought back. Keeper Vaughan was thrown to the ground – allegedly – by a strong man named Spilsbury, who knelt on his chest and proceeded to strangle him almost to death. The other keeper, Beech, had a cutlass but this was taken off him and rammed through his skull so that he died; it later took three men to pull it out again. Vaughan survived to give evidence against two men, but both were acquitted as identities were said to have been in doubt.[19] Cooke, owner of the Wheatley Park estate, complained that 'the poacher is favoured at both York [the assizes] and the sessions, and every pains are taken to convict the keeper'.[20]

In 1843 poachers from Liverpool shot Lord Derby's keeper who died from his wounds. Five were tried in December 1843, with one turning Queen's Evidence – the very one who allegedly had cried 'Blast them!' just before the shots were fired. All four of the others were sentenced to death, but the Home Secretary commuted the sentences of three and only John Roberts went to the gallows. Despite this, the following year was one of the worst for murders of gamekeepers, such as Lord Coventry's keeper at Croome Court in February 1845.

Though poaching attracted young men and habitual poachers, it also involved some who were hungry. One of the most infamous cases of this is described by Hopkins in *The Long Affray*: an unemployed labourer and father of five was committed for stealing pheasant eggs which he had picked up under a hedge at Henham Park, Suffolk. As this was a first offence, he was sent to prison for three months hard labour. However, the landlord of the family's cottage, fearing non-payment of rent, seized the furniture and the wife set fire to the cottage in despair. She went to prison for a year and the children were placed in the workhouse, where they became a charge on the parish ratepayers. The head keeper, William Easy, shot himself in a covert on 30 August 1844 and the assistant keeper shot himself the following day in his own cottage, more or less in front of his wife and children. A third keeper was 'placed under restraint owing to the alarming excitement ... created in the man's mind'.[21] Though Hopkins implies the deaths were due to the imprisonment of the poor man, *The Times* of 3 September suggested it might be due to the depredations of Earl Stradbrooke's prize pheasants by poachers.

From about 1844 there was strong opposition to the game laws. A sporting landowner, Sir Harry Verney, was disgusted when a labourer was given thirty-two weeks in gaol for picking up an empty snare – which he had not put down: 'any system which renders our rural population criminal must be highly injudicious to the best interest of society,' he said.[22] In 1872 an Anti-Game Law league was founded.

The police were never capable of controlling poaching, and in some areas avoided doing so – they left it to the army of keepers. The Chief Constable of Worcestershire in the 1850s thought that he had 815 professional poachers within his area.

Around Sheffield and Doncaster miners often went poaching and the Wheatley Park estate suffered especially during economic depressions.[23] When a group of unemployed mill workers were given three-month sentences for poaching at Blackburn in 1862, it provoked a serious riot.[24]

With juries increasingly inclined to give the benefit of doubt to the poachers, keepers continued to die, but even the judges took sides. In 1859 at Bishop

A poacher, trapping rabbits, is surprised by a gamekeeper.

Burton, Yorkshire, poachers beat a keeper to death after he shot their dog; the judge at York ruled that the keepers had used excessive force themselves and changed the charge to manslaughter. Forty Staffordshire keepers were injured just in 1860–61.[25]

The result was the Poaching Prevention Act or 'Night Poaching Act' of 1862. This was also a failure; according to Hopkins, 'far from stamping out the poaching war, it re-fuelled it'. After a keeper was beaten to death at Silverwood near Rotherham in 1865, the coroner observed: 'I think it is a pity that any man should lose his life for the sake of game.' The jury at the trial agreed and found only for manslaughter.[26] Even the historian of the criminal law, J. Fitzjames Stephen, noted in 1883 that assault on a policeman was punishable with two years penal servitude, but it was seven years for assaulting a keeper. Stephen's view was perhaps shared by the judge who heard the case at Nottingham after the death of a keeper, Daykin, at Clifton in June 1893; the defence argued that the poachers had been afraid of the keepers' dogs and had shot the keeper instead by accident – the other keeper had then shot one of the poachers in the legs. In summing up, the judge made clear his views, blaming those who allowed 'keepers to go out armed with firearms and other weapons, and accompanied by savage dogs, for the purpose of protecting game [which is] eminently calculated to lead to violence and bloodshed'.[27] Not surprisingly, the poachers were found not guilty of murder.

The vast majority of poaching convictions were for minor offences. The Report of the Game Law Committee, published in 1874, noted that convictions in England and Wales in 1871 included 7,713 for day poaching, 429 for night poaching, 26 for illegal buying and selling and 721 for offences under the Poaching Prevention Act; the total showed a fall of about 10 per cent from the previous year.

Game caused trouble between landowners and neighbours. In 1858 a small-holder, Thomas Birkett, shot dead a game watcher, Watmore (or Watmough), at Barnby in the Willows near Newark. Birkett told the policeman: 'I did shoot him; it's a bad job.' Birkett had often placed rabbit traps on his own land but men from the adjoining estate of Mr Thorpe repeatedly came on to his land and sprang them. Attempts by Birkett to prosecute them were thrown out by the magistrates, as a result of which 'much indignation was felt and expressed in Newark'. A game watcher from Thorpe's estate had also been charged with manslaughter after a supposed poacher had been shot only a few weeks earlier. Evidence was produced to show that local bets had been laid that Watmore would be dead in six months – and now he was. When Birkett's case reached Newark magistrates, they closed the doors against press and public. At Nottingham, Birkett was found guilty of murder largely on the basis of having made many threats, though the Home Secretary then recommended life transportation rather than execution. When his sentence was read out, Birkett shouted: 'And so much for the game laws!'

In 1891 two keepers, William Puddephatt and Joseph Crawley, were killed at Aldbury, Buckinghamshire. The defence argued that the keepers had violently assaulted the poachers but two men, Rayner and Eggleton, were found guilty of wilful murder and Smith of manslaughter. Eggleton's defence, that he had been knocked out in the fight and was insensible at the time the keepers died, did not save him.[28] The Home Secretary was questioned in the Commons but said that the keepers had been killed 'with frightful violence inflicted with formidable weapons'. Mr Conybeare complained that executing Eggleton would mean that he had been 'judicially murdered by the right honourable gentleman', the Home Secretary. But The Times thought that Conybeare's language was 'a public scandal'. Nonetheless, the two men were executed at Oxford on 17 March 1892. The case further contributed to the disenchantment of some landowners with the whole business of keeping game,[29] but The Times thought that two brutal murders in which men had been repeatedly battered had nothing to do with the game laws at all.

The markets of London were well supplied with game, plenty of which was clearly netted rather than shot. The ironically named Fox twins of Hitchin had accumulated 202 game convictions between them in the 1890s, having largely avoided any battles against keepers. The pattern of poaching in the 1890s was for well-organised gangs to go out with nets, catching rabbits which could readily be sold. This was easy work and not dangerous if shotguns were not involved: at Arderne Park, Tarporley, poachers who tried to fight off keepers were armed only with sticks and a few stones.

Lord Haddington's keepers clearly knew an organised gang was at work for they hid under a hedge until the poachers were spotted, then pounced on them. Some of the poachers had sticks, stones and two rabbits – they told the magistrates that the stones 'were for fear they met dogs'.[30] This was a possible reference to the Clifton case, which had been only two months before, and was met with laughter in court. The prosecution complained that the two men arrested 'found a market for thousands of rabbits' and they were fined £2; they clearly felt the risk was worth it.

Grouse were also attractive, and a book published in 1893 complained that poaching grouse using nets 'had increased to an enormous extent' in Yorkshire and Westmorland. A gang of seven was surprised on the estate of the High Sheriff of Cheshire in January 1896, although only one poacher was captured and taken to court; he was given eighteen months hard labour. This gang was again armed with just sticks and stones.

By the end of the Victorian era the poacher had changed his character. The lone and hungry labourer was no longer typical, instead he had almost been squeezed out by large and organised groups who often had game licences and even used the railways to send their 'produce' to market. But at least the decline in deaths had begun.

SHEEP & ANIMAL STEALING

Of the three typical 'countryside crimes' of the era, the least commented on was the theft of sheep. This was a crime of the starving and desperate because the theft of a single sheep usually took place for food and rarely for money, though it was not always so: 'sheep stealers ranged from inadequate or hard-pressed or greedy farmers or butchers, to literally starving labourers'.[31] A man, or woman, could easily kill a sheep under cover of darkness and then skin and gut it in the field. However, it was an offence that was punishable by death until 1832.

An example of this crime was committed by Thomas Drew at East Peckham in the winter of 1837/38. Drew stole a sheep from a nearby field to feed his daughters; his mistake was committing the offence close to home. His home was searched and small pieces of mutton were discovered hidden in nooks and crannies around it – there were pieces under the stone floor and even in his pocket. Drew was transported to Australia for fifteen years.

Similar punishment was handed out to two labourers in Herefordshire who stole sheep at Little Dewchurch in 1838; they received ten and fifteen years transportation. The following year James Chaplin of Feering, Essex, was given seven years transportation for stealing two pigs, which he rather foolishly hid in his rabbit pen.

Punishment did become less severe, especially for a first offence. Although a gang from Whitchurch all received at least seven years transportation in 1849, a lone man convicted for a first offence at Welsh Bicknor five years later received only a year's hard labour. In 1853 George Whitworth and his son were arrested for sheep stealing in Derbyshire; the elder man received a sentence of eight years penal servitude, but strangled himself in Derby gaol in January 1854.

Opportunistic thieving also occurred. When one sheep disappeared from a field at Kensington near Liverpool in 1855, it was not a man trying to feed his family that was responsible; the passing thief had killed and skinned it behind a nearby beer house and tried to sell the carcass to the beer house keeper, who was rightly suspicious!

In December 1850 a cattle dealer at Hulme near Manchester needed to move some sheep into a field, so he took on a young unemployed lad named Richard Warren to help him drive them. When he returned to the field the next day, the sheep had vanished – and so had Warren. Warren had driven the sheep to Stockport where he hawked some to the butchers, then sold more to other butchers in Hazel Grove and Whaley Bridge. He then stopped to spend some of his earnings in a public house and was arrested there, still with six of the sheep.[32]

The real worry for the farmer was systematic depredation. Common land was always at risk, such as the 'sheepwalks' of the Forest of Dean, which in 1854 suffered severely. One man lost 50 sheep, another had only 50 left out of 150, and John Priest saw his flocks cut from 238 animals to only one. The crimes were the result of a 'large and organised band of sheep stealers' who sold the animals at nearby markets.[33] On the Yorkshire Moors farmers clipped the ears of their sheep so they could be identified. A 'round-up' in January 1864 revealed that Charles Bedford of Bickley had lost the most, but closer inspection proved that Peter Fletcher – Bedford's neighbour – had cut out Bedford's marks and replaced them with his own. He was sent to York Assizes on six counts of sheep stealing.

The Hatfield Broad Oak and Debden gangs in Essex systematically stole mainly fowl, such as ducks, led by Francis Clark, who had been in custody fifteen times. The 'fence', Mrs Marshall, was unable to explain how she had pillows stuffed with duck feathers and three of the men in the gang were transported – Clark for fourteen years. James Dodd, a small farmer at Hatfield Broad Oak, stole three cattle from a neighbour and was transported for life after the hides were discovered buried on his farm; they had distinctive markings. His brother was also transported, for twenty-nine years.

Some butchers cut out the middle men and did their own stealing. Christopher Horwood was a butcher in Slough in 1843, where he was 'ruining the fair dealing butchers' with his very low prices; he had employed a gang of young men who he paid 1s a head for stolen sheep. They were caught after they stole sixteen sheep from a field near Chesham and drove them to Slough, where a police raid uncovered carcasses with the Chesham farmer's mark on them. An attempt to set up an alibi among the young men by doubling back out of town failed because they had gone to the pub to spend their earnings. Sentences varied between ten and fourteen years transportation, though the youngest lad was only given a year in prison.

A similar crime involving more butchers took place near Chester in 1883. Two of the town's butchers borrowed a sheepdog on the pretext that they needed to drive some animals from the station, but in fact they went to Upton where they stole seven sheep and two lambs, which they drove back to the Chester slaughterhouse. They managed to sell the carcasses for £14 and dispatch the skins to a hide dealer in Liverpool before the police arrived.

Horses could be stolen in many different ways. In March 1841 an 11-year-old boy was sent out on his father's mare to visit Stilton on the Great North Road. On the way he was stopped by a 15-year-old who told him to 'deliver your money'. On finding there was no money to be had, the youthful highwayman pulled out a pistol and demanded the horse, telling the boy that it would be available for collection in York. The boy's father soon gave chase and caught up with his horse and its rider approaching Stamford; rather than risk an assault, the older man started a conversation with the lad, suggested 'a glass' at Stamford, and then found it easy to overpower him. The youth got ten years transportation.

William Hotham was a 'sporting gentleman' who frequented Newmarket. After an unfortunate series of betting events, he was without the means of getting home so began walking. At Six Mile Bottom he knocked another man off his horse and took it. This was a relatively easy crime for the police, who guessed he would be going to London and sent a man ahead by train. Meanwhile, Hotham tried to pass a fraudulent cheque at Newport and was eventually arrested at Bishops Stortford. It then transpired there was a summons against him for debt at Newmarket. In custody, he was violent and twice attempted to escape. Intriguingly, a William Hotham had been acquitted of taking and selling a horse from a London livery yard in 1844.

Horses were often taken from their owner's stable at night. Thomas Salmon was one of two men who took a horse from a farmer's stable at Bexwell, Norfolk. The two then rode off at a gallop, bareback, surprising a servant of the farmer who was coming up the lane back from the fair. He managed to grab the bridle and the men ran off. Salmon was arrested at Liverpool, where he had booked a passage to New York. Instead he was transported in a different direction for fifteen years.

Notes

1 T. Makesheff, *Rural Conflict, Crime & Protest: Herefordshire 1800–1860*, Woodbridge, 2003, p. 87.
2 H. Hopkins, *The Long Affray*, London, 1986, p. 221.
3 Ibid., p. 180.
4 G. Rude, *Protest and Punishment*, Oxford, 1978, p. 4.
5 F. Engels, *The Condition of the English Working Class*, 1958 edition, p. 300.
6 Makesheff, p. 186.
7 David Jones, 'Rural Crime and Protest' in G.E. Mingay (ed.), *Victorian Countryside*, vol. II, London, 1981.
8 Malcolm Baker, *The Revolt of the Field in North Essex*, 1979, publisher unknown.
9 *The Times*, 4 July 1844.
10 *The Times*, 14 June 1844.
11 *Hansard*, 22 March 1844.
12 Makesheff, p. 186.
13 *Journal of the Royal Statistical Society*, vol. 8, p. 354.
14 David Jones in *Victorian Countryside*, vol. II, p. 571.
15 *Hansard*, 27 February 1845.
16 Stephen, *Criminal Law*, p. 100.
17 Hopkins, *The Long Affray*, p. 72.
18 Ibid., p. 208.
19 *The Observer*, 7 January 1844.
20 Hopkins, *The Long Affray*, p. 206.
21 *The Times*, 9 September 1844.
22 Hopkins, *The Long Affray*, p. 221.
23 Ibid., p. 203.
24 Ibid., pp. 238–9.
25 Ibid., p. 236.
26 Ibid., p. 241.
27 *Manchester Guardian*, 18 July 1893.
28 *The Times*, 17 March 1892.
29 Hopkins, *The Long Affray*, pp. 278–80.
30 *Manchester Guardian*, 22 August 1893.
31 Rule & Wells, p. 171.
32 *The Observer*, 14 December 1850.
33 *The Observer*, 16 December 1854.

7

Crimes on Rail & Road

The new railways were well protected by private legislation and bye-laws. The Railway Regulation Act of 1840[1] allowed for fines of up to £5 for criminal trespass, but in 1843 seventeen trespassers were still killed on railways and 313 by 1899. The laws were extended again in 1868 and 1871. Some early offences were due to sheer ignorance, like the man caught riding his horse along the new railway at Sheffield Brightside in 1839, who was fined £2. A shareholder of the North Midland Railway seemed to have difficulty understanding that this did not give him the right to walk along it near Oakenshaw, and he was fined 5s in May 1841. A man and his wife were fined 5s for walking along the railway at Dukinfield while drunk in 1844. Three boys who walked through the lengthy Bramhope Tunnel near Leeds in 1867 were fined 50s – or three months in prison.

The Offences Against the Person Act, 1861, could be applied to people who threw stones at trains, and the Malicious Damage Act of the same year was used to prosecute vandals. Punishment could be quite severe even before this: at Abingdon in 1841 a young man was given three months for throwing stones at a train, and a boy who pushed a coping stone on to the tracks at Baldock in 1862 got a nine-month sentence.

Both acts could also be used for attempts to derail trains, which included a punishment of up to life imprisonment. Offenders were often boys: two of whom put timbers across the tracks between Bradford and Shipley in 1874 and were given a month in the house of correction and four years at the reformatory. However, as early as January 1844 a coroner's court reached a verdict of 'manslaughter by an unknown person' after an Eastern Counties train was derailed in Essex causing the death of its driver and stoker. In 1855 a train between Brighton and Lewes was derailed by a pile of sleepers put across the track and five people were killed. A 10-year-old boy, James Boakes, was suspected of having been playing 'see-saw' but evidence was inconclusive. A year later he was reputedly struck by lightning at the same spot.[2]

The act of 1840 and a further act of 1842 included provision for recklessness by railway staff. Nevertheless, the concept of 'corporate manslaughter' was never fully developed as 'the Judges made it repeatedly clear that they were not going to hold employers and superior employees vicariously liable in criminal law for the deaths of employees in accidents', or, indeed, of passengers.[3]

When the railway caused death, the law of deodand came into effect – until 1846, when the Deodands Abolition Act was passed. Deodand was a sum that could be levied against any moving body that caused the death of a human being, but also anything attached to it, therefore an engine and all the carriages. However, the sum was not payable to the injured or the families of the deceased, but to the Lord of the Manor or the Queen; as a result, when railways caused an enormous upsurge in deodands, it caused many complaints. After one accident at Selby in 1840, a deodand of £500 was levied on engine and carriages, but a few months later there was another accident nearby and this time the coroner's jury came to violent blows with each other as to whether it should be £10 or £1,050!

Railway employees could be found guilty of manslaughter. On 5 June 1857, seven people were killed in a collision at Wolverton after an express was diverted into a coal siding. The signalman was found guilty of manslaughter due to carelessness. While the judge commented severely on his poor work, the jury had other ideas: 'We find the prisoner guilty, but we blame the company for not keeping two men at the points.'

In July 1853 a verdict of manslaughter was returned by a coroner's court against the chairman of the York & North Midland following a derailment caused by a defective engine; Judge Earle, however, said it could only be manslaughter if the chairman had known about the problem. Even when there was a conviction, the penalty was slight; nearly thirty people were killed in a terrible collision near Norwich Thorpe station in 1874 and Inspector Cooper was found guilty of manslaughter, yet he received only an eight-month sentence.

James Holmes, signalman at Manor House in north Yorkshire in 1892, worked a twelve-hour night shift and then spent most of the day tramping the countryside looking for a doctor to tend his sick child. By the time he got home, the child was dead and it was time to go back to work. He reported in as unfit for duty but was told there was no 'relief' so he would have to work. He made an error and eight people died. Though he was found guilty of manslaughter, the judge released him without further punishment.

THE DISCOMFORT OF STRANGERS

The close proximity of passengers in railway compartments led to many reports of indecencies being committed. At the Great Exhibition of 1851 a device allowing passengers to raise an alarm was demonstrated; a handle could be turned to blow a whistle and coloured glasses showed a guard which compartment featured a woman in distress. Some railway companies began to introduce ladies-only compartments and there were calls for a fixed system of communicating with the guard, though it was only the Regulation of Railways Act of 1868 that made this compulsory for trains travelling over a prescribed distance.

This act followed the killing of banker Thomas Briggs in a North London Railway train in 1864. Briggs was battered and thrown out between Hackney

Scenes depicting the crime of Franz Muller, the first railway murderer, including the fatal 'Death' jewellery box.

Wick and Bow; he died of head injuries later. The compartment was left blood-spattered but containing a hat that did not belong to the dead man. Two days later a gold watch chain was offered to a jeweller – ironically named Death – by a man with a German accent. The hat was recognised and led to Franz Muller, who had had a jewellery box with the name 'Death' on it. By this time Muller had left for New York but police took a different ship from Liverpool and got there first. He was arrested and brought back to England, stimulating the formation of the German Legal Protection Society amidst xenophobic frenzy. Muller's girlfriend, a part-time prostitute, and her landlady vouched for his whereabouts on the night of the murder. It did not save him, however, and he was hung on 14 November.

The other famous railway murder of the era was by Percy Mapleton, who murdered Frederick Gold in a Brighton train whilst passing through Merstham Tunnel. In Balcombe Tunnel he bundled the body out of the carriage, and emerged spattered with blood at Preston Park station to say that there had been a terrible fight. By the time the body was found, Mapleton had disappeared, but he became the first man to have his picture in a national newspaper wanted for murder. An attempt to arrest him in Wallington failed when he escaped out of the back door. He was eventually arrested in Stepney and was hanged at Lewes on 29 November 1881.

One of the most extraordinary stories of railway survival was told by 'H.S.' in a letter to *The Times* in 1864. Passing through Surrey at about 40mph, H.S. looked out to see a young woman hanging out of the next compartment by one hand. Unable to stop the train as there was no communication cord, H.S. leant out and held the girl on the running board. After about 5 miles the guard's attention was attracted and the train was stopped. The girl, Mary Moody, was rescued and her attacker, Henry Nash, arrested. She told police that he had grabbed her round the waist and 'I also felt my dress greatly raised in front'.

Fearing a fate worse than death, Miss Moody compromised her sense of legal values: 'I knew that if I got out of the carriage I was liable to be fined … [but] … if my character had been gone then my life would have had no value.' After she had climbed out, Nash closed the door behind her – no gentleman, clearly. An attempt to prosecute Nash before Hampshire magistrates fell apart as the offence had been committed in Surrey, although he was arrested in Hampshire. He was eventually found guilty of common assault at Surrey Assizes and sentenced to nine months, a disgrace for a yeoman farmer.

The same line witnessed the most famous train-based sexual assault, involving Colonel Valentine Baker of the 10th Hussars. On 17 June 1875 men in a first-class compartment heard frantic screaming outside the carriage of a Portsmouth to London express; a young woman was clinging to the outside of the speeding train. The communication cord was not working, but some track workers saw

The murder of Mr Gold on a Brighton express train was one of the great sensations of 1881; these views include a woman who saw a struggle in the passing train, scenes of the tunnel where the body was found, and one of the houses being watched by police where the suspect escaped out of the back door.

the girl and attracted the driver's attention enough for the train to be brought to a halt. 'Half dead with terror', the girl explained that she had been 'grossly and persistently insulted' by an officer who was found with his trousers 'unfastened at the front'.

Baker had entered Kate Dickinson's compartment at Liphook and 'violently forced her back into the corner, sank down close in front of her, and violently kissed her'. He tried to put his hand up her skirts. Miss Dickinson had a barrister, an army officer and a doctor for brothers, who were determined to take the errant officer to court. Rumours then began to circulate that he had had similar brushes with notoriety in the past. In his trial at Croydon, there was much interest in whether Baker had attempted to rape the young lady, but in the end he was found guilty of the lesser charge of indecent assault and fined £500 plus twelve months in prison. Disgraced, Baker took up military posts in Turkey and Egypt.

In January 1892 it was again the woman who climbed outside. Passengers between Tamworth and Burton were astonished to find a woman outside the window, knocking. Clinging on for dear life, she slipped and fell, and was found badly injured at the foot of an embankment. She told a story of how a man in black had assaulted her, but she had fought him off, crying: 'You want to take my character from me.' John Goodall was charged with assault and grievous bodily harm, and then two other female railway passengers came forward to lay charges. He was given two years hard labour.

There were also cases of women who deliberately sought out men on their own in compartments. In 1866 a woman alleged that Dr Alexander Moseley had tried to rape her on a train between Watford and London. Moseley denied it, saying the woman had got into the compartment after him and started a free conversation. However, Inspector Fowey of London Bridge station recognised the accuser as a woman who often 'went off with male passengers'. The woman, Ellen Allen, was given five years hard labour for demanding money with menaces.

In 1867 a clergyman, Rev. George Capel, had a similar narrow escape after a woman accused him of putting his hand on her in a railway carriage; the chief witness turned out to be the woman's boyfriend, with the couple making regular attempts to extract money from false allegations.

You could also be robbed by fellow passengers, but few incidents were as bizarre as in December 1849 when George Lambert travelled from Rotherham to Doncaster. A fellow passenger gave him a lozenge, after which he lost consciousness. He was later dragged out of the train by railway staff who assumed he was drunk and charged him for travelling beyond his booked station. However, it became clear he was unwell and had difficulty seeing, and he discovered he had been robbed of £5.

In December 1874 an ex-convict stole the watch off a sleeping passenger on a train near Newark, but when the passenger awoke he jumped out of the speeding train near Tuxford. The signalman there was astonished by the blood-soaked apparition who appeared out of the night and said he had fallen out of the train. Telegraph messages to Retford soon revealed the truth and the ex-convict, Price, was found to be in possession of a dagger, false whiskers and pieces of sandpaper. He was judged to be insane.

THE PROFESSIONALS

Railway companies employed their own detective forces against criminal gangs, with the Great Western Railway making use of Mr C. Nash. One trick was to steal goods then offer to 'return' them for a consideration. In July 1845 a Mr Prance lost a case containing £2,000 at Paddington but then received anonymous letters offering to return it for a reward. Nash's work on this case led to the discovery of a similar case involving £40,000 worth of scrip stolen at Euston which had been returned for £150. Nash identified members of the gang as Garratt, Maynard and Miss Wareham, and some cloak and dagger work led to the discovery of burned documents from the Euston case in their fire grate. On 5 August 1845 Maynard and Garratt were arrested, followed by Wareham a few days later – then released again after a Great Western Railway director misguidedly intervened in fear of damage to the company's 'reputation'.

The thieves brought an action for wrongful arrest against Nash and others in an attempt to intimidate them, but Nash continued to gather evidence. Garratt started to liquidate his resources ready for escape. After he was re-arrested, he used others to try and intimidate Nash's family. In November 1845 Garratt and Maynard were transported for fourteen years. Nash resigned in January 1846, feeling that he and his family had not been properly supported.[4] Wareham had not been convicted, so she pursued the wrongful arrest case against Nash and won, but received only a farthing's damages. Although this was something to encourage Nash, he was bankrupted by £800 legal bills; meanwhile, Garratt escaped from custody as soon as he got to Australia.

Another powerful group uncovered by Nash was that run by John Farr. Their offences included a series of robberies at London Bridge and Euston, but also Post Office robberies at places such as Gravesend in 1845–46. The takings were 'laundered' through a Sloane Square lodging house run by Farr's mistress, Newland. Farr was transported for twenty-one years and Newland got six months hard labour; if they had been married rather than cohabiting, she would not have been convicted.

Organised criminals soon progressed to robbing trains. On 2 January 1849 between Bristol and Exeter, mail trains in both directions were robbed in an operation that depended on the knowledge of a former railway guard, Henry

The three main characters from the famous train robbery: railway clerk, professional thief and railway guard.

Poole. The gang climbed into the mail compartment during the journey, rifled the contents and then resealed the bags with string and wax. On both journeys, the stolen goods were placed in bags and dropped out of the window to waiting accomplices. Poole was caught almost immediately because the robberies could only have been done by people in the adjacent compartment, and he had string and wax stuck to his heel. Rumours that they had stolen £80,000 were unfounded but Poole had used his railway contacts for a number of other robberies, including theft of £1,500 in gold sovereigns. He received fifteen years transportation.

In May 1851 forty-six boxes of gold dust were delivered at Southampton by steamer for onward delivery to London. Three boxes were stolen before the train had reached Winchester in a meticulously planned crime. William Pamplin was arrested and sentenced to ten years, but this was reduced to two years after he agreed to give evidence about the method of robbery.

The most famous gold robbery was planned by Edward Agar, perhaps the leading 'professional criminal' of his day. Agar was said to have netted £45,000 from a raid on Rogers' Bank but lived in unostentatious style with Fanny Kay. He recruited William Pierce, who had been sacked from the South Eastern Railway's ticket-printing office, and two SER staff – Burgess, a guard, and Tester, the clerk who arranged the guards' rosters. Agar wanted to steal the gold bullion that was sent between London and Paris while it was on the train through Kent, and needed to have the guard on duty to help him.

The plan was to copy the keys of the chests and replace the gold with lead, which would have to be carried on to the train in bags. In May 1855 Agar and Pierce bought tickets to Ostend and joined the train. At Redhill one bag of gold was handed out to Pierce and Tester joined the train; at Folkestone the 'gold bullion' was unloaded, although by this time the safes contained only lead shot, whilst Pierce and Agar continued to Dover. The crime was only discovered when the 'gold' reached Paris.

Pierce and Agar took the gold back to London and began selling it via the disreputable barrister James Saward (whom we encountered in Chapter 4). Saward bought the gold for £3 2s 6d an ounce, charging between 6d and 1s an ounce commission. Agar then separated from Fanny Kay, though he gave her £2,500 to support herself and their child.

The crime might never have been solved had not Agar been sentenced to life over a forged cheque. He gave Pierce £7,000 to look after Fanny Kay and his child, but since Pierce decided to keep the money, Agar confessed the whole story. Pierce was sentenced to only two years because he was not a railway employee and had not burgled a house, but the press condemned him as 'the greatest rogue of the lot and, for his conduct to the woman, Kay, a blackhearted wretch'.[5] By contrast, Tester and Burgess were both transported for fourteen years.

ROAD CRIMES

By Victorian times the highwayman already belonged to a bygone age, but this did not mean the roads were safe. Indeed, the country lanes were often dark and uninviting places, especially to those who had to travel by foot, particularly at night.

Urban fears about 'garrotters' extended to country lanes. Thomas Cooper, a poor bricklayer from Clerkenwell, decided in 1842 to arm himself with two pistols and go out into the country on the edge of Hornsey to prey on travellers on the Great North Road. Being on foot and without shoes, he hardly counted as a highwayman but was more of a footpad. He attempted several robberies before the police spotted him following a man on foot. PC Moss gave chase, but Cooper shot him in the arm. Then PC Mallet and a passing baker, Charles Mott, came up, but Cooper shot Mott in the shoulder and ran off to Highbury Cottage. There he was trapped in by PC Daley, but he shot Daley dead. Surrounded by several others, he gave himself up with the words: 'I'm done; now I give myself up.' Cooper was hung in July 1842, one of the last of the 'highwaymen' who preyed on travellers at the edge of town.

It was unusual to be stopped at gunpoint, although a carter was stopped by men with pistols and robbed of £5 in 1847 near Fyfield, Essex. At this stage highway robbery was technically still a capital offence. A young man who demanded money from a carrier near Mucking in 1847 only got sixpence, for which he received a fifteen-year sentence of transportation.

Sabino Piazintine, an Italian pedlar of religious images, was attacked near Ingatestone in 1866. Two young men attacked him with a 'life preserver' — a strip of leather or canvas containing lead – and a screwdriver. He was beaten and robbed before the approach of other travellers caused the attackers to hide. One of them, James Rutland, was found in a ditch with the life preserver, while the other, Henry Guy, was trapped nearby. Both were given eighteen months hard labour, and Guy an additional twenty lashes with the cat o' nine tails.

The farmer returning from market was a classic victim of highway crime, especially 'small' farmers such as James Simpson of Ashover in Derbyshire, who walked rather than taking a ride. Simpson was coming home from the market at Alfreton when he was shot at a road junction near Ashover Hill Top. He was found by a mine owner and carried to a house on a board, but died soon afterwards. It was reported that 'a tramp' had been seen with him.

Market towns were where the banks were. Elderly gardener Thomas Hurst went into Saffron Walden in December 1898 to deposit his life's savings of £130; he was unable to make the deposit, so he went to the pubs instead and met two troublemakers who offered to accompany him home. They stole the money, but were easily caught as they had been seen in the pubs with Hurst. By the 1890s the charge of highway robbery was often laid against London street robbers; men such as Henry Pope, convicted of highway robbery in Aldgate, London, in 1898, were given nine months in prison and twenty strokes of the 'cat'. Edward Barnett, who leapt out of a field near Clifton, Rugby, knocked his victim to the ground and beat him around the head with a stone, was sentenced to fifteen lashes plus five years penal servitude.

DRIVING OFFENCES

Before motor cars, roads were not as safe as is often assumed: in London most years saw more than sixty people killed on the roads. Typical was the death of 5-year-old Henry Godwin in 1840, run over in Hampstead Road, London, by one of Mr Hansom's 'patent cabriolets'. The cabman was exonerated but a deodand of £5 levied on the cab. The country roads were also dangerous and there were fatalities; for example, in 1843 William Ford was tried for 'riding against and killing' Elizabeth Clemence, one of a group of women in the road near Wadebridge. The jury took the view that this was an accident and acquitted him. In 1846 George Cook was indicted for knocking down and killing James Briggs whilst driving his horse and cart along Miller Street, Ducie Bridge; when arrested he was found 'much the worse for liquor', thus showing that drink driving is not a new problem.

The Victorians had their own concept of dangerous driving, one common trick landing William Weselby of Dorrington, Lincolnshire, with a 1s fine in 1855 – this was riding on the shafts of the wagon of which he was supposedly in charge. Similar to this was driving a team of horses without reins, which earned George Richardson of Gayton-le-Wold a hefty 17s fine in 1855, the offence having been committed on the turnpike.

Under the Offences Against the Person Act of 1861, 'wanton or furious driving' could be punished with up to two years in prison. Two successive cases at the City Police Court in London in September 1882 illustrate this. Firstly, Edward Hudson, a carman of the Lion Brewery, was brought in after colliding with a horse and carriage, 'frightening' two ladies. His defence argued it was not his fault as 'his horse was such a poor one that it could scarcely put one foot in front of the other', which the brewery manager denied. He was fined 40s and was sacked, but lacking the money went to gaol for a month. He was followed in court by two drivers from rival omnibus companies, who had been racing in King William Street; they were only fined 2s each.

The RSPCA brought many cases for cruelty to cab horses, such as that against James Peppett, a London cabman, in 1857 for excessive cruelty to a worn-out horse. Peppett had been beating it with a whip which had a nail attached to the end. He was fined 40s but was unable to pay, so Clerkenwell magistrates sent him to prison for a month. There was also an offence of 'leading a diseased horse on the highway', which led to a £5 fine in Wandsworth in 1881.

The arrival of steam vehicles and later motor cars on the streets created further problems. The Locomotives on Highways Act of 1861 set a 10mph speed limit and the 1865 Locomotives Act introduced the 'red flag man'. The Highways and Locomotives (Amendment) Act of 1878 abolished the red flag, but was used against vehicles which it had not been designed for, so that motorists were fined under local bye-laws for exceeding 2mph or not having a man in front as was still required. Licences under this law cost £10. Sir Thomas Parkyns, inventor of a 'motor tricycle', was summonsed for five offences under these laws at Greenwich in 1881, including not having a man in front, or three drivers, and with tyres narrower than permitted; the magistrates fined him a nominal 1s on each count.

The London Commissioner of Police said he would 'not countenance a general use of cars in the streets' and that a maximum permitted speed of 14mph 'would of course be intolerable'. On 17 October 1895 James Pullinger was stopped while driving a motor car in Farnham; he and the car's owner, John Knight,[6] were both fined for using a locomotive without a licence. The first Englishman to be fined for speeding was Walter Arnold, who appeared before Tonbridge magistrates on four charges under the Locomotives Act; he argued that his motor car was not a locomotive and had not been envisaged by the act, but he was fined 32s plus over £2 costs.[7]

A campaigner against the laws was Walter Bersey, who was repeatedly fined under the 1878 act. Throughout 1896 he was regularly in trouble, often deliberately so; driving his car around Parliament Square at more than 2mph and without a flagman twice was simple provocation. As the law was about to be changed, he felt he was unjustly treated. So perhaps were Hunt & Co., who took a new motor car across Tower Bridge without the licence that it still needed under the old laws – which had two weeks to run at that point.

The Locomotives on the Highway Act of 1896 liberalised the situation from 14 November.

Notes

1   Also known as Lord Seymour's Act.
2   L. James, *The Law of the Railway*, London, 1980, p. 72.
3   D. Phillips, *Crime and Authority in Victorian England*, p. 259.
4   *Herapath's Railway Magazine*, 30 October 1847.
5   Ibid.
6   Knight built Britain's first petrol-powered road motor vehicle, and collected its first fine.
7   *Manchester Guardian*, 30 January 1896; this is usually assumed to be the very first speeding offence, but the article refers to one previous in Glasgow.

8

The Cruelties of the Sea

As a nation that depended for its trade and defence on the sea, England had many maritime laws. For example, the powers of the Master Servant Act had their maritime equivalent in the Merchant Shipping Act of 1854, under which seamen brought cases for non-payment of wages. Duncan McPhail, after working for months on the *Pernambuco*, was dumped off in Japan after badly injuring his leg in the hold; his hospital costs and the cost of returning him home were deducted from his wages, leaving almost nothing. When he got back to London in 1877 he complained to the Lord Mayor who forced the owners to pay the full amount plus costs.

Maritime law was, as the *Franconia* case demonstrated at great length, often rather unclear. Very complex rules governed desertion or the refusal of a seaman to serve on a ship which he considered unseaworthy; in this case, a magistrate had to decide whether this was the case, and the seaman could not then be tried for desertion. Over the period, regulation was extended to control merchant shipping, such as the Merchant Shipping Act of 1876, which introduced the 'Plimsoll line' and the Merchant Shipping (Life Saving Appliances) Act, as well as the Saving of Life at Sea Act, both in 1888.

CRUELTY & MUTINY

Few mutiny cases were as spectacular as the *Flowery Land* and *Lennie* cases, described below, or the *Globe* case, in which there was a mutiny in the Black Sea; the Turkish authorities assisted in the arrest of the offenders, three of whom were hung at Winchester on 23 December 1856 for the murder of two officers.

In January 1857 a group of black seamen were taken out into the Mersey at night, most of them under the impression that they were joining the *Robin Hood*, bound for Antigua. In the morning they discovered they were on a different ship, bound for Mobile. Some refused to work, but Second Mate Peter Campbell decided that a mutiny was taking place and drew a revolver; he started to shoot at the black men, wounding one named Christie. The others started fighting back and the first mate was felled by Jeremiah Jones. The distress flags were run up and the revolt soon quelled, with sixteen being taken to court in Birkenhead and two seriously injured white crewmen being taken to hospital. Of the sixteen, only three were charged, but it rapidly became evident that they had acted in self-defence and Campbell was tried for attempted murder and other offences in April. He was transported for life.

Some of the largest ships of the era had crew problems, though to call these 'mutiny' was stretching the definition at times. In September 1859 the authorities in Weymouth had to deal with thirty men accused of 'mutinous conduct' on board the *Great Eastern*; they had refused to wash the deck on a Sunday because they did not consider it 'necessary work' for the Sabbath. The court sent many to the cells, for periods up to four weeks.

THE CASE OF THE *FLOWERY LAND*

The two most significant 'mass executions' at Newgate in central London during the Victorian period both involved mutinies on merchant ships.

The *Flowery Land* left London for Singapore on 28 July 1863 with a crew of Captain John Smith, Karswell the mate and approximately eighteen others, plus the captain's brother George as a passenger. The names and nationalities of the crew caused confusion throughout the subsequent events: three of the crew were variously described as Chinese or Malay and typically were given nicknames in the ship's articles of Afu, Abo and Agou.[1]

Bad feelings developed during the voyage and there were mutterings about killing the captain. In early September a crewman, Carlos, refused to do his watch and the mate, Karswell, dragged him out of his berth, strapping him to a bulwark for about five minutes. On another occasion, Carlos and Blanco had a fight which the mate separated by striking Carlos.

James Early reported that on 10 September, at about 2 a.m., Mauritio Duranna struck Karswell with handspikes. They 'belaboured him with their weapons about the head and face until every feature was obliterated'. He was then thrown overboard, still alive, while the carpenter, Anderson, was hit on the back of the neck with a capstan bar. Fearing for their lives, Early and Anderson went and hid below. Later, the captain was found by Taffir lying in a pool of blood. Lyons told Early that they had killed the captain and the mate.

By the time Early returned to the deck at about 3.30 a.m., there was no sign of the mate or the captain's brother. 'There was a good deal of blood about the

In preparation for execution convicts were pinioned, as can be seen as the *Flowery Land* 'pirates' await their turns at Newgate in 1864.

decks and the men washed it way,' Early later commented. One of the witnesses described seeing the captain's brother dying on the companion ladder, and he was dumped overboard.

At about 5 a.m. Early went to the captain's cabin and saw that he was dead, surrounded by Second Mate Taffir, who was naked and crying, and some of the other men, with one of them wrapping the body up in canvas. He saw Lopez, helped by Watto, throw it overboard. The mutineers collected together all the money on board and made a great show of dividing it between all the survivors. Taffir was directed to navigate the *Flowery Land* to the River Plate, continuing for twenty-two days until land came into sight on 2 October.

Anderson, the carpenter, was ordered to prepare the ship for sinking. He had to drill eight holes in the hold using a 2-inch augur and plug them with oakum. He was then told to nail down the hatches with long nails but suspected that this was to imprison some crew members and send them down with the ship, so in his later testimony he said that he used only short nails and set timber loose so that it would float.

Early, the steward, the cook, Cassap the lamp trimmer, Taffir, Frank Powell and Watto got into one of the boats and began to set off before being ordered back to the *Flowery Land*. The steward, rightly sensing that this could be his last chance to escape, resisted but was pelted with missiles such as bottles and fell into the water. Lyons refused to help him out of the water, saying that he had betrayed them, and the steward drowned. Cassap, a Chinese man, was forced to go back to the ship after being beaten with champagne bottles, but pleaded to Canderan, 'Finish me quickly'; he did not want to be left to drown.

The *Flowery Land* sank about two and a half hours after the initial attempt on the boats, and the cook and the lamp trimmer went down with it. Early affectingly described the *Flowery Land's* last moments: 'As it went down I saw the cook in the rigging, to which he clung until the waves closed round and over him.'

The mutineers claimed to be from the wrecked *Maria*. However, Taffir reported that the 'shipwrecked sailors' were actually mutineers and murderers. The mutineers were judged too dangerous to be shipped back to London together. Five were brought back from Montevideo in the Brazilian *Parana*, landing at Southampton with two of the witnesses on 2 January 1864. Five others returned on the *Uruguay* to Liverpool a week later than the others, being rushed on to London for the first hearings.

Charges included mutiny, the murder of six people[2] and piracy. The press openly spoke of them as 'pirates', but they were mutineers. Eight were sent to the Old Bailey – Lyons, Blanco, Lopez, Mauritio Duranna, Santos, Marsolino, Carlos and Watto or 'Varto'.

The trial in February 1864 was principally on a charge of murder on the high seas. Not surprisingly, there was a good deal of confusion made worse by the need to translate everything into Spanish, which six of them spoke. Press attention focused on Blanco, saying that he 'is as remarkable for apparent ferocity, as he is also for height and personal strength'. The accused defended themselves by arguing that they had been nearly starved by the captain and had been allowed only a pint of water a day in tropical conditions.

Seven were found guilty of murder and sentenced to death. Georges Carlos was acquitted of murder but was found guilty of assisting in the scuttling of the ship, for which he received ten years penal servitude. The execution of seven men at once was expected to be the biggest such event at the Old Bailey for thirty-six years. Basilio de los Santos and Marsolino, whose roles in the violence seem to have been limited to striking Anderson once, were reprieved on the orders of the Home Secretary, but he refused the proposal to disperse the executions.

Only five of them were taken out to be hung outside Newgate on the morning of Monday 22 February 1864, in front of at least 20,000 onlookers

A cheap souvenir produced for the execution of the *Flowery Land* 'pirates', rendered even less accurate by the late reprieve of two of them.

and 500–1,000 law enforcement officers. The scene was described by a contemporary:

> The simultaneous hanging of five men was without parallel since the execution of the Cato Street conspirators in 1828, and immense crowds assembled and made the vicinity of Newgate a bear-garden from the previous Sunday evening and onward through the night. Calcraft was the hangman – a short, thickset shabby man, whose venerable white locks, beard and sinister face belied the cringing and fawning deference of his behaviour.
>
> It was well stage-managed. There were five ropes on the gibbet, to which Calcraft brought out the culprits one by one, adjusting the noose on No. 1 and then going back into the prison for No. 2, and so on. When all appeared to be ready a cry went round the mob, 'Hats off!' and a great groan arose when the drop fell and left all five men struggling in the air. The fall then given was short; necks were seldom dislocated, and strangulation was the usual result.

Blanco, the most 'aggressive' in the public mind, carried two holy pictures to the scaffold with him and, once standing on the scaffold with the noose around his neck, fainted. To prevent early death by strangulation, warders propped him up with a chair.

After the 'drop' had taken place, they were left to hang until the warders cut them down at 9 a.m., the bodies falling into a 'shell'. They were certified dead at 2 p.m., all the clothes cut off, the shells filled with quicklime and, at 3 p.m., buried beneath the stones of a corridor in Newgate – at the end of a row of famous murderers. Their memorial was a rough carved mark on the wall: 'B L D L W Ship Flowery Land Feb 22.'

THE *LENNIE* CASE

On 23 October 1876 the *Lennie* took on crew at Antwerp; most were Greek, but Captain Hatfield also signed on a young Belgian steward, Constant von Hoydonk, and a Dutch-Belgian cabin boy, Henri Trusselot. Later the same day, they sailed for New Orleans.

By 31 October the men were grumbling that the captain kicked them and swore at them; they wanted him to share his tobacco but he had refused. By 4.25 a.m. Hatfield was irritated at the poor work with the braces and shouted at them that they were more like soldiers than sailors. The steward, Hoydonk, then heard a lot of shouting and running on deck but, when he attempted to go up the ladder, found his way blocked by Caludis and Kaida. Hoydonk went to the captain's cabin and took his two loaded pistols, hiding them away. Still held below, Hoydonk heard five shots. The captain died just above his head – Hoydonk thought that Hatfield's throat must have been cut as he heard a 'gurgling sound'. Blood there must have been: some was found in the rigging, 8ft above the deck, from where the mate had been shot down.

One of the mutineers, 'Jonny Moore', told Hoydonk later that Carcaris shot the mate and Petersen struck down the second mate with a marlin spike, hitting him five times. Moore, whose real name was Moros, appears to have been a simple soul who joined the mutiny in exchange for peppermint and brandy.

They threw overboard the bodies of the ship's officers – Hatfield, Wortley and McDonald – tying a pump to the captain, a mooring chain to the 'chief' and a ring bolt to the second mate. They tried to sail to Greece, forcing Hoydonk to navigate, but eventually fled into France where they were arrested, having been convinced by the steward that republican France had no police.

On 27 February 1876 Bow Street magistrates court saw one of its most unusual days when a motley band of seamen from the *Lennie* were brought in on charges of murder and piracy. In all, eleven were charged that day: six Greeks, one Englishman, an Austrian, an Italian, a Dane and a Turk. Two were soon discharged – the Dane, Petersen and Lettis. Moros, it was said, had been in his bunk the whole time, while Petersen had been hiding in the coal bunker with Renken.

Eight were tried for murder at the Old Bailey on 2 May 1876. *The Times* thought the case a poor alternative to romantic pirate tales of old: 'Not a gleam of even misdirected intelligence, not a stirring of any manly passion, is to be

VON HOYDONCK STEWARD OF THE LENNIE

Von Hoydonk, the steward on the *Lennie*, was the hero of the story; the first hearing of the case at Bow Street attracted huge crowds.

discerned among the commonplace brutalities of this mutiny.' Renken, whose role was always unclear, was charged as an accessory to murder but then released on a technicality to do with extradition – all had been extradited on a murder charge, so could not be held on a different one; this caused much indignation. Leosis and Green were acquitted by the jury. Cargalis, Caludis, Kaida and Carcaris were all sentenced to death. 'To my mind,' the judge said, 'there is no possibility of pardon for any one of you on earth.' He then asked Hoydonk to step forward and awarded him £50 from the public purse.

The four mutineers were executed within Newgate prison on 23 May 1876.

The Times editorial drew two conclusions from the case: firstly, that British shipowners should be more careful in choosing their crews, and secondly, that foreign sailors should think twice before risking the vengeance of British justice. An unexpected consequence of the case was destitution for some Greek sailors who were trapped in Newcastle with no one prepared to sign them on for another voyage.

OTHER MARINE OFFENCES

The sea was a cruel place, not only because of the harsh conditions of the environment, but also because of the way ships were run. Cases occurring almost anywhere in the world usually ended up in British courts, often in the Thames Court in London.

One of the strangest cases of the era was the 'mutiny' on the *Tory*. Returning from China under Captain Johnstone, she put into Deal in November 1845 with three men in irons; the captain reported an attempted mutiny on board and for the trip to London, sixteen were put in irons out of a crew of thirty or so. In London, Johnstone reported injuries to his head and legs and the sixteen were charged with murder and mutiny. However, there was a sensation when Johnstone was arrested whilst planning to leave the country.

The sixteen were released and Johnstone was charged with wilful murder. Evidence was uncovered that the deaths of three men were due to Johnstone's tyranny, including that of William Mars, the first officer. Johnstone repeatedly hit him and slashed at him with a cutlass, cutting him while he was fastened in irons. Eventually he ordered the crew to take him up on deck and 'squeeze' him – by fastening a rope around 'his loins' and then pulling on both ends. Shortly after this he was propped up on deck and a worm came from his mouth, taken by the crew to be an evil spirit; then he died. Two others similarly died after being repeatedly slashed with the cutlass.

Johnstone had been a poor captain, miscalculating the amount of food and water needed for the voyage and drinking excessively. The jury decided on a verdict of not guilty by reason of insanity, since there was no reason for his actions in cutting and killing his crew. *The Times* was aghast at this verdict: 'It is difficult to restrain one's indignation, it is impossible to abstain from bitterness,' its editorial thundered.[3] Johnstone was sent to the Bethlem hospital and later Broadmoor; a journalist who visited the institution in 1865 rather mistakenly described him as having 'killed all the crew of his ship'.[4]

One of the most appalling stories of suffering from the period befell Andrew Rose, who signed on with the barque *Martha Jane* in Barbados for the trip back to Liverpool in April 1857. Rose, who was probably physically and mentally ill when he joined, was badly beaten by the second mate on his first day at work; the other crew members advised him to run away before the ship set sail, which he did. However, he was captured, brought back and put in irons; from then on he was a marked man.

Once the *Martha Jane* sailed, he was subjected to endless cruelty by the captain, Henry Rogers, and the two senior mates. He was often strung up in irons for hours at a time, but despite this continued to sing 'Oh that will be joyful', to the annoyance of Rogers. The captain got an iron bolt, forced it into Rose's mouth and tied it in a fixed position with yarn round the back of his head. The ship's dog was trained to bite him, tearing pieces of flesh from his hands and legs, including when he was in irons. He was sent up into the rigging naked and, while there, whipped by the second mate so that his blood dripped on to the decks. On several occasions Rose fouled the decks while in irons, and the captain forced the excrement into his mouth and nose with a spoon. He was put in a water cask and rolled endlessly round the decks without food or water for twenty-four hours; a crew member who tried to feed Rose some soup was also placed in irons. Finally, a noose was placed around his neck and he was hung for several minutes, being cut down almost dead.

Rose died on 5 June. His body, with many maggot-infested wounds, was such that many of the crew refused to touch it, so the corpse was 'dragged aft with a rope' and heaved overboard without any ceremony. When the *Martha Jane* reached Liverpool on 9 June, several of the crew immediately went to the authorities to lay charges against Rogers and his assistants, Miles and Seymour. They received wide press coverage: 'a series of the most atrocious and horrible cruelties perpetrated.'[5] All three were tried for murder, the jury rejecting any claims that Rose had died of natural causes; they were all sentenced to death, but the Home Secretary reprieved Miles and Seymour, leaving Rogers to go alone to the scaffold in front of an enormous crowd of 50,000. He left a wife and five children.

Captain Wilson of the *Express* was committed at Liverpool for the manslaughter of the steward William Henderson, at Brass River in Africa, in January 1861. He was also charged with the ill-treatment of others on the *Express*, 'principally men of colour'.[6] He often knocked Henderson down, once with his fists, then jumped on his chest; he threw a knife and a handspike, and beat him with a knotted rope. 'It makes no material difference to you what time, what day, or how you die, for you shall never see England again,' he told him. When they reached Africa, Henderson was ill with African fever, and the doctor noticed his face blackened with ugly bruises. Henderson died on the ship at Brass River. Wilson was brought back to Liverpool and tried for manslaughter before a jury including foreigners, since Wilson was Prussian. He was sentenced to twenty years.

When there were accidental deaths the law tried to identify a man responsible, as with the *Josephine Willis* case. In February 1856 this emigrant ship set sail from London with 105 people on board, but in the Channel it was run down by the steamer *Mangerton* and seventy drowned. The latter's captain, George Boucher, was charged with manslaughter.

One of the crew of the *Josephine Willis* had saved himself by leaping from the deck of his own doomed ship on to that of its assailant, and reported that no officer had been on duty or lookout. In fact, Boucher had been in his cabin examining charts, and the wheel had been left to an illiterate boatswain. Although he had clearly failed to ensure the proper navigation of his ship, Boucher was found not guilty of manslaughter.

On 17 February 1875 the German steamer *Franconia* collided with the British *Strathclyde* about 1.9 miles off Admiralty Pier, Dover. The British ship sank with the loss of thirty-nine lives. *Franconia's* Captain Keyn was tried for manslaughter in that he had failed to 'render assistance'. It was generally believed that Britain had jurisdiction for 3 miles out to sea and Captain Keyn was found guilty, but released on bail to appeal. After a lengthy process the appeal judges were divided, but there was a small majority who agreed that British authority extended no further than the low-water mark. This limitation of the imperial powers caused some apoplexy in the press; one man wrote to *The Times* to complain that 'if the judgement in the *Franconia* case is right, a foreigner passing our shores might deliberately take a pot shot at an Englishman on shore and kill him without being within our jurisdiction'.

The slave trade was of course illegal, but cases occurred occasionally. A Parliamentary Committee investigated Britain's continuing interest in the slave trade during 1842. One case involved Thomas Jennings and Pedro Zulueta of the *Augusta*, trading from Sierra Leone in 1843.

Although Jennings was the nominal captain of the *Augusta*, it was Pedro Zulueta who was in the spotlight. The Zulueta firm was of Spanish origin but 'eminent' and 'of high standing' in the City of London. The firm had suspiciously close links with other firms at Havana known to be involved in slavery. The *Augusta* had been bought in 1840 at Portsmouth and was actually the slave ship *Golupchick*, which had previously been captured by the British navy off the coast of West Africa. As sold, she still had slave decks only 32 inches apart. She then loaded at Liverpool with illegal goods but under the name of Captain Jennings rather than Zulueta; later implications were that the goods included such items as slave shackles, made in Birmingham.

The *Augusta* then set sail for Sierra Leone and her appearance off the African coast came as a surprise to Captain Hill of the Royal Navy, who recognised her as the same *Golupchick* that he had captured previously. Hill stopped the ship, searched it and took Jennings into custody, but he also found some letters that were of such interest that they were sent back to London.

Zulueta and Captain Jennings were charged with preparing a ship for the slave trade, but Jennings disappeared. It was 1843 before Zulueta could be tried, largely because those involved in the case were scattered around the world, and in October that year he was found not guilty. Nonetheless, many thought that there was considerable doubt about Zulueta & Co.'s innocence.

WRECKING

The Merchant Shipping Act prohibited 'wrecking' – most commonly the removal of goods from wrecks without permission. Wrecking was much reduced after the creation of the coastguard, which provided a visible presence around the coast. However, the 1843 Select Committee on wrecks found that the coastguard was not always effective as it had 'no authority to interfere, excepting where the articles from the wreck are subject to customs duty'. The committee was partly prompted by the events of 13 January that year, when a severe gale led to several wrecks, some of which were plundered. At Boscastle in Cornwall, 130 wreckers battled with coastguard and revenue officers for goods from the *Jessie Logan*, whilst there was another wreck further north off Braunton. A correspondent from Braunton reported: 'scenes of audacious plunder ... which have continued up to the present time, are of the most revolting description.' The cargo, worth £35,000, was much depleted by the time the owner arrived from Liverpool, although nine arrests had been made. Two of these were found guilty at Bodmin in March 1843.

In November 1861 the *Regina*, carrying a cargo of tallow worth £17,000, was wrecked on the Middle Swin Sands off the coast of Essex. Its crew were rescued by the *Effort*, which took them miles away to Whitstable in Kent. The Lloyds agent set out from Whitstable to the wreck, but when he got there a number of fishing smacks were already plundering it. The marines came from Sheerness to assist and two of the smacks were captured. The Kent courts charged six Brightlingsea fishermen with wrecking and they were each fined £100.

The *North* stuck on the Goodwin Sands on the wild night of 30 August 1866. The wreck was soon surrounded by boats from Deal, who stripped it of anything that could be taken. Lloyds engaged a detective to trace some of the stolen property and he found that a large quantity of rope from the rigging had been sold at a good price to a paper mill for turning into brown paper. A marine store dealer was arrested for the crime and *The Times* reported that wrecking was the actual profession of the Deal boatmen. However, the local jury found its citizens not guilty and the MP and the vicar both wrote letters to defend the local men.

The *Deutschland* got stuck on sands off the Thames estuary for more than thirty hours in December 1875, during which no fishing smacks came by to help her; but as soon as the captain abandoned the ship there were fourteen smacks gathered there. As a 'derelict' abandoned by captain and crew, a ship was regarded as a total loss and seen as legitimate spoil, but there was also evidence that fishermen robbed the luggage of passengers – and worse. Of twenty bodies landed at Harwich, all but one had been robbed, with clear marks on the fingers where rings had been removed; the only one who had not, had somehow been wedged down a funnel of the ship. Despite this, the owners declined to prosecute anyone.

SMUGGLING

Everyone knew about smugglers, but water-borne sheep rustlers must have been unusual. In January 1840 the crew of a ship travelling up the Thames were attracted by some sheep grazing on the marshes at Allhallows, and two of them thought it would be a simple job to nip to the shore in a boat, load up a sheep, and get back to their ship; a good plan – except they were spotted by the coastguard and arrested with the sheep still in their boat.

Much smuggling was small scale: the lone traveller who would be recognised in smuggling statistics in the twenty-first century. A core smuggling trade was of cigars from Europe into London; they were small, light and high value, and easy to carry or take in luggage. In March 1872 George Martin was arrested after arriving in London from Hamburg on the *Osprey*. He declared a box of sixty cigars, but was then found to have a trunk loaded with 4½lb of cigars and tried to bribe a policeman with £6. He was fined £6 15s. Five months later another man was arrested on the same route, from the same ship and similarly made a 'declaration' as a feint; he was found to have 4lb of cigars and snuff, and was fined £4 10s.

It is plain that some people lived by tobacco smuggling. Charles Coutaile was arrested getting off a boat from France at London Bridge in September 1857, because the position of his hat made him look suspicious; underneath it was 2lb of tobacco and a pint of brandy, and he had more brandy in a pocket. Coutaile evidently travelled regularly between Boulogne and London, and paid the £4 fine without hesitation.

Brandy was the second most popular trade. In July 1871 Bodora Gesselin was found to have six 'bladders' of brandy hidden beneath coal on the Gravelines lugger *Progress* at Hartlepool. As Revenue officers arrived, he got a knife out and slashed at three of the bladders so brandy ran across the decks; the brandy then caught fire, temporarily engulfing one of the officers. He was fined £100 or six months in prison. Gesselin was typical of the many seamen who supplemented their wages with a little smuggling, often done by groups working together, such as the engine room crew of the *Osprey* (again) on the Hamburg to

A crowded dockyard in London offered many opportunities for a little smuggling.

London run. At least some of these men were responsible for the 105lb of cigars found beneath the engine room planking in 1878. Six were accused, but some absconded, and the others were fined £100 each. Others tried to bribe their way out – a Spanish man was fined £100 at North Shields in 1873 for trying to bribe the Customs 'tide surveyor'.

A vessel used for smuggling could be seized by Customs, so illicit trade by the crew could place its owners at risk. The *Director*, a ferry used for the Guernsey to London run, nearly met this fate in 1850 having been found with 25lb of tobacco hidden beneath the engine room floor when it arrived at Brewer's Wharf. The responsible individual was identified and fined £100, so in this case the vessel could be released to its owners. In December 1854 the owners of a ship sailing from India to England, who had discovered that it was being used to smuggle women, went to the magistrates to report it themselves. The risks for a captain-owner were considerable. Captain Muggeridge of Portsmouth arrived at Arundel in 1874 with tobacco worth over £2,000 on board; he was fined £5,997, but went to gaol in default and lost his boat.

Large-scale smuggling operations were seemingly in decline by the 1850s. Substantial 'runs' were often known about by Revenue and Customs officers, especially if there was a regular pattern, and they would eventually be traced and stopped. In September 1844 Excise officers heard of a cargo being landed at

Huttoft, a remote spot in Lincolnshire; they tracked a cart going inland towards Lincoln, but when they attempted to seize it the young man in charge put up a fight and escaped into the night, leaving the officers with the haul – 730lb of tobacco. In a bizarre postscript to this event, the authorities sold the horse and cart and locked the tobacco up at the Monson Arms in Lincoln, from where it was immediately stolen. In August 1846 the same Excise team captured 5 tons of tobacco.

One technique was to hide contraband goods in with normal deliveries. In April 1874, 317lb of tobacco were found hidden between strips of glass in a packing case being delivered to Liverpool from Europe.

Shopkeepers were often charged with selling contraband goods, but seem to have got away with it frequently. Samuel Dewhurst, a Manchester grocer, was prosecuted for having 10cwt of contraband soap for sale; he had bought it 'off the street' for about a third less than normal, delivered in a sugar cask – so he plainly knew it was illicit. However, he was let off the charge on the grounds that the duty should have been paid by the importer, not the retailer. Usually such goods were simply seized.

Notes

1 Charged with mutiny: John Lyons (Manila); Francisco Blanco; Ambrosio dios Mauritio Duranna; Basilio de los Santos; Georges Carlos (Greece); Marcus Vartos – 'Varto' or 'Watto' (Ionian Isles/Turkish); Marcellino de la Croix – Marsolino (Greece); Marco Raduck – Paul or Powell; Miguel Lopez, also known as Joseph Chancis or 'the Catalan' (Malaya). All were aged between 20 and 32. Joseph Williams, 17, was initially a prisoner but was later released and became a witness at the trial.

   Other significant crew members included William Taffir (second mate); Frank Canderan (French); Michael Anderson (carpenter, Norwegian); Frank Powell and James Early (ship's boy).

2 The murder victims included: Captain John Smith; George Smith (passenger); Karswell (mate); 'Abo' (steward, Chinese or Malay); 'Afu' (cook, Chinese); Cassap or 'Agou' (lamp trimmer, Chinese).

3 *The Times*, 7 February 1846.

4 *The Times*, 13 January 1865.

5 The full account of the evidence, printed in the *Manchester Guardian* on 20 August 1857 and repeated in papers across the country, is perhaps one of the most moving and terrible accounts of needless suffering in the Victorian press.

6 *Illustrated Times*, 20 July 1861.

9

Riot, Revolt & Disorder

Gradually the police became both more numerous and more adept at handling disorder on the streets. Railways and the electric telegraph enabled the authorities to respond to problems by moving their forces – whether constables or soldiers – around the national network. However, it was the late 1860s before every police station had the electric telegraph.

Almost anything could cause a riot: the spread of 'ritualism' or 'Puseyism' in the Church of England led to a number of riotous disturbances, and at St George's in the East in London anti-ritualists flocked to the services to disrupt them. On one occasion, over 4,000 tried to get in and in February 1860 police had to clear one church during a service.

The new technology was used to good effect during the Chartist disturbances in 1839. In July 1839 a corps of riflemen was sent by train from Birmingham – reportedly at 60mph – to help control a Chartist disturbance in Coventry.[1] Authorities soon saw the advantages: in 1841 the Derbyshire sessions considered building their new police station by the railway station 'for the preservation of the peace of the county in the event of any popular commotion'.[2]

The Riot Act had first come into effect in 1715; magistrates were expected to read out the Riot Act and give an order for a crowd to disperse; if they did not obey within an hour the military could be deployed.[3] The improved police forces were meant to be able to control crowds without military support, but occasionally they failed. In the London riot of 1886, the police were in the charge of a 74-year-old district superintendent who, wearing plain clothes, was engulfed in the crowd and had his pockets picked.

Disorder was seen as a legitimate form of protest. The visit of the Hungarian General Haynau to a brewery on Bankside, London, in September 1850 caused a riot which was widely seen as reflecting the high sentiments of true Englishmen. Haynau, who was accused of summary executions and flogging women, boldly signed the visitors' book and went on a brewery tour, but by the time he reached the stables, a large crowd of brewery workers and labourers from Borough market had assembled. A tress of straw was dropped on him, knocking him to the ground, followed by 'missiles of the most offensive character'. Carters attempted to flog him with their whips but he ran to The George Inn, where the rioters found him hiding in a dustbin. 'No Englishman, bearing the heart of a man in his bosom, can feel otherwise than satisfied at the deep seated national sense of right which the conduct of the crowd on that occasion manifested,' *The Observer* concluded.[4]

Many towns had their rivalries that occasionally burst into something more substantial. In February 1848 Cambridge saw an outburst of 'Proctorial Riots' fought out between 'younger members of the University and the lower order of townsmen'. Although the proctors' main purpose was student discipline, they had powers that affected the townspeople, such as apprehending prostitutes. The riots were sparked by the townsmen's dislike of the university proctors, who had the power to take a person to a custodial hall called the Spinning House. The town mob took to following the proctors and trying to release any captives, following which students started joining in on the side of the proctors. On 17 February the young 'gownsmen' planned a takeover of the streets, linking arms and wielding various weapons, but two days later the townsmen returned with support from bargees and butchers. A Magdalene student was felled with a sheep hook by butchers from Swavesey. In 1856 Oxford endured several nights of rioting in celebration of the end of the Crimean War, in which the university marshal was struck in the eye.

Another famous riot in Cambridge occurred in May 1897, when the university was voting on the issue of degrees for women at the Senate House. Disturbances were orchestrated from nearby Gonville and Caius College, starting with the crowing of a cock and involving much throwing of missiles and setting off of rockets. Although the male students were pleased by the 3–1 vote against women's degrees, the problems continued into the evening with a disturbance in the marketplace and the hijacking of a cab.

CHARTIST & OTHER POLITICAL DEMONSTRATIONS

Riots associated with Chartism were widespread, but perhaps less so than the authorities feared. Some of the early problems, such as the Birmingham riots of July 1839, were partly due to poor preparation by the authorities and this improved in the 1840s.

The first serious riots in Birmingham were on 4 July 1839, which the Chartists blamed on a detachment of sixty London police officers who had arrived that day, but riotous behaviour had continued until nearly four in the morning. The need for outside help was evident: the Birmingham commissioners had twenty-three street keepers who were 'chiefly decrepit old men' and a few constables. The police complained that they had been set on when trying to arrest a speaker at Nelson's monument and all the police had been injured. Earl Stanhope read out a statement in the House of Lords, alleging that a small crowd of about 500 had actually been peacefully listening to one of them reading a newspaper when the police had been sent in amongst them. In the midst of this William Lovett, one of the Chartist leaders, was brought to court for issuing a seditious libel about the police on a placard, and was sentenced to a year in gaol.

The Birmingham riots were due, at least in part, to 'over confidence of magistrates', according to *The Times* editorial of 19 July. There was undoubtedly some agitation and a warrant was issued for the arrest of the Chartist Brown for 'sedition and inflammatory language'. Much of the trouble was blamed on a one-legged man named Jeremiah Howell, who led a crowd through the Bull Ring on 15 July. Nelson's Hotel was attacked and Mr Bourne's premises set on fire in trouble that lasted from 8 p.m. until at least 3 a.m. An eyewitness reported:

> Birmingham would not be kept in order by London police, though they were at least their own countrymen, and the Chartists broke down the iron palings around Nelson, and drove the London contingent out of the Bull Ring. I have often wondered what Irishmen must think of having their heads broken by alien ruffians of order, sent over from England, when Birmingham men treated London policemen as aliens. Some frenzied men set fire to houses in revenge. Soldiers were brought out, and a neighbour of mine, who happened to be standing unarmed and looking on at the corner of Edgbaston Street, had his nose chopped off. Soldiers, like policemen, soon know when outrages are expected of them. There was no resistance after the police were driven away. At four o'clock next morning I went with my wife, who wished to see whether Mr. Belcher, whose house had been fired, needed aid in his household, as she had great respect for him. Although we alone crossed the Bull Ring, the soldiers rushed at us, and tried to cut me down. I did not like them. Until then I thought the duty of a policeman or soldier was to keep his head, protect the people, and keep the peace except in self-defence.[5]

The rioters were tried before the attorney general at Warwick on 1 August. Howell and four others were charged with riotously tearing down Bourne's premises along with 2,000 others unknown. Three of the Birmingham rioters, including Howell, were sentenced to death but reprieved.

One of those who went to prison was Rev. Joseph Stephens, who was arrested on 27 December 1838 for seditious speeches, riot and unlawful assembly. He was tried at Chester in August 1839 and incarcerated for eighteen months. On

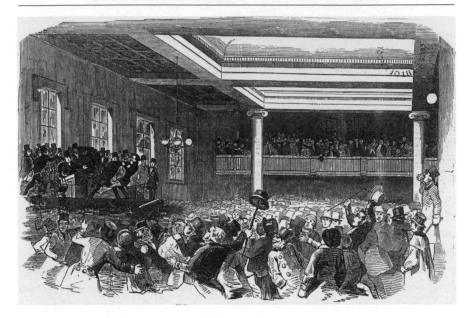

A political meeting at Lincoln in 1849 descended into violence and fisticuffs, but this was not unusual.

17 March 1840 Fergus O'Connor, the nearest Chartism had to an overall leader, was found guilty at York of seditious libel and also given eighteen months. One of the results was the introduction of a bill to set up police forces in Birmingham, Bolton and Manchester.

In August 1842 there was widespread rioting in the north in connection with the Chartist strike, especially in Lancashire. Violence flared when Chartists attempted to force the strike on to mills where work was continuing, and in Blackburn the crowd stoned soldiers defending a mill; the soldiers opened fire and killed two with forty arrests. An attack on the Nova Scotia mill resulted in eighty arrests. In Preston two were shot dead on 12 August after the Riot Act had been read and the coroner's jury recorded a verdict of justifiable homicide. In Burslem, three men were shot dead by the yeomanry and the mob decamped to Hanley, plundering shops. They destroyed Shelton Hall, set it on fire and turned an old clergyman out of his house[6] – their hatred of the Church of England was intense. The houses of stipendiary magistrates were pulled down. On 12 August a mob of several thousand attacked the mills at Bollington, raked the fire out of the boilers and proclaimed triumph.

The riots underlined the inability of the police to keep order, largely because parsimonious authorities employed too few: Wigan, a town of 32,000, had nine PCs, one sergeant and a superintendent. Nonetheless, arrests were made and trials held, including those of two women in Lancaster who attacked the carriages carrying prisoners to the castle; they were each given six months. Fifty-eight others were also tried at this session.

The year 1848 was one of international revolutions. In London, the prospect of political trouble seems to have brought out more youths intent on taking advantage than genuine revolutionaries; Mr Cochrane's appearance in Trafalgar Square on 6 March resulted in scuffles and stones thrown, but also several arrests for theft. One journalist brought an action against a policeman after his head was 'split open' by a truncheon. A gang of youths ransacked some bakers' shops in Tothill Street, crying out: 'We shall have bread or we shall have blood.' Instead they got six months in gaol. The police generally had the upper hand and controlled the crowds effectively.

There were further Chartist riots in Manchester in 1848, starting at Tib Street workhouse when a mob tried to 'turn out' the inmates. They then toured the city attempting to 'turn out' the workers of various mills, with mixed success and a few injuries; eventually they were cornered by the police, who 'gave them a thorough good thrashing'.[7]

The most famous Chartist demonstration took place in London on 10 April 1848. Seven thousand regular troops and thousands of special constables were deployed but, apart from a brief fight on Blackfriars Bridge, there was little trouble. A further demonstration on 29 May was more threatening – not least because it was on the north side of the river – but there were so many spies at work that the police always knew what would be happening. On 15 August a group of conspirators meeting at the Orange Tree in Bloomsbury suffered a police raid. As they were caught in possession of 'weapons', such as a sword, the head of a pike, a pair of pistols, a rusty bayonet and a shoemaker's knife, four of the group were sentenced to life transportation.

One of the most famous Victorian riots was caused by arguments about Sunday trading. In 1855 Lord Robert Grosvenor brought in a bill to severely limit trading on Sundays – the only day off for the working class, who already felt insulted by the 1854 Sale of Beer Act which had restricted drinking hours. Opposition to Grosvenor's Bill was led by a member of the working class who quickly identified that the aristocracy out in their carriages in Hyde Park were both hypocrites and an easy target. The leisure of the working class was being attacked, but the leisure of the aristocracy depended on their servants working on the Sabbath. At the end of June 1855 groups started gathering in Hyde Park to 'hiss' the aristocracy.

Sir Richard Mayne, the police commissioner, decided on a policy of repression, the result being that 150,000 or so gathered to flout a ban on public meetings in the park. When one man stood up to speak, police tried to arrest him, and attacking the constables soon proved a better sport than hissing the nobility. Allegations of police brutality were covered in the press, and indeed some tried to escape the

The authorities were reasonably well prepared for the reform demonstration in Hyde Park in 1867 – or so these images of police and soldiers would indicate. The police, in particular, seem very relaxed and even chat with women and children.

Police attempt to make arrests during the Trafalgar Square demonstration in 1886.

flying truncheons by swimming the Serpentine, only to be picked up by police in a boat. A total of 104 arrests were made but when some of the accused were taken to Marlborough Street magistrates' court on 2 July, a crowd gathered outside and began stoning it. Lord Grosvenor abandoned his idea: 'Nobody likes to be mobbed and bullied out of a measure,' he whined. However, *The Times* saw it differently: 'the sympathies of nine-tenths of the educated population are on the side of the rioters,' it opined.

The year 1866 also saw significant reform riots in London. In July the police closed Hyde Park rather than allow a huge meeting there, accidentally closing the gates with people still inside. The mob promptly turned access to the park into a symbol of their struggle, and not even 1,600 officers could do much to prevent the railings being pulled down. Matters degenerated into a pitched and running battle between the two sides, during which Commissioner Sir Richard Mayne was pelted with stones. By the time the Grenadier Guards arrived, the park had been claimed by the people. Problems continued over the next few days, with windows being broken in Pall Mall. The Carlton Club was a popular target. Over forty people were arrested and mostly fined about 40s. Eventually the government gave in and permitted the use of the park for meetings.

Later in the century disturbances were often associated with extreme radical views. In 1886 there were problems with the London Workmen's Committee, a branch of the Social Democratic Federation. A crowd of over 10,000, described by the *Morning Chronicle* as 'composed of a few fanatics, a great amount of loafers and idlers, and [a] huge contingent of professional thieves', massed in Trafalgar

Square. Although the actual meeting was peaceful, gangs went off looking for trouble afterwards into Pall Mall. After smashing the windows of clubland, starting inevitably at the Carlton, the mob moved into shopping districts and looted many items including wine, cigars and a small bath. Some of the socialist leaders like Henry Hyndman were arrested, but they had had even less control of events than the police.[8] Twenty went to court, with one receiving five years for breaking and entering. In November 1887 the police banned the use of Trafalgar Square for a meeting of the unemployed, leading to violence in which one man died.

LABOUR DISPUTES

The relationship between employer and employees gradually became the centre of much legislation during the Victorian era. Trade and labour disputes routinely gave rise to tensions in communities, and sometimes between those who were on strike and those who weren't. The Molestation of Workmen Act, passed in 1859, was meant to give some protection to the latter. It had only limited effect – only the following year, there were riots in the Black Country around Coseley when striking nail workers attempted to prevent others returning to work.

The most famous series of violent labour disputes have come to be known as the 'Sheffield outrages', though they did spread over a slightly wider area.[9] There were sixty different trade unions in Sheffield and at least twelve used violence and intimidation, which was known as 'rattening', in a period between 1853 and 1866. The clerk to Sheffield magistrates reckoned on 166 cases of rattening and twenty-one of sending threatening letters.

The violence commenced in July 1853 when a horse belonging to Elisha Parker was hamstrung. His house was slightly damaged by a gunpowder explosion and the nearby house of another man similarly attacked. Parker was woken by stones being thrown on his roof, and when he went outside he was shot at three times and wounded. These attacks, like nearly all of the others, were paid for directly from union funds – in this case the Saw Grinders' funds dispensed by William Broadhead.

In 1857 James Linley was shot with an airgun. Broadhead had provided £3 to buy a revolver, but Linley's assailants had found this too difficult and so used a weapon that they practised with on rabbits. Linley died from wounds to the head in February 1858. Linley had lived with his brother-in-law Poole, and gunpowder was also thrown into Poole's house.

In the late 1850s gunpowder became the standard weapon. Joseph Helliwell was blown up in October 1859 by putting gunpowder in the trough of his grinding lathe; he was blind for two weeks. The cellar of Joseph Wilson's house was blown up on 24 November 1859 and attempts were made to bring down the chimneys at several workshops. After an explosion in Mr Fearnehough's cellar on 3 October 1866, a reward of £1,100 was offered without success.

Men from the File Grinders' Union caused an explosion at George Gillott's house, and the Sickle Grinders fought a war of attrition against Christopher Rotherham at Dronfield; after his boiler had been blown up, his house at Troway targeted with gunpowder and his warehouse attacked, he agreed to join the union in 1865. The Brickmakers disliked James Robinson so they stabbed one of his cows, destroyed 17,000 bricks, bombed his house with three ginger beer bottles full of gunpowder and killed a horse, but failed to set fire to his haystacks.

The worst incident was when the Fender Grinders attacked George Wastridge's house in 1861 with gunpowder. The fire spread and the nightdress of his lodger, Bridget O'Rourke, caught fire; she threw herself out of the garret window but died a few weeks later in 1862.[10] A man named Thompson was tried for her murder at York, but acquitted; in 1867 it was revealed that Robert Renshaw had been paid £6 for this attack.

The trouble spread to Rotherham, where nail workshops were blown up by suspending tin can gunpowder bombs down the chimneys on string. Three men were tried at York for this and given fourteen-year sentences, but then pardoned after an outcry.

These outrages were well known but it took almost a decade for any concerted response. In January 1862 a letter to the *Manchester Guardian* complained of the 'system of terrorism that prevails in Sheffield', and one to the *Daily News* complained of 'trade assassins'.[11] In November 1866 a deputation of trade union leaders asked the Home Secretary for an inquiry, worried that general violence would undermine their cause. The inquiry granted immunity to its witnesses and very quickly men like 'Putty' Shaw told how they had been paid by Broadhead and others to cause explosions – using gunpowder stored in Broadhead's bedroom. The evidence given by William Broadhead was sensational, but he was immune from prosecution.

The bitterest disputes were often in the mining industry, because families all lived closely together and often in houses provided by the mining company. There were notable riots in Staffordshire in 1842 and in the Black Country in 1855. In 1857 there were riots at Hanley, started when Earl Granville's mining agents announced a 6d cut in wages. A large crowd assembled in Hanley marketplace and then toured the local pits trying to 'turn out' other men. Although the crowd numbered 1,500, the police tried to arrest the three ringleaders, which they managed briefly, until the crowd captured them back and inflicted injuries on the leading police officers. The next day troops were brought in to calm the situation.

It was not always so confrontational, however. In October 1864 the authorities learnt that colliers were gathering at Tipton to 'thrash the bobbies', so the

Coalminers fought with the military around Tankersley and Westwood in 1870.

12th Lancers and yeoman cavalry were called in with the Lord Lieutenant and sundry other dignitaries in attendance. Imagine their chagrin when they were faced with a drummer and barely a dozen men.

A significant riot occurred at Thorncliffe and Tankersley pit in January 1870. A group of over 300 men, armed with guns and bludgeons, with faces blackened or covered by masks, attacked the police and two groups of houses used by the police and by strike-breakers. The mob forced the police back into Westwood railway station and then smashed the houses, pausing only to release a man they found handcuffed there. The rioters, said to be mainly from Barnsley or Mexborough, were eventually repulsed by a detachment of Barnsley police who used cutlasses.

In a similar incident, twelve colliers from Fryston near Pontefract were tried at Leeds in 1886 following riots at Newton and Brotherton that January. Miners from other areas had been brought in to take the place of those on strike, so forty gathered with revolvers and other weapons and engaged the police in combat. Enoch Jones received nine months for having a revolver and firing it, and six others received custodial sentences.

One of the classic mining disputes occurred in the Durham coalfield in February 1891, particularly affecting Lord Londonderry's pit at Silksworth but eventually spreading to stop every one of his pits in the county – more than twenty in total. Londonderry, who was active in the Coalowners' Association, was keen to break the power of unionism and began a process to evict hundreds of families at Silksworth. Bailiffs – known as 'candymen' – were brought in from Leeds and kept in 'barracks' under police protection. When the bailiffs started work they were 'assailed by jeers and reproaches'[12] and protected by 350 police. After the first few evictions, the miners began barricading their houses from the inside so the bailiffs had to force their way in with crowbars and progress became very slow.

After one morning's work on 25 February, the bailiffs had only dealt with eight houses before a huge crowd began to assemble. The police tried to clear them and up to fifty of the crowd, including a number of bystanders, were injured. John Wilson MP, secretary to the Durham Miners' Association, was hit by stones. The next day the mob attacked the houses of 'blackleg' pit deputies, tearing them apart, and one man fired twice at the mob with a revolver.

Wilson's colleague, Samuel Storey MP, attempted to interject with the bailiffs and police and was roughly thrown out of a cottage kitchen at Newlands Farm. Storey brought a charge of assault against the police, but the magistrates' bench was packed with his opponents and the case was thrown out. He then launched an unsuccessful adjournment debate in the Commons: 'it seems to be the theory of that gentleman … that whenever a policeman hits anyone other than an armed burglar, they are entitled to bully the Home Secretary and obstruct the business of the House of Commons,' the *Manchester Guardian* complained.

Six striking miners from nearby Thornley were sent to prison for two weeks after refusing to pay fines for damages. Storey's fury increased when Durham police brought a charge of perjury against him following the collapse of the assault case, which was enthusiastically taken up by the county magistrates even though the offence had supposedly occurred in the borough of Sunderland. Though the magistrates committed him for trial, the case was dismissed by the Court of Queen's Bench as the Durham magistrates had exceeded their powers. Finally, Storey won a libel case against a Sunderland newspaper which had alleged he tried to bribe the police and the candymen to 'go away'.

There were further problems in the coal industry in 1892, especially in the north-east. Striking miners attempted to prevent others going to work to do the pumping or the loading of coal into wagons. There was violence at Morpeth, Burnhope, Harraton and many other places in late March and trouble was so common at Hebburn that *The Times*' correspondent reported: 'The usual riot took place this evening at Hebburn.'[13] A large number of police were sent to Hebburn to protect the enginemen who manned the pumps, but a crowd of 3,000 gathered at dusk and police had to extract the enginemen from their threatened homes. A riot ensued, in which the police gave as good as they got, and 'many of the mob fell, deserving their punishment richly', *The Times* correspondent noted with a lack of balance. The authorities sent ninety-two soldiers from Newcastle to Hebburn with calming effect and cavalry were stationed at Newcastle and Durham.

There were also periodic disturbances in the textile districts, such as that in north-east Lancashire in 1878 which resulted in sixty-eight cases at the Lancashire Assizes after strikes lasted nineteen weeks. Blackburn suffered the most, but there were also problems in smaller places such as Great Harwood. The house of the employers' leader, Ransford Jackson, was burnt down.[14] During a police charge in Blackburn, a group of strikers took shelter in a hotel where they demanded a gallon of beer. Robert Forrest held a bottle of acid up to the face of the landlord and either threw it or spilled it; the landlord lost an eye and Forrest was given five years in prison.

The Master Servant Act dated from 1823 and meant that a man who withdrew his labour could be sent to prison for six months. In 1864, according to Ernest Jones, 10,246 men were sent to prison under its powers in Britain.[15] When this law was revised in 1867, it only applied to aggravated breaches of contract. The act severely restricted the powers of trade unions which, until 1871, could be seen as criminal in some of their activities.

TROUBLE AT THE POLLS

The death of William IV and the ascent of Victoria to the throne forced an election in 1837, which was attended by typical turbulence. Famous riots associated with 'great occasions' have attracted much attention, but English elections often featured riotous behaviour until late in the century. None were as serious, however, as the outbreak at Six Mile Bridge in Ireland in 1852, when soldiers who had been attacked opened fire on a crowd and killed at least eight. In fact, the law allowed for an election result to be set aside if there had been rioting and intimidation, though most of the trouble occurred after polls had closed. The law also allowed for property owners to bring actions for damages against local magistrates in connection with the reading of the Riot Act; an offence committed before the act was read was a misdemeanour, but afterwards it was a felony.

In Canterbury there was rioting in the streets in 1837 and John Constant was assaulted by George Green, who beat him about the head with a flagstaff. Constant died and Green was arrested for manslaughter. The same election also saw a man killed at Wakefield, when a Tory was knocked down and beaten with a blue stave, during a time when the 'Yellows' were throwing large numbers of missiles about.

John Godding died at Banwell, Bristol, after being injured during polling for East Somerset in July 1852; he was wounded by a pike and died of tetanus. The same year there was chaos in the streets of Colchester, where the presence of county police at the declaration of the polls was seen as provocative, with 6,000 people packed into the high street. There were some 'pugilistic encounters', banners were torn down and attacks made on the Tory party, but as soon as the result was declared, the Essex police waded into the crowd with heavy wooden staves. The *Essex Standard* condemned the 'onslaught of the Police on

An election tussle at Liverpool, 1880.

the assembled electors' which had inflicted 'wounds alike on the obstreperous and the peaceable'.

The election riots at Blackburn (a borough with a lengthy history of rioting) in 1853 show that such problems were far from spontaneous. The election was a bitter contest between Fielden, a Liberal, and Hornby, a Conservative mill owner in the town. Before the election, navvies, colliers and other 'roughs' who were 'willing to fight for five shillings a day and their rations' were brought in from such places as Accrington. Once in Blackburn they 'proceeded to the practice of street fighting with truly professional deliberation'. The trouble was carefully planned and included night raids on the homes of known Liberals such as Daniel Milner, who was beaten in his own home and then abducted to prevent him from voting – this was called 'bottling'. Another gang took over the bridge which joined Whalley Banks to the nearest polling booths to stop the Liberals there from voting; a pitched battle then took place and eighty soldiers had to be summoned from Burnley to supplement the eleven constables in the town.

Fielden won the election and the soldiers went home, but Hornby's supporters were not finished. They had a carefully planned revenge strategy which included marking the houses of Liberals with chalk crosses and then attacking them with the mob. The son of one Liberal was beaten insensible in the street and over fifty houses were attacked, many of them within the vicinity of Hornby's mill and belonging to Scottish drapers who were known to have voted for Fielden en masse. Several shots were fired by people defending their homes and one man received eleven pellets in the face and head – tellingly, he was a labourer at Hornby's mill. Four hundred special constables were sworn in and the soldiers brought back, but there were pitiably few arrests; in fact, those arrested tended to be simply the ones who were too drunk or injured to run away. The press soundly criticised the town's authorities for maintaining an entirely inadequate police force: 11 in a town of 46,000.

There was trouble in another Lancashire town – Bury – in 1859 when both sides took to bottling. Three Tories packed a Liberal into a cab and took him out of town to Astley Bridge, a trick made easier as one of the Tories was a cab proprietor. Three Liberals similarly got a Tory drunk and put him in a cab, having laced his drink with laudanum; by the time he woke up he had missed the election.

In 1865 there was a serious riot at Ripley in Derbyshire, started by a man sending his dog into a crowd with a blue ribbon tied round its tail, after which the crowd attacked the dog's owner with stones and bricks. This set the mood alight, and every cart or cab coming into the town was attacked. One man fired a pistol from a shop to keep the crowd away and a man was wounded. The Riot Act was read in the marketplace, but it was said that all the trouble was caused by 'out of towners' from Clay Cross Side. During the same year there were election riots in Loughborough, Syston and Ashby de la Zouch in Leicestershire; in the latter, rioters had control of the town for several hours.

Nottingham had one of the worst reputations for election violence, though most notorious of all was the riot during the Reform crisis when Nottingham Castle was destroyed. In June 1865 some framework knitters from Sutton and Kirkby in Ashfield arranged a train trip to Nottingham during an election, but were set upon by a mob as soon as they arrived at the station and were beaten back into the train. The candidates Morley and Paget went into hiding as the hustings were set on fire and destroyed. The police were conspicuous by their absence, but some soldiers from Sheffield made twenty arrests. In 1868 Liberal agents were said to have come from London and paid villains to bludgeon the Conservatives.[16] In 1870 and 1886 there were again serious riots in the town.

RACE & RELIGION

The most common form of 'race riot' in the Victorian era was trouble between the English and the Irish, and it was perhaps worse in the north-west than elsewhere. 'Fierce and violent Protestantism and anti-Catholicism' was 'a significant element of popular Englishness in the mid nineteenth century'.[17]

The building of the North Midland and Manchester & Leeds Railways in 1838–41 prompted anti-Irish riots in several places so that detachments of Metropolitan Police had to be stationed at Clay Cross, Wakefield and Rotherham. In October 1838 Irish navvies were actually forced off the works at Masborough Common and English navvies attacked the house of the contractor. The same contractor, John Stephenson, was injured in an anti-Irish riot at Methley in 1840 – Metropolitan Police commandeered a canal barge to take their prisoners to Wakefield. A number of English navvies were sent to prison for two months at Oakham in July 1840 for having rioted against the Irish. Some of the worst violence was at Penrith and Kendal in 1846, when English and Irish navvies fought pitched battles. In 1866 a contractor in Kent brought in French and Belgian navvies to undercut the rates being paid to English workers; this caused a riot at Mark Beech, directed mainly against the French. Seven men received one-year sentences.

'Orange' riots were common in areas with high Irish populations. In July 1850 there was trouble in Liverpool when Irish demonstrators gathered outside the house of Henry Wright, a leading Orangeman who lived in the 'Irish' area. When his house was attacked, Wright yelled: 'Now, you bloody Papists, come on, and we will blow your brains out.' He shot out from the windows and killed John Sangster. Stockport was especially notorious, with almost endemic violence in the early 1850s, where the issue of race was obscured by a focus on the

Catholicism of the detested Irish. On 29 June 1852 the Irish Catholic population planned a procession between the three Catholic chapels in the town, despite a national ban on processions involving religious symbols. The march passed off peacefully and offending religious items were kept to a minimum, but the next evening a fight broke out at the Bishop Blaise public house, as a result of which the street of Hillgate became almost a war zone.[18]

As Stockport only had ten constables, the Riot Act was read and the infantry called out – but it was too late. An enraged Protestant (that is, English) mob sacked the Catholic chapel at Edgeley and the adjoining priest's house; the priest took refuge up the bell tower, prudently pulling up the rope so that he could not be reached. Rioting continued until 4 a.m. A child in one house was nearly killed when a stolen Catholic candlestick came through the window.

This prompted some revenge attacks by the Irish, who set upon the house of surgeon Mr Graham and the St James' Sunday School building. Irishman Darby Scarle, who had wounded several with a pitchfork, was beaten to death and Irish houses in Rock Row were wrecked. One man lost his finger during a fight in a cellar, went to the surgeon for repairs and then returned to the cellar to collect his finger.

Rioting continued the next night with fears that people would arrive from other towns, and 500 special constables were sworn in amidst fears that hundreds of Irish would arrive from Manchester. Troops were stationed in the National School.

The matter was debated in the House of Commons on 2 July and the town clerk was summoned to the Home Office in London. Sentences of up to two years were deployed, leading to weeping amongst many who had previously led blameless lives. Matthew Mulligan was charged with the murder of Michael Moran, but received fifteen years transportation for manslaughter.

During the early 1860s there was widespread antipathy towards Irish Catholics; there was a dislike of the Pope and ritualistic practice in general, and for some there were strong feelings of support for the Italian nationalist Garibaldi who was opposed to the power of the Pope. Baron de Camin, an anti-Catholic speaker, attracted violent opposition from Irishmen wherever he spoke, such as in Hull in 1860. In 1862 there were riots in a number of places, with Hyde Park in particular featuring battles between Garibaldi supporters and largely Irish Catholics. These spilled over into other parts of London: there was a riot at Holborn Hill where the police 'were shamefully assaulted by adherents of the Pope'. In the same year there were riots at Wakefield, where the Catholic chapel and school were badly damaged. At Birkenhead, the local debating society's meeting on Garibaldi precipitated a huge riot, supposedly orchestrated by Catholic priests. The authorities lost control of the streets for several hours, during which the correspondent for *The Times* was injured.

The 'Murphy riots' were a cause of major disturbance in many places across Britain, before Murphy was badly beaten in Whitehaven from which he never recovered.

In the later 1860s there were widespread riots which became known as 'Murphy riots', as they were mainly stimulated by William Murphy, an anti-Catholic speaker. Wherever he performed, trainloads of Irish Catholics would be organised to disrupt events. During several days of rioting at Ashton under Lyne in 1868, a Catholic chapel and fifty-one houses were wrecked as English and Irish fought each other. Despite debates in the House, Murphy continued to speak across the country at places such as North Shields, always attracting opposition. In April 1869 the Home Secretary banned him from speaking in Tynemouth and he became a symbol of free speech. Two years later he was attacked in Whitehaven and badly injured, leading to his death in March 1872.

Such problems occurred on occasions throughout the period, but few were as blatantly provoked as the Cleator Moor riot in July 1884. There was already bad feeling in the area following the attack at Whitehaven in 1871 on William Murphy; Murphy's subsequent death in Birmingham had been blamed on this assault by Irish Catholics.[19] Cleator Moor had grown as a centre of the haematite mining industry and had a large Irish Roman Catholic population – it was a provocative choice, therefore, for a celebration of the 'Glorious 12th July' by the Orangemen. The decision caused 'grave fears' and the Roman Catholic priest wrote to the Home Secretary, but received no reply. The Orangemen arrived by train with bands and banners, marching deliberately past the Catholic church. The route back to the station was subsequently blocked at the marketplace by a large Irish group, with the police sandwiched between. The police were stoned by the Irish and then general fighting broke out. Some alleged that it was one of the police, PC Hamilton, who shouted out 'Fire men, fire!' but it was the Orangemen who drew revolvers and began shooting. Others used swords and pikes.

At first it seemed that blank cartridges were being fired, but then people began to fall. Henry Tumelty was shot in the head and died, the owner of the Ironworks Hotel was shot in the arm and a bystander received two bullets in the leg. Fighting continued all the way back to the station and the Orangemen even continued firing from the train windows as they left. A few Orangemen were left behind and had to be guarded at the Haematite schools.

Recriminations continued for some time. The windows of the Conservative Association were smashed, PC Hamilton could not be let out without protection and John Bawden, sexton of the Anglican church and president of the Band of Hope, was arrested, suspected of having fired the first shot. A man named Robinson denied having shot Tumelty, and the mines supervisor sacked some of the rioters, following which his house was dynamited in the middle of the night, with Patrick France being arrested for this.

France was first up in court and found not guilty as most of the evidence was circumstantial. Bawden was found not guilty, although seven others pleaded guilty to minor offences and were let off with a promise to 'enter into their own recognizances'. The whole thing was a shabby episode from which no party, including the government, emerged with any credit.

SALVATION ARMY

The Salvation Army was unpopular with brewing interests and 'Skeleton Armies' were formed to try to disrupt its activities. According to one history, these had four common features: 'the backing of the breweries, the sympathy of the magistrates, the conservative attitude of the local population and the relatively small size of the towns in which the "skeletons" operated'.[20]

The Salvationists' public demonstrations and noisy music was seen as provocative by some, especially when, in Sheffield at Easter in 1882, the decision to hold a 'monster meeting' coincided with a large racing festival. Magistrates were uneasy, having already had a riot in January. The Salvationists had a champion wrestler mounted on a white horse at the head of their procession, who became a target for the opposition, and who was struck violently on the head as the procession tried to continue through crowds of baying 'roughs'. That year General Booth claimed the 'Army' had suffered 669 injuries and damage to fifty-six buildings. There was repeated trouble in Harwich involving 'a number of roughs, and some disgraceful scenes' which led to some of the roughs being charged with assault; one young man deliberately rode his horse into the Army's marchers, and sentences of a month in prison were handed out to the miscreants.

During August 1884 a mob surrounded the ironmonger's shop run in Worthing by George Head, a Salvationist who had built a 'citadel' nearby. The police remained at the police station fearing that they were outnumbered. As the mob became angrier, a pistol was fired from inside the shop after which tempers flared further; the mob began to break in to ransack the place and more shots were fired. Three were wounded. The Worthing riots were only quelled when thirty-six soldiers were brought in from Brighton, prompted by the threats of the 'Skeletons' to attack the homes of magistrates.

More than twenty rioters and George Head were taken to the assizes at Maidstone. The case against Head was dropped due to the overwhelming evidence that he had suffered hours of intimidation and provocation, as well as being in imminent danger of a lynching. Three of the 'skeletons' were not so lucky: they got three months hard labour.

In Eastbourne, the Eastbourne Improvement Act of 1885 had banned Sunday processions, which the Army eventually attempted to overturn by promoting a private bill of its own in 1891. The Salvationists regularly tested the resolution of the authorities, and were often abused by large crowds of youths and other characters, to the extent that Rev. Cooper of Eastbourne's Emmanuel church condemned William Booth for 'letting helpless women and girls fight an illegal battle … in the face of howling mobs'. Nine Salvationists were arrested for unlawful conspiracy to process in July 1891 – most of the band – and General Booth claimed over 1,000 Salvationists had already been sent to gaol by this time. The 'Eastbourne Nine' caused an interesting legal debate: everyone agreed that processing with a band was illegal, but if they were only singing the position was less clear.

At one point Eastbourne's mayor threatened to sue Bramwell Booth, who had alleged that the mayor and corporation watched placidly as women were beaten in their streets in November 1891. Justice Hawkins tried to engineer a compromise but the situation worsened, with fireworks being thrown at the Salvationists and police being assaulted as 'Salvation Army protectors'. The mayor complained that 'a gospel of disorder had been preached at Eastbourne by the Salvation Army'.

SPORT & DISORDER

The difference between public entertainment and disorder became a common subject of debate in the Victorian era. In particular, many forms of 'street sport' came to be seen as a threat to decent society and bye-laws were increasingly used to limit or even kill off such activities.

One example was the Shrove Tuesday tradition of 'football' which gave rise to turbulence in a number of towns. In the 1840s the council of Derby attempted to stop their version of the game because it disrupted work and caused chaos. The game survived in Ashbourne because it was moved out of the town centre in 1861. At Kingston in Surrey, police reinforcements were drafted into the town in 1867 to stop the game amidst considerable chaos. In Dorking the proceedings were usually initiated by a procession, with a man carrying a pole from which hung two or three painted footballs, several other characters in fancy dress and at least one man dressed as a woman. In April 1897 fifty people were brought up before magistrates on charges of obstructing the highway, although there was a steadfast defence that the traditional football 'match' was an ancient right that predated the restrictions imposed by the 1835 Highways Act.[21] The example of the Lord Mayor's Parade in London was cited – this also blocked the streets every year! The magistrates were unimpressed and imposed fines of 1s with 4s costs on everyone involved. Although the sport continued fitfully for a few more years, the local authority more or less succeeded in killing it off.

Animals were central to English sport, some of which was cruel: cockfighting, the use of dogs to kill rats and bull-running; bear-baiting had run its course by 1837. Also seemingly forgotten by this date was the Shrove Tuesday tradition of cock shying, which did at one time include live birds. Some of these sports were associated with disorder, and cockfighting and bear-baiting were made criminal by the Cruelty to Animals Act of 1835, which was partly the result of lobbying by the Society for the Prevention of Cruelty to Animals (SPCA), although the first modern cruelty legislation dated from 1822.

The SPCA was involved in the famous campaign against bull-running in Stamford, Lincolnshire, which took place every year on 13 November. In 1837 charges were brought against a number of the previous year's 'runners' and there was some lobbying of the Home Office. Eight 'bullards' were sent for trial in Lincoln, where the defence argued that they were practising an ancient tradition dating back to King John. The judge had a low opinion of the SPCA and it was suggested they had subsidised the bull so they would be able to get people arrested. Nonetheless, three bullards were found guilty of riotous behaviour.

Special constables brought in to control the proceedings later in 1837 showed no interest in preventing bull-running, only protecting property. In 1838 and again in 1839 locals managed to ensure that a bull was run through the town.

The officials had thought that all the bulls for miles around had been taken into custody, but one surprisingly appeared in the street as if from nowhere. What killed off this practice in the end were the views of the local shopkeepers and ratepayers, who found that it intervened with their trade; they also found that the extra policing put up their rates.[22]

The next target was cockfighting, with a number of prosecutions between 1838 and 1841, although a SPCA official was killed in a brawl which started when he tried to stop a cockfight in 1839.[23] The 'sport' attracted a mixed clientele of sporting gentry, the betting fraternity and profit-minded publicans. A mixture of these people were caught up in an operation engineered by the SPCA at Hillingdon on 11 May 1839, which resulted in a mass hearing at Uxbridge sessions. Those prosecuted for aiding and abetting a cockfight included the Earl of Berkeley, George Berkeley MP for Bristol, George Dashwood who was also an MP, and the legendary 'Tom Spring' of the Castle Tavern in Holborn. A publican at Hillingdon had rented his barn to George Berkeley, who fitted it up with seats for the purpose and admitted 100 clients at a sovereign each; those convicted were fined £5 each. Legislation of 1849 and 1854 effectively outlawed the sport.

Cockfighting went underground and there were seven prosecutions in Northumberland in 1850 alone; those arrested at a cockfight in Southwark in 1865 were using the upper room behind a public house, which made it more difficult to escape when the police arrived. Some leapt out of windows, but thirty-four were fined £5 each, the magistrates considering that anyone who could afford half a sovereign admission for such entertainment could afford the full penalty of the law. At Aintree in 1875 over 100 people attended a cockfight and there were bets as high as £3,000. When the police arrived there was the usual scramble to escape, leaving behind 'numerous empty champagne bottles', but twenty were caught, including a number of Liverpool publicans. The Marquis of Hastings, Henry Plantagenet Rawdon, and three of his keepers were prosecuted at Loughborough magistrates' court for a cockfight at Donington Hall in 1863; he was a noted sporting gentleman of the era with a reckless enthusiasm for gambling.

There were periodic attempts to ban other sports, including pigeon shooting which was apparently popular at Shepherd's Bush and Fulham in 1871. Attempts were made in Parliament to increase the penalty for cockfighting in 1875. In contrast, dog fighting was not specifically banned until 1911.

Prize fighting was disliked because of the crime and disorder linked to it. Between 1839 and 1867 the sport was actively encouraged by railway companies and steamboat owners, surviving because it still enjoyed some aristocratic patronage. Unlike cockfighting, it was almost impossible to hold an illegal prize fight in the backyard of a pub because top fights were national events and attracted large crowds. Fights needed to finish before magistrates could intervene; it was

The prize fight between Sayers and Heenan near Farnborough on 17 April 1860 was one of several that earned the South Eastern Railway a rebuke from the Home Secretary; the excursion train waits in the background to take supporters back to London.

believed that a quiet spot on a county border was a good choice, but in fact magistrates regularly pursued their quarry across a border.

In October 1839 a fight was arranged between Ward and Bailey at Ditton Marsh in Surrey, with spectators travelling by train from Nine Elms. Imagine their horror to see the Surrey magistrates on the same train – although the latter all got out at Kingston. When police intervened, everyone caught a train to Woking, a desolate area at that time. The same year Charles Rudge, who held the money during a fight in Somerset, and two other men were convicted of manslaughter at Bridgewater after the death of one of the fighters; sentences were up to one year. A fight at Throstle Nest near Manchester, in August 1850, resulted in the death of one of the pugilists. The other fighter, Middleton, his bottle-holder and several others were tried for manslaughter but were only sentenced to ten days in gaol.

A fight was organised in December 1842 between William Perry, the 'Tipton Slasher', and Charles Freeman, a 7ft-tall American. Spectators travelled by scheduled train to Sawbridgeworth but the fight had to be relocated because the poorer class of sporting fans had assembled in the area the night before and magistrates had intervened. The fight ended after seventy rounds because it was dark, and continued the next week further north at Littlebury; again police intervened.

One member of the betting fraternity must have concluded that they would have more chance of success if they hired their own train, which could move around to avoid the police. One run by the London & South Western Railway in 1849 involved the driver starting from London with 'sealed orders' and stopping at three different parts of Hampshire for the contest; one stop was well hidden, if inconvenient, as it was at the bottom of a deep cutting, up the sides of which everyone had to clamber.

In May 1852 special trains were run for a fight between Orme and Jones, which actually used a railway between Great Chesterford and Newmarket that was otherwise disused.[24] Some sources suggest that Orme sat on the tender, guiding the train to the best spot. After several interventions by the police and moves to different spots, Jones refused to get out of the train.

The police put good intelligence to limited effect. The 1860 fight between Sayers and Heenan attracted huge crowds and two trainloads from London Bridge, which passed through the countryside watching police in the fields with cutlasses drawn. In December 1863 the Home Secretary was rather shocked to discover that the Metropolitan Police had attended London Bridge station to help with excursion crowds – who were going to see King vs Heenan at Wadhurst! Commissioner Mayne defended his action in sending men to help:

> The noise of the mob could be heard at a long distance off all of the morning, and the violence of the ruffians composing it was such that foot passengers were violently assaulted and plundered, cabs seized and the passengers plundered before they could alight, windows of the railway station were wilfully broken … murder would have been committed had not prompt and energetic arrangements of Police been made.

The Home Secretary wrote to the South Eastern Railway, which had promised to stop such trains in 1859 but had been tempted by the £3,000 profit it made from this fight alone.

What killed off this alarming excursion trade was the exploitation of the spectators. Trains were put on and exorbitant ticket prices charged, but the intention was to make a profit off the train without a real fight at all. The sporting press soon wised up to this and the trade dwindled away.

Also unpopular was the ritual celebration of Guy Fawkes' night. An act of William III had banned the sale of fireworks in London altogether, but the law was not adhered to after 1830 for many years.[25] Then, in 1854 the authorities started bringing prosecutions; by this stage there were 350 shops selling them, some of which received nominal fines of 5s. In the 1870s the editor of the *Bedfordshire Times* complained that 'stupid customs die hard, and the greater their absurdity the longer they live'.

Guy Fawkes' night was especially notorious in the town of Lewes, where the 'gross mistreatment' of magistrate Mr Blackman in 1846 led to an attempt to ban any events in 1847. Around 170 special constables were sworn in and 80 Metropolitan Police imported, but the locals offered £10 reward for the first tar barrel to be 'run'. As soon as the clock chimed midnight to mark 5 November, a tar barrel was run through the streets, however its supporters were upended by a chain that police had stretched across Rotten Row. Eight were arrested, although a few more fireworks and tar balls were thrown. One man was injured when his horse was startled by a squib.

In Bedford in 1878 there was the usual procession and squibs were thrown about. One went through the window of a florist's shop and set the curtains alight; people in the street formed a human pyramid to reach the burning curtains and pull them out into the road. The following year's celebrations included a man firing a gun; he was arrested, but police attempts to stop others throwing fireworks were practically hopeless.

Notes

1   *Railway Times*, 3 August 1840.
2   *Railway Times*, 10 April 1841.
3   The Riot Act was repealed in 1911.
4   *The Observer*, 9 September 1850.
5   G.J. Holyoake, *Sixty Years of an Agitator's Life*, London, 1892, p. 84.
6   *The Times* mistakenly reported that this was because it was a bishop's house, but it actually belonged to the Bishop family.
7   *The Times*, 11 March 1848.
8   Leaders did not always escape: John Burns got six weeks for trying to enter Trafalgar Square during troubles in 1887.
9   Most of this account is based on the report of the Trades Unions Parliamentary Commission reproduced in full in the *Annual Register*, vol. 109, pp. 245–53, and additional details from the press.
10   The problems with initial press reports are well illustrated in this case: the *Manchester Guardian*, 1 December 1861, reported the family names as Westnidge and that it was Mrs Westnidge who had jumped out of the window.
11   *Manchester Guardian*, 15 January 1862.
12   *Manchester Guardian*, 21 February 1891.
13   *The Times*, 25 March 1892.
14   The house was Clayton Grange.
15   Ernest Jones, *Democracy Vindicated*, Edinburgh, 1867.
16   C. Emsley, *The English and Violence since 1750*, London, 2005, p. 124.
17   Ibid., p. 82.
18   W. Astle, *Stockport Advertiser History of Stockport*, 1922, pp. 137–45.

19   Emsley, p. 82.

20   R. Hattersley, *Blood and Fire*, London, 1999, p. 273.

21   This act banned street football, with a 40s fine.

22   R. Holt, *Sport and the British*, Oxford, 1989, p. 34 and A. Gray, *Tales of Old Lincolnshire*, Newbury, 1990, pp. 123–5.

23   Ibid., p. 35.

24   The line had been replaced by a route via Cambridge in October 1851.

25   *The Times*, 5 November 1854.

10

The Rise of Terrorism

The idea of organised, covert political violence has been a dominant feature of British and world politics for the last fifty years, but the origins of this trend can be traced back to the Victorian era. During this period the idea of a secret campaign of almost random violence took root as a way of exerting political pressure on a government. It has proved to be one of the most enduring legacies of Victorian criminal activity.

One of the most extraordinary 'terrorist' incidents was the 'raid' on Chester Castle on 11 February 1867. A group of Irishmen planned to seize the weapons there, hijack a train back to Holyhead and escape across the Irish Sea. However, the plot was infiltrated by the authorities, notably by John Croydon,[1] and the train carrying one of its leaders, Captain John McCafferty, was shunted into a siding to allow a trainload of troops to be rushed to Chester. Around 1,500–1,600 Fenians arrived in the town to find it full of soldiers and volunteers. This botched raid is most significant for the chain of events it set off, leading to the terrible events in Clerkenwell ten months later.

Two Fenians, Thomas Kelly and Thomas Deasy, were arrested in Manchester and kept in Belle Vue gaol; on 18 September 1867 an attempt was made to capture their prison van by opening fire upon it. Having scattered its police guards, a group of men forced open the doors of the van. Sergeant Brett was fatally shot by William Allen and a bystander was injured. Allen, Michael Larkin and Michael O'Brien were executed for the murder of Brett. Despite several police raids and a large reward, Kelly and Deasy escaped. The three executed became known as the 'Manchester Martyrs' since at least two of them were unconnected with the death of Brett, and the third – Allen – probably did not intend to kill him. Two others were also sentenced to death but their sentences commuted or reprieved.

Two leading nationalists, Burke – who was believed to have planned the Manchester coup – and Casey, were arrested in London on 20 November 1867

The famous attack on the prison van carrying Fenian prisoners in central Manchester; the death of a policeman in the attack led to executions and created the story of the 'Manchester Martyrs'.

and taken to the gaol at Clerkenwell. On 13 December 1867 a barrel of gunpowder was wheeled down Corporation Lane by associates of the Irish Revolutionary Brotherhood and placed against the prison wall. A ball was thrown over the wall as a signal to Burke and Casey, who it was intended to rescue from the exercise yard. A tall man with a beard lit the fuse, 'the wall heaved and shook, and then fell inwards with a crash'. Houses opposite were badly damaged, but the Fenian prisoners were helpless spectators still locked in their cells.

Some reports suggested that forty died but it is usually assumed now to have been about twelve.[2] PC Moriarty had most of his clothes blown off; at least two children were killed and over a hundred injured. The devastation was because the plotters seriously underestimated the power of their explosives.

Sergeant Bunce had got to know the conspirators of the rescue plot by donning plain clothes and watching them in their favourite pub.[3] However, police had failed to notice the rescue attempt the previous day, where the gunpowder had failed to ignite, or spotted the barrel being wheeled along the street, because they expected the wall to be mined from beneath. Patrick Mullaney was arrested for the plot and turned 'approver'. The defence counsel for the others argued that it was Mullaney who had led the plot and was now trying to earn the reward money. Only Michael Barrett was found guilty and he steadfastly insisted that he had been sleeping rough in Glasgow at the time. His execution outside Newgate

Scenes of the 'Clerkenwell Outrage' in 1867, showing how crude the method of setting the explosion was.

in May 1868 was the last public execution in England, and the justice of his punishment is hotly disputed to this day. Burke was given fifteen years for illegal arms trading.

The Explosives Act of 1875, which especially concentrated on the manufacture of gunpowder, was a major step forward in the control of explosive substances.[4] But dynamite, invented in 1867 by Alfred Nobel, was soon adopted because it was more stable than nitro-glycerine so could be more easily transported. The potential of dynamite was emphasised by the Irish-Americans who took part in the Great Dynamite Convention of 1881, which chose to support a campaign of bombing in Britain. The Convention was dismissed as 'a mass of gibberish too extravagant to be seriously considered',[5] but it did propose the dynamiting of British shipping and at least one attempt was made to sink the *Queen* in this way by Thomas Kearney in 1883.

The serious phase of dynamite terrorism began in 1882, inspired by O'Donovan Rossa and partly led by Dr Thomas Gallagher, who linked up with a group established in Glasgow in July 1882. Some explosions in Scotland in January 1883 were the precursor to a campaign in England, which was launched with an explosion at the Local Government Board on 15 March, causing 'the immense destruction of glass' but little other damage. An attempt to bomb the offices of *The Times* the same night failed, 'by the providential accident of the vessel containing the explosive falling over'.

A few days later there was a strange attack on Lady Florence Dixie at her house, The Fishery, between Windsor and Maidenhead. Lady Dixie was an intrepid explorer but also a critic of the Irish Land League, and she reported how two 'very tall women' – which she said were men in disguise – had attacked her with a knife. 'The man who bent over me with the dagger had an awful look of determination stamped on his face.'[6] She fought them off, sustaining cuts to her hands, until they were scared away by the dog Hubert. Sir William Harcourt, the Home Secretary, was strangely uncommitted in responding to the suggestion that these were Irish assassins sent to vanquish an enemy, and Dixie was troubled by rumours that she had invented the attack.[7]

In Birmingham, Sergeant Price heard reports of chemicals being delivered to a rented shop in Ledsam Street. They had been ordered from retailers such as Philip Harris & Co., though Harris' could not provide the type of rubber bag needed to get the explosives to London.[8] Instead, explosives were taken away in rubber fishing stockings.

Price found carboys of acid stored in the shop on Ledsam Street and on 5 April the premises were raided, uncovering stores of nitric and sulphuric acid that were ingredients of nitro-glycerine. Just before this, one of the conspirators had been arrested in a London hotel room with a huge amount of explosive. Four hundred pounds of nitro-glycerine had been transported by express train from Birmingham.

In this striking image of the devastation caused by the 'Clerkenwell Outrage' in 1867, police look out from the prison yard as rescue attempts continue in the street outside.

1. The Fishery: Residence of Sir Beaumont and Lady Florence Dixie. 2. Lady Florence Dixie. 3. Wicket-gate where Lady Florence was followed. 4. Spot where the attack took place.

SCENE OF THE ATTACK ON LADY FLORENCE DIXIE.

In 1883 Lady Florence Dixie claimed she had been attacked by Irish nationalists dressed as women – only to be saved by a dog. However, not all were convinced that the attack ever occurred.

The gang leader, Dr Thomas Gallagher, was staying at the Charing Cross Hotel. One detective even shared a breakfast table at the hotel with another conspirator, Curtin. On 5 April 1883 more were arrested and premises in London were raided, nitro-glycerine being found in India rubber fishing stockings. Four were sentenced to penal servitude for life. The Explosive Substances Act of 1883 was passed hastily; life imprisonment could be given for causing or conspiring to cause an explosion, as well as possession of explosives with intent.

The rise of terrorism forced a reallocation of police resources. The threats of the Irish–American dynamite gangs led to the creation of the Special Irish Branch in 1883, which included a high proportion of Irish officers. Prominent amongst these officers was William Melville. After the Irish threat declined, this unit was reconfigured as Special Branch and became a key feature of the 1890s struggle against the anarchists.

The capture of the Gallagher group did not stop the threat. Attempts were made to bomb the underground railways on 30 October 1883 by dropping bombs from the windows of forward carriages on a piece of string. At least thirty-two people were initially reported as injured by an explosion near Praed Street station (now Paddington) and sixteen minutes later there was another blast between Charing Cross and Westminster stations.[9] On 17 January 1884 five bags of explosives were found in Primrose Hill Tunnel near Euston. On 26 February 1884 there was a serious explosion in the middle of the night at the Victoria station left luggage office, but only two men were injured, plus a photographer who fell into the hole. A search of stations uncovered devices at Charing Cross and Paddington and, a week later, at Ludgate Hill. The dynamite involved came from America, through Customs, brought in by Harry Burton.

These bombs used an alarm clock mechanism which did not work very well and some key evidence survived, including a quartz button that later convicted Burton. Nevertheless, the bombers were adept at leaving and entering the country, and they returned on 30 May to score a spectacular success with bombs that damaged Scotland Yard, the Junior Carlton Club and Carlton Square. A bomb at Nelson's Column failed to explode and was picked up by a boy, yielding vital evidence. The Scotland Yard bomb was in a public urinal which badly damaged Special Branch's base.

On 11 April 1884 John Daly was arrested at Birkenhead railway station, carrying three parcels of bombs and a fourth of chemicals. He was the 'messenger' who linked groups in Birmingham and Liverpool, though some Irish nationalists suspected him of being an informer. Police raided a house at Grafton Road, Birmingham, where Daly had lived with James Egan. Nitro-glycerine was found buried in the garden, although there were persistent claims that it had been 'planted' there.[10] Daly received a life sentence and Egan twenty years, but both were released in the early 1890s; their plot apparently was to throw a bomb from the Stranger's Gallery in the Commons.[11]

There was an ill-fated attempt to bomb London Bridge on the night of 12/13 December 1884. Three men[12] hired a boat and attempted to hang a bomb on the side of the bridge, but it went off prematurely and killed them: 'the men were blown to atoms by the premature exploding of the explosive agent used,' Robert Anderson noted in a report. This setback did not deter the gangs, who exploded a bomb on a Metropolitan railway train near Gower Street on 2 January 1885.

On 24 January 1885 small and ineffective devices were planted at the Tower of London, Westminster Hall and inside the House of Commons. One of the bombs was delivered by underground train in the skirts of Mrs Dillon. The Tower bomber, Cunningham, was trapped inside when a bugle cry gave the signal to close the gates, and his associate Harry Burton was soon also in custody, where evidence linked him to the quartz buttons. Cunningham was found to have hidden detonators in his socks at his lodgings. Both were known to have been involved in the railway bombs at Victoria and Gower Street and were sent to prison for life, bringing the total number of bombers in prison by this time to twenty-four.

Following the attacks of January 1885, there was widespread fear that the bombers would attack other historical buildings. The authorities at St Paul's

Westminster in 1884: a scene of devastation after one of the dynamite explosions.

Cathedral, York Minster and the Castle Art Museum in Nottingham were all fearful. An explosion at the Admiralty on 1 June may have been one effort. However, there was a lull in the explosions between 1885 and 1887 because Clan na Gael, the main Irish-American organisation, had split into factions following claims that one faction had embezzled the funds.[13]

As early as February 1886 there was talk in nationalist circles of 'celebrating' Queen Victoria's jubilee.[14] John Monroney (also known as Melville) was sent to England on the *City of Chester* in June 1887. Joseph Cohen brought explosives. However, Cohen died in London, two others were arrested and no bombs were set off. The fiasco has given rise to arguments that it was all a secret service plot and that one of the conspirators, Millen, was a double agent in any case.

One of the star witnesses at the Parnell Commission hearings in 1889 was Major le Caron,[15] who had been a British secret agent in the Irish-American nationalist network for many years. Le Caron said that he had been the son of a Colchester rate collector, had an early career as a banker in France and had gone to America in 1861, from where he had supplied intelligence about Irish nationalist activity to his father largely from a base in Detroit. After his father's death in 1888, he had supplied information directly to British government figures like Robert Anderson. Anderson, who was appointed as assistant commissioner with the CID in 1886, had a long history of involvement in secret work against the Irish nationalists, although he was described by Lord Harcourt as 'utterly careless … a weak creature in every respect'.[16]

By the late 1890s Britain had a counter-terrorism operation capable of tracking suspects across Europe at least; this led to a series of major arrests – and equally spectacular failure – in 1896–97. Assistant Commissioner Robert Anderson, and Melville, had long wanted to arrest Patrick Tynan, allegedly the 'Number 1' at the centre of the murder of Lord Frederick Cavendish. During 1896 they tracked Tynan to France and Belgium, and claimed they had discovered a dynamite plot based in a house in Antwerp. In September they arranged a series of arrests in Glasgow, Rotterdam, Antwerp and Boulogne, where Tynan was dragged from his bed at 4 a.m. At first the plot was said to have been an attempt to murder Nicholas II, Tsar of Russia, on his visit to England, and the house at Antwerp was reportedly stashed full of explosives. However, the French press thought the arrests had been orchestrated by Melville, 'whereby he might have some right to the gratitude of the Russian Government'.[17]

What should have been a great success for Anderson and Melville turned to disaster. The French government refused to extradite Tynan and only Edward Ivory,[18] who was arrested in Glasgow, was brought to court. The case against him collapsed because it seemed his visit to the house in Antwerp was before the explosives arrived. A group of Irish MPs alleged the whole thing was a fraud, got up by Robert Anderson in particular, and Ivory returned to a hero's welcome in America.

THE ANARCHISTS

By the 1890s, the problem had changed. The Social Democratic Federation were holding meetings in November 1891 in public, despite being banned from doing so. When these spilled over into the King's Road in Chelsea, the police arrested the leaders for blocking the highway, attracting many more keen on a challenge. When John Moore stood up to speak on 9 November, he was arrested and taken to the police station – which was promptly besieged by the mob. Despite the arrest of one of the crowd with a loaded revolver, actual revolt did not break out. In summer 1894 the police suppressed similar anarchist meetings at Beckton and Canning Town.

A bigger worry was what the foreign 'anarchists' might do; they had often used Britain – the bombs that nearly killed Louis Napoleon in 1858 were made in Birmingham. The anarchist editor of *Freiheit*, Johann Most, had been given eighteen months in 1881. In 1884 there was a conspiracy to bomb the German embassy, to plant evidence on an innocent person and to claim the reward offered, causing the Home Secretary, Sir William Harcourt, to stop offering large rewards.[19] In 1892 six men were arrested in Walsall and charged under the Explosive Substances Act with conspiring to cause explosions. Five of them, including a Frenchman called Cailes, were members of an anarchist club in Walsall and the sixth was an Italian who came up from London to help them prepare bombs. The police raided the house of a man named Ditchfield and found bomb-making equipment. They then raided the club and found a revolver and anarchist pamphlets. There was some dispute as to the intended target, but the anarchists insisted they were making bombs for Russians to use. They received sentences of between five and ten years. This case brought Inspector Melville up from London and he became the leading police authority on terrorist bomb plots.

There have been some suggestions that the Walsall plot was instigated by an agent provocateur, Auguste Coulon of London, linked to Melville.[20] The arrests and trial certainly made Melville's name and career, and by 1893 he was head of Special Branch. Sergeant MacIntryre[21] subsequently denounced the Walsall plot as a sham, but Melville was too well established to be shaken.[22] Certainly Battolla, one of the Walsall plotters, was angry about Coulon: 'Coulon it was who ought to be tried and who ordered the bombs. He was a great intriguer and very clever,' the Italian complained at his trial.[23]

The editor of the anarchist journal *Commonweal* and its printer were arrested for inciting the murder of the Home Secretary and Inspector Melville after the Walsall verdicts. The editor, Nicholl, was convicted and sentenced to eighteen months but the printer was acquitted after claiming he had not read the article.

On 15 February 1894 a bomb slightly damaged the Royal Observatory and left a young man with his left hand blown off; he died thirty minutes later. He was a French anarchist, Martial Bourdin, who had been carrying a bomb which had exploded in his hands. Bourdin's lodgings were raided and explosives found there. The police then raided the foreign radicals' Club Autonomie and expelled most of its members.

Club Autonomie was already notorious. Almost a year earlier the French government had sought extradition of one of its members, Francois, an anarchist linked to bomb explosions in Paris. The Club had started in Fitzroy Square but then moved to Windmill Street after a riot in which members used knives and firearms against a police raid. In 1890 two members were charged with assaulting a policeman who went to the Club to arrest an offender; they got two weeks in gaol, but the offender escaped. The Club was believed to have 700 members, including Russian nihilists from Hammersmith, Armenians from Shepherd's Bush, and other anarchists from Forest Hill and Camden Town.

There was also a group of Italian anarchists in London, clustered round Saffron Hill. In April 1894 Francis Polti, a youth of 19, was seized by police while walking

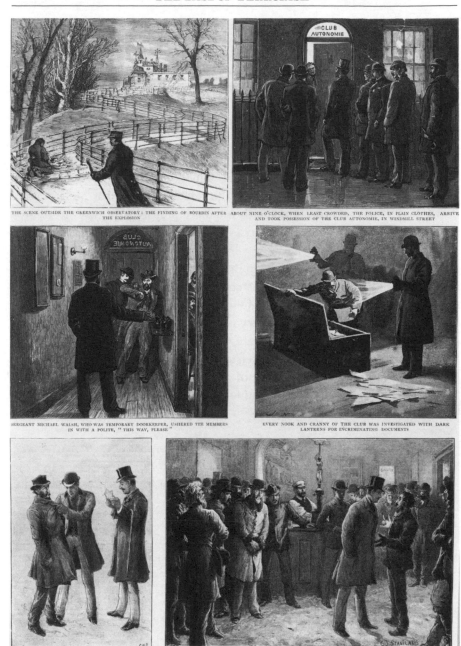

THE SCENE OUTSIDE THE GREENWICH OBSERVATORY: THE FINDING OF BOURDIN AFTER
THE EXPLOSION

ABOUT NINE O'CLOCK, WHEN LEAST CROWDED, THE POLICE, IN PLAIN CLOTHES, ARRIVE
AND TOOK POSSESSION OF THE CLUB AUTONOMIE, IN WINDMILL STREET

SERGEANT MICHAEL WALSH, WHO WAS TEMPORARY DOORKEEPER, USHERED THE MEMBERS
IN WITH A POLITE, " THIS WAY, PLEASE "

EVERY NOOK AND CRANNY OF THE CLUB WAS INVESTIGATED WITH DARK
LANTERNS FOR INCRIMINATING DOCUMENTS

SEARCHING THE POCKETS OF THE CAPTURED ANARCHISTS

ALL THE MEN WHOM CHIEF INSPECTOR MELVILLE SUSPECTED WERE TAKEN INTO THE BAR OF THE CLUB AND
CLOSELY INTERROGATED

In 1894 the anarchist Bourdin attempted to blow up the Royal Observatory with a bomb,
but it exploded in his hands. The police, led by Melville, raided the premises of the anarchist
Club Autonomie in search for more anarchist weapons.

along Farringdon Road carrying a parcel – an iron cylinder intended to be used for a bomb. Polti had arranged for similar shells to be made at the iron founders in Lancaster Road and Blackfriars Road, but clearly had been watched by the police. At his lodgings in Clerkenwell they found sulphuric acid and potash for making explosives. Next they arrested a man known as 'Carnot', who was really Giuseppe Farnara, allegedly the 'Head Centre' of a large anarchist network who was arrested at night in east London.

Both men were tried for conspiracy in May 1894. It was believed that they intended to blow up the Stock Exchange. It took the jury only four minutes to find both men guilty, following which the judge inveighed that 'a man cannot come here to this country and with impunity prepare explosives to destroy people and property in other countries'.[24] Farnara was given twenty years and Polti – despite Farnara saying he was innocent – ten years. As they were taken from the dock, Farnara yelled at the judge: 'Today you make the law; another day we shall make the laws.' People in the courtroom laughed.

Also in custody was Theodore Meunier, a French cabinetmaker accused of having set off a bomb at the Café Very in Paris in 1892, which killed two people. Meunier and an associate Ricken were arrested on their way out of the country by Inspector Melville. The French started extradition proceedings for Meunier but Ricken was released with a fine of £5. Meunier was sent to France in June 1894, where he received penal servitude for life.

Notes

1 R. Swift, *Irish Migrants in Britain 1815–1914: a documentary history*, Cork, 2002, p. 183: the evidence is from the Chief Constable of Chester.

2 Even a brief survey of the internet references shows claims varying between seven and thirteen dead. K.R.M. Short, *The Dynamite War*, gives twelve dead and five others 'indirectly'.

3 *Illustrated London News*, 24 March 1868.

4 It was also a step forward in the social control of Guy Fawkes celebrations, introducing a fine for throwing fireworks in a public place.

5 *Manchester Guardian*, 24 August 1881.

6 Lady Dixie's account in *The Times*, 19 March 1883.

7 *The Times*, 16 April 1883.

8 Short, *The Dynamite War*, Dublin, 1979, p. 136.

9 However, seventy-two claimed for injuries.

10 Short, p. 236.

11 Ibid., p. 181. A third man was also convicted.

12 Lomasney, Malon and Fleming.

13 Short, p. 230.

14 Ibid., p. 232.

15 His real name was Thomas Beach.
16 Short, p. 234.
17 *The Times*, 17 September 1896.
18 Also known as Bell.
19 *The Times*, 29 October 1887.
20 www.kerrymuseum.ie/forum_1.html.
21 This officer may be the same as was involved in the arrest of Thomas Cream, the 'Lambeth poisoner'.
22 Melville's meteoric career went even further in 1903 when he moved into international intelligence work for the War Office.
23 *The Times*, 5 April 1892.
24 *Manchester Guardian*, 5 May 1894.

11

Passion, Love & Lust

SEXUAL CRIMES

Over the period the law was gradually extended, giving greater protection to women – though it was a slow process. Although prosecutions for rape and other offences against women began to rise in the 1820s, this was as much due to cases coming to court as to any rise in actual offences.[1] The judicial statistics for 1846 showed the largest increase in the area of rape and attempted rape,[2] but may not represent the true trend in crimes committed. 'The removal of rape from the list of capital offences in 1841 unburdened prosecutors, juries and judges alike of the guilt of sending a man to his death.'[3] Trials for sexual assaults continued to increase in the period after 1856, although other crimes of violence fell.[4] Nonetheless, 'the nineteenth century saw sexual assault much more clearly defined in the courtroom as violence'.[5] Jackson identifies increases in the 1840s, the 1860s (after the Offences Against the Person Act), and peaking in 1885 in an atmosphere of moral panic.[6]

This was also the classic era for blackmail connected to sexual issues. Apart from the criminality of homosexuality, discussed below, many men or women of social standing feared being unmasked for adultery. Joseph Robson, a partner in a retail business at Saffron Walden, was a happily married and respectable Quaker when two women made allegations that he had committed 'immoral acts' with them both. They sent threatening letters but he resisted, even fighting a slander case to try to clear his name – which he won. He eventually received a letter from his blackmailers asking him to meet them on the common at night; he went but ensured the police were watching. The two women were given nine months each.

At the start of the Victorian era, the 'age of consent' was only 12 (which it had been since 1576) and it was raised to 13 in 1875. Intercourse with a child under 10 had been a felony since 1828, although with a 10- to 12-year-old it was only a misdemeanour.[7] 'Indecent assault' included 'attempted carnal knowledge' with someone under 12. The landmark was the Criminal Law Amendment Act of 1885 which raised the age of consent from 13 to 16 and made it an offence to encourage any girl under 18 to leave home – which was regarded as abduction. Penalties included up to two years imprisonment or twenty-five lashes if the perpetrator was under 16. There was also a host of organisations which fought against immorality and attempted to help unfortunate young women.

The criminalisation of intercourse with girls is one of the most prominent – and hard-fought – examples of how changing moral expectations influenced the law of the time. Lord Millburn complained in the debate over the 1885 bill that it would make a crime out of what 'had hitherto been only considered a moral offence', which was exactly the position with incest more than twenty years later.

An act of 1849 was intended to protect young women from the use of 'fraudulent practices' to secure their 'defilement', aimed primarily at seducers who promised marriage.[8] This was replaced with clauses in the Offences Against the Person Act of 1861, which made it an offence to use such methods with a woman under 21. This act 'failed to address effectively the issue of sexual violence',[9] while the Criminal Law Amendment Act of 1885 has been seen as more protective of men from women than the other way round, though it was partly motivated by the worries over 'white slavery'.

Girls were also protected by the laws which prohibited taking a girl away without her parents' consent if under 16, and organisations such as the Society for the Suppression of Vice helped to bring such cases. In 1872 a girl from Silvertown, Catherine Pusey, was introduced to John Ross by a gatekeeper who undoubtedly received something for his troubles from Ross. Ross, a practised rake, took her to North Woolwich Gardens and then into London by first-class train. After an evening at a music hall, they shared a bed at a coffee house and then she went home. He did not turn up for the next appointment so, fearing pregnancy, the story came out. Ross was found guilty but his sentence was not recorded.

Under the laws of seduction, a father could sue a person for seduction, 'criminal intimacy' and taking away his daughter. John Naylor, a stonemason of Merrick, north Yorkshire, sued Richard Ellerton in 1846. The Naylors lived in an estate cottage belonging to Ellerton's mother, and during this time Ellerton – who was 32 – became attracted to the girl, who was 14. He seduced her when she was 16, first in the woods, then in a field, then in a lane and also in her parents' house. It was alleged that he slept with her at the house 'with the connivance of the parents', and old Mrs Ellerton evicted them from the cottage. The girl gave birth to a stillborn child, but there was also much evidence that Ellerton had promised marriage, so he was made to pay £300 damages.

Rape was a notoriously difficult charge to prove. As a capital offence until 1841, it was often difficult to secure a conviction by a jury. In the debate on it in 1840, it was noted that no one had been executed for four years for rape, but then Mr Serjeant Jackson said that 'Nothing was more frequent than for charges of this nature to be preferred for the mere purpose of forcing a marriage'.[10]

Rape was a common offence, with several cases occurring in the larger assizes: at Stafford in 1849, 20 of the 105 cases were rape. There was a 14 per cent increase in committals for rape in 1848, but it is difficult to identify whether this was because there were more rapes, better policing or greater confidence in bringing charges. The changes of 1861 left the law hopelessly vague, and a number of cases were left to consider whether a rape conviction could be secured if the woman was drunk, asleep or deceived.

It was still a capital offence when Constantine Sullivan raped Sarah Congdon, a 14-year-old girl who had gone to buy cement from the works in Stratford, Essex, where Sullivan worked. A sentence of death was 'recorded' but the judge noted it was unlikely to be carried out. Opportunistic rapes were common but hard to prove; a typical case is the rape of Ann Williams, who was 13, by John Unwin near Worksop in 1848. Williams and another girl were walking from Worksop workhouse to Mansfield when they were stopped by two men. A shepherd saw Unwin throw the girl down and assault her, after which she returned to Worksop and went to the workhouse surgeon. The other girl corroborated her story, yet the evidence of the surgeon 'appeared to be some reason, however slight, to doubt as to the actual completion of the offence'.[11] Thus Unwin received only two months for assault.

In February 1840 a Slough farmer, John Atkins, was tried before magistrates for raping his servant girl. Atkins, who habitually treated her cruelly, had suddenly started treating her more kindly – just before his wife and children went away. He plied her with drink and then assaulted her in a room upstairs; her attempts to escape out of the window proved futile. Afterwards, he told her to go down and make his tea, but she ran off. However, during an adjournment of the proceedings, the witnesses – the girl and her family – all disappeared, leading the magistrates to conclude that they had been 'interfered with'. The rape of servants was not unusual: in 1855 a married earthenware dealer from Liverpool was sentenced to fifteen years transportation for raping a 14-year-old servant girl, but there were many other servant girls who had similar experiences that they were not able to bring to court.

The case in 1842, when seven young men from the village of Hougham in Kent were convicted of raping a girl in a field at three o'clock in the morning in April 1841, was exceptional; all seven were transported and, given how small the village was, the impact must have been considerable.

Cases such as that of Maria O'Grady tended to undermine the women who had a genuine grievance. In early 1849 Robert Bartlett, an Epsom solicitor who had been previously taken to Horsemonger Lane gaol for debt, was brought before Epsom magistrates on a charge of raping O'Grady, a young girl who he and his wife had 'rescued' from the workhouse. A charge was brought by the girl's mother that he had raped her in her bedroom, but one of the servants whose room was above O'Grady's said she had heard nothing. More to the point, she said that Bartlett's bed had been slept in and the sheets then washed; he had even asked for them to be ironed before his wife came home.

Bartlett's defence was that he had had intercourse with the girl willingly in the dining room and then again in his bedroom, but he had then received menacing messages demanding £700. Bartlett was cleared, but then taken back to prison for debt, and his household furniture – including the bed – was sold.

The Protection of Females Act of 1849 proved inefficient partly because the absence of consent had to be proved if a man were to be found guilty. The Offences Against the Person Act failed to resolve this. In December 1856 William White was tried for assault and indecent assault on Martha Appleby. The crime had been committed in February 1854 and two men had already been sent to prison. Appleby had gone to a public house, said she had been knocked on the head by one of a group of four men, but that she knew nothing else. Witnesses told how a policeman had seen the four men carrying her down the street and had made them take her to her house. After he had gone, they returned and carried her to a field at Dallington Moor where two had held her down and at least one 'outraged her'. She was clearly intoxicated at the time, and afterwards was carried to the police station by some passers-by. Mr Justice Willes, in his summing up, told the jury that 'some doubts are entertained whether the offence of rape could be committed upon the person of a woman who had rendered herself perfectly insensible by drink so as to be unable to give any signs of resistance'.

This view certainly prevailed in the case of Ann Eades of Bocking in 1852, who alleged that George Metson dragged her into his house and raped her after walking her back from the pub. The jury recorded a verdict of not guilty, to the disgust of many in the court, arguing that the girl could have consented to intercourse while affected by drink.

When Stephen Rudland was found guilty of breaking into Jane Marriott's house at Great Chesterford and raping her, the jury asked the judge for a merciful sentence. When the judge queried this, the foreman of the jury reasoned: 'The Jury thinks the prosecutrix might have used more resistance.'

A serious rape case was that of Charles Wiltshire, who was sentenced to be hung at Gloucester after the rape and murder of a woman after a night out drinking at St George's Bristol. It was a winter night and the woman left the pub at about ten or eleven o'clock, but she collapsed in the mud and wet. At about one in the morning, Wiltshire came by and dragged her to a haystack where he raped her. She was found dead the next morning and he was found guilty of her murder, though the medical evidence suggested she had died of cold and exposure. The Home Secretary, therefore, reprieved Wiltshire from the gallows.

There was also a steady stream through the courts of men charged with minor indecencies. Railway compartments were a favourite venue, one of the earliest cases being that of James Thompson on the London & Greenwich Railway in 1841. Thompson tried to take hold of Emily Stacey and 'hold her in an improper manner'; then he used 'vile language'. He was fined £5 for this. In October 1841 a railway guard on the London & Brighton Railway offered a young woman travelling second class the chance to go first, but then 'commenced taking indecent liberties' with her. When she resisted, he put her off the train at the next station. He was fined 40s and sacked, but the Home Secretary Sir James Graham wrote to Croydon magistrates to say the punishment was too lenient. The ex-guard circulated a leaflet making allegations about the girl's character.

The idea of a paedophile was unknown in Victorian England, but the crimes associated with it were not. In 1857 Henry Hills, who was acting chief clerk to the Poplar Board of Guardians, was arrested for having systematically abused the girls who attended a school run by his wife; it was said that he had 'contaminated in a greater or lesser degree nearly all of his wife's charges'. He was charged with unlawfully assaulting Hannah Stamp, a girl under 12, though it was mentioned in court that there were up to seventeen others. Hills pleaded guilty and was sentenced to one year's hard labour. A very similar case was that of Robert Skillings, who was charged with five indecent assaults against girls who attended his wife's school at Leyton in 1882; he was given eighteen months hard labour.

In 1865, 9-year-old Caroline Hawkins disappeared from near her father's grocery shop in London, reappearing several days later in London hospital. She had been taken away by William Hubbard, who took her to various lodging houses and then asked for a double bed in another lodging house. The landlady refused and other lodgers attacked him. The child seemed ill, so was taken to the hospital by the people from the lodging house.

Henry Ashbee, a noted Victorian collector of pornography, made his own commentary in a work entitled *Little Miss Curious's Tale* which was reprinted in 1865. This described the seduction of a 12-year-old by a manservant, with little evidence of disapproval.[12]

In December 1874 Sergeant Richard Coate of the Royal Artillery, who taught in the army school at Purfleet, killed a 6-year-old girl and dumped her body in the marshes nearby. 'The appearance of the body led to the conclusion that a murder had been committed, after an outrage of a horrible nature had been attempted,' the local press reported; Coate was executed at Chelmsford.

Frederick Baker murdered 8-year-old Fanny Adams near Alton in 1867, for which he was hung on Christmas Eve.

Another murder linked to sexual crime was that of 5-year-old Ernest Packer, who was persuaded to go into a copse with a man when he left school at Catteshall near Goldalming, Surrey, on 8 March 1897. The man was Ernest Travers, who had been an inmate of several asylums and had only been released from Cambridge asylum a few weeks before. The cries of the boy attracted women and a man who was out shooting, but they were too late to save the boy from having his throat cut. Travers was found lying down next to the naked body of the child, and was held there at gunpoint. 'An attempt had been made at outrage,' it was reported. Travers was detained 'at Her Majesty's Pleasure'.

The understanding of the 'crime' of incest in Victorian England was very different. In the 1830s and early 1840s the discussion was all about whether a man might marry his widow's sister, which Lord Francis Egerton proposed in 1842.[13] Later that year, when Charles Simpkins was brought up before parish authorities in London for failure to maintain his wife, 'a very pretty looking woman', it was reported that she had committed 'adultery *and* incest' with his brother. A rare prosecution was in 1856 when George Chapman, a bricklayer from Wrotham in Kent, was charged with assaulting and 'carnally knowing' his 13-year-old daughter; however, the fact that she was his daughter did not add to the criminal charge. The defence that the girl had consented was rejected and Chapman was transported for life.

In a sensational case, John Cooke brought a case for damages for criminal conversation against Rev. Charles Wetherell, rector of Byfield, Northamptonshire, at

Croydon Assizes in 1845. Wetherell was his stepfather-in-law and Cooke alleged adultery and incest was committed both before and after his marriage to Miss Wetherell. Charles had married a rich woman who, clearly not entirely trusting her husband, had settled most of her wealth on her daughter. After her death, Charles had taken the daughter to his bed and her bank account for his own – the servants openly admitted in court that 'they were in the habit of continually sleeping together'. Miss Wetherell had become 'stout', following which she disappeared to the countryside and returned much slimmer. Not knowing the true story, Cooke proposed marriage and, seemingly against her father's wishes, succeeded in marrying what he took to be a rich woman; shortly after his marriage, he was asked to pay a debt of hers for £500, and then others followed. When he protested she left him and went back to her father; he had only the debts which, as her husband, he was now legally liable for.

Cooke, an attorney, sued and won £3,000 damages. Meanwhile, Charles Wetherell was taken to the debtors' prison where he remained for several years. Nevertheless, he could not be charged with incest and neither could the Bishop of Peterborough remove him from his living, although its income was sequestrated.

The crime of incest, in the modern understanding, did not enter the statute book until 1908 with the Punishment of Incest Act. Throughout the Victorian era it was only punishable under the ecclesiastical courts and not under criminal law. In contrast, Scottish law had made it criminal in 1857 and it was a capital offence there until 1887.[14] The resultant act made it an offence within state jurisdiction, although the Criminal Law Amendment Act of 1885 had given some protection for children by raising the age of consent from 13 to 16.

Finally in this section, we can briefly mention bestiality. This offence appeared regularly on the calendar for assizes, but only very rarely received any press comment. Unsurprisingly, it was sheep that featured in two cases from Lincolnshire. In 1839 William Robinson of Spalding was given eighteen months hard labour for bestiality with a sheep. In 1859 Thomas Bett of Potterhanworth was indicted for 'feloniously diabolically and against the order of nature' having a 'venereal affair [with] a certain ewe sheep' – in the words of the *Lincolnshire Chronicle*.

HOMOSEXUALITY

Male homosexuality[15] was criminal throughout the Victorian era and the death penalty existed for sodomy[16] until 1861, when it was removed by the Offences Against the Person Act, even though it had not been used since 1835. Its use had been regular in the recent past – five were executed for sodomy at Lancaster in two weeks in 1806. The ultimate penalty was then repealed as part of the

Offences Against the Person Act. The Criminal Law Amendment Act of 1885 had as its main purpose the protection of young girls, raising the age of consent from 13 to 16, but Henry Labouchere MP introduced an amendment which made any sexual contact between men illegal with a punishment of up to two years imprisonment.

The criminality of homosexual practice made it an open opportunity for blackmail. In December 1838 in London, James Norton was transported for fifteen years for assaulting Rev. Gilbert Chestnutt, robbing him and threatening blackmail. Norton accused Chestnutt of abominable offences and his defence tried to insinuate that they were on 'terms of the greatest intimacy'.[17] Another example involved Edward Protheroe, MP for Halifax, who brought a case against his former valet James Newbery for demanding money and blackmail. Newbery had threatened to unmask Protheroe for an 'abominable offence'; Newbery circulated letters, one of which claimed that the steward of one of Protheroe's clubs had been dismissed for making a similar allegation. Newbery was given twenty years transportation but the following year Protheroe was himself in court – this time accused of assaulting a man who had made allegations about his behaviour. The case was dismissed, but Protheroe was also mentioned in the case of Henry Tiddiman in 1850, when some of those accused stated in court that Tiddiman had procured 'lads' for money and taken them to Protheroe's bedroom.[18]

In 1868 Buckinghamshire painter Robert Watson pleaded guilty to a charge of sending threatening letters to Corbett Whitton, who he had accused of 'an unnatural offence'. The judge said this crime 'was more heinous than murder' and sentenced him to penal servitude for life. In 1871 Henry Spencer was blackmailed by a man, Parker, after using a London urinal. The magistrate, Mr Tyrwhitt, sided with Spencer: 'It is well known that urinals were visited by such scoundrels as Parker either for the purpose of robbery or worse.'[19]

Another man to be named in the courts for such an apparent offence was Robert King, otherwise known as the Irish peer, the Earl of Kingston. Aged about 60 at the time, King was accused of indecent assault with intent to commit an unnatural offence upon a young man named Cull. The event apparently took place behind Marylebone police station, and seemingly involved much suggestive discussion about the merits of cigars. Cull had allowed himself to be 'picked up' and accompanied the noble lord to a public house in Oxford Street afterwards. However, when Lord Kingston left, Cull went straight to get a policeman and Kingston was arrested in the street. At the magistrates' court, the complainant 'described acts of a filthy and disgusting nature'. Kingston was bailed for £5,000 but he did not appear for his trial and his bail was forfeited. In 1860 he was arrested for drunkenness and assault, and in 1861 declared to be 'of unsound mind'. The soliciting of an offence was punishable and, in the case of George Whitehurst in 1862, it was argued that soliciting the offence by letter – even if

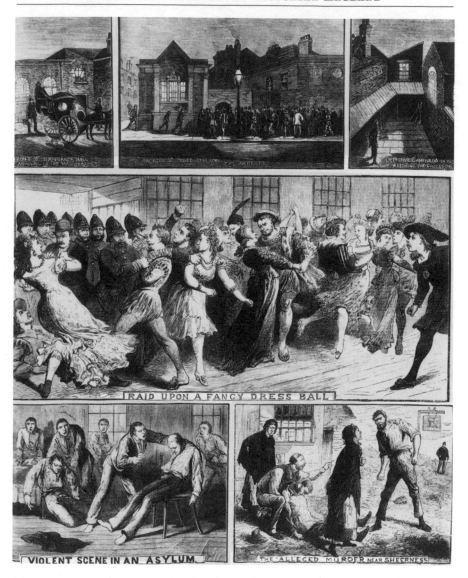

The Manchester fancy dress ball police raid exposed the city's homosexual subculture to public scrutiny in a way that was unusual for the era. (S. Webb)

not intending to commit it – was an offence; Whitehurst had been planning to lure another man to a meeting at Constitution Hill in order to gather evidence against him.

Parts of the West End of London were known for their culture of 'theatrical pubs' and 'gentlemen's clubs'. When Ernest Boulton and Frederick Park were arrested outside the Strand Theatre in 1870, they were charged for the misdemeanour of wearing women's clothes. However, the case then escalated into the more serious charge of conspiring to commit a felony: sodomy. The police searched a house in Wakefield Street and a large quantity of women's clothing was removed. Lord Arthur Pelham Clinton MP, son of the Duke of Newcastle, was implicated when it was known that one of the two men arrested had introduced himself as 'Stella, Lady Arthur Clinton'. The day before the trial was due to start, Lord Arthur died, apparently of scarlet fever, though many assumed suicide. All the defendants were acquitted on the charge of conspiracy as it depended on a felony having actually been committed – for which there was no evidence.

Dressing up in women's clothes was not only a feature of London life, such as at the Holborn Casino, but also occurred elsewhere, such as in Manchester. In September 1880 Inspector Caminada led a police raid on the Temperance Hall in Hulme, where a number of men had gathered for a fancy dress ball.[20] The windows were covered over with paper but police watched from nearby rooftops as guests went to an ante-hall, 'in which illicit activity took place'. Caminada was aware of similar previous events and got admission to the hall using the password 'Sister'. A police raid led to forty-seven arrests, with most of the men being bound over – more of a problem for the working men involved than the more professional ones who could afford the payments.

The most infamous homosexual scandal of the Victorian era resulted by chance from an investigation in 1889 as to how young telegraph boys employed at the London central telegraph office had money to spare. Disappearances of cash were being investigated when Thomas Swinscow[21] was found with the unlikely sum of 18s, which he said was actually obtained from providing services to men at a house at 19 Cleveland Street. Inspector Abberline attempted to arrest its 'manager', Charles Hammond, but only Henry Newlove could be secured. Newlove, 18,[22] was a clerk at the telegraph office and the procurer of the boys. What made the scandal significant was the gradual leaking out of the names of upper-class gentry who were the customers of the telegraph boys, including the Earl of Euston and Lord Arthur Somerset. Even Prince Albert Victor, son of the Prince of Wales, was implicated.[23] Also involved was George Veck, who had been sacked from the telegraph office for 'improper conduct' with the messenger boys; he later took to posing as a clergyman. Newlove and Veck were given four and nine months for indecency but Hammond went to America, his passage being attributed to funds from Somerset.[24]

In all probability the convictions of Newlove and Veck should have been followed by the arrest of the key establishment figures involved, but Somerset enjoyed high-level protection and after a brief visit to England was able to escape to France. Not until 12 November 1889 was a warrant for Somerset's arrest issued. However, the *North London Press* got hold of the story and named Lord Euston, who sued; Euston claimed that he had only visited the house because he had assumed it featured female nudes, and the newspaper lost the case. Its editor Parke went to prison.

In December 1889 the solicitor who had represented Veck and Newlove – Arthur Newton – was tried for attempting to pervert the course of justice by offering the telegraph boys money to leave the country. He received six weeks in prison, but some commentators have alleged that it was Newton who spread the rumours about the prince.

MARRIAGE

Where a husband and wife were concerned, the law went through a period of transition in the Victorian era. A wife could not stand as a witness against her husband, but the law increasingly gave some protection to married women, although this was only fitful in the case of protection against often endemic marital violence. The law also decreed that a husband was liable for his wife's crimes and debts, saving only treason and murder; this was the principle of 'coverture' which assumed a wife acted under the direction of her husband being one person with him. Up to 1884 she could be imprisoned for refusing intercourse: 'However brutal a tyrant she may unfortunately be chained to … he can claim from her and enforce the lowest degradation of a human being, that of being the instrument of an animal function contrary to her inclinations.'[25]

A wife was not even free to walk the streets. Until 1891, she could be legally imprisoned in her own home, although not in the unlimited fashion implied by some commentators. In the early Victorian era she certainly could not use her own possessions as she felt; indeed, from the time of her engagement she could not dispose of her own things without consulting her fiancé. This meant that a wife who ran away from a cruel husband could be prosecuted for wearing her own clothes.

The Married Women's Property Bill of 1857 was an attempt to free wives from this peculiar form of 'crime', but it was lost in the wider discussion of divorce through the Matrimonial Causes Act. However, acts were passed in 1870, 1882 and 1893 which gave women some control of their own income and property. The coverture principle was further reduced by the Matrimonial Causes Act of 1878, which allowed magistrates to grant a separation order due to assault.

The Staunton murder case of 1877 'undoubtedly aided the passing through Parliament in 1882 of the Married Women's Property Act'.[26]

The Cochrane case in 1840 ruled that a husband's rights included enforcing a 'common residence'. After several years of apparently happy marriage, Mrs Cochrane left her husband and went abroad with her mother; she was tricked into returning in 1840 and kept in a house by her husband until a writ had been issued upon her. In court, the judge found no evidence that she had left her husband because of abuse and indeed said that the law would protect a woman whose husband's intentions were improper or excessive. Despite this, quoting from an old text, he said that 'a husband hath by law a right to the custody of his wife, and may, if he think fit, confine but not imprison her'. This ruling was later condemned by Lord Esher as 'absolutely wrong'.

The Leggatt case of 1852 proved that a husband's right to detain his wife was not the same as a father's right over a child, but it did not cover a woman who was already detained[27] and this was further clarified in the Clitheroe Abduction Case. Mr E. Jackson, a relative of Colonel Jackson of Clitheroe Castle, married a wealthy local heiress, Miss Hall, in 1887 without the knowledge of her family. He then immediately went to Australia to seek his fortune. When he returned in 1889 she refused to see him or live with him, so Jackson took out a writ for restitution of conjugal rights.

He had no luck with this, so in March 1891 he, his brother and a friend abducted her as she was attending church at Clitheroe, assaulting her sister, the wife of a solicitor, in the process. They sped off to Blackburn where she was imprisoned in a house. The writs started flying immediately and a large crowd convened outside, tending to favour those in the house against the police gathered outside with a writ to release the woman. Milk and newspapers were hoisted through an upstairs window, but the house otherwise was stoutly defended. At the time, Mrs Jackson told the crowd she was content to live with her husband but it was her family who had set her against it.

After three days they surrendered. The subsequent legal battle dealt with Jackson's right to abduct his wife, starting with a victory when the High Court ruled that detaining his wife was not illegal as long as it was not cruel. However, the Court of Appeal then demanded he produce his wife in court, following which three lords, including the Lord Chancellor, decided that in fact there was no legal right to detain a wife, otherwise she would be a mere slave.

Wives could provoke assaults by men on each other. A great sensation in early Victorian years was the Heaviside elopement. It involved the wife of Captain Heaviside, a Brighton Railway director who lived in that town, and Dr Dionysius Lardner, a leading scientist of the day. Lardner made a fortune from a popular science book explaining how steam engines worked. He already had a 'reputation', having been divorced in 1839. Nonetheless, Heaviside invited Lardner to dine

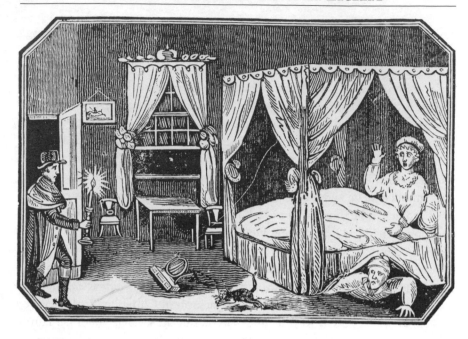

A classic scene of Victorian life: the husband returns home unexpectedly, the lover hides under the bed, the cat runs away in fear of what might happen next.

several times until, on 13 March 1840, Mrs Heaviside disappeared, booking into the Adelaide Hotel in London for a night of passion with Lardner. The imputation was that she had been a happily married woman until Lardner arrived: Heaviside's counsel said, 'she was a person on quiet, gentle and retired habits [but] … in an evil hour [Lardner] made his appearance at Brighton'.[28]

The couple were tracked to Paris by Heaviside and his father-in-law, and confronted them over breakfast. Lardner was beaten, his wig thrown on the fire and attempts were made to recapture Mrs Heaviside.[29] The court was told that Heaviside 'inflicted on him the most severe and well-merited punishment'. Heaviside then sued Lardner for 'criminal conversation' in August 1840 and won £8,000 damages, but Lardner earned £40,000 from a lecture tour in America to replace it.

Since all property in a marriage belonged to the husband in the early part of the period, a married woman could not hold any property of her own. If she eloped, she was technically stealing from her husband – or her new lover was. In 1881 Walter Walford was enjoying life as the lodger of Mr and Mrs Pickmore of Canvey Island, and enjoying additional care from his landlady. The couple decided to run off together and take all the contents of the house to start a new life in Mitcham, Surrey, hiring a railway container to help them move. They were traced to their new home and Walford was sentenced to six months in prison, at which point his paramour rushed across the court to kiss him, much to the judge's annoyance.

Communities had their own ways of expressing disapproval of marital or extramarital relationships, with the process of 'ran-tanning' being well known but in decline by the mid-1800s. It was made technically illegal by the Highways Act of 1882 because it often took place in the street outside. In February 1882 the wife of the publican in the small Essex village of Ardleigh left home and went to stay with an unmarried man, Charles Gardiner, in order to escape – she said – a beating. After a brief return to her husband, she fled back to Gardiner. This offended local morals and a large crowd gathered outside Gardiner's house, lit a bonfire and watched as the sparks set Gardiner's thatched roof alight. Then the house was pelted with missiles, and effigies of Gardiner and the errant wife were burnt. The publican and his brother were fined only £5 for this organised terror campaign.

BIGAMY

Elopement and divorce were rare, but at a time of travel opportunity it was easy for a man or woman to 'move on' and start a new life. A famous biga-mist was 'Lola Montez', who in reality was an Irishwoman named Elizabeth Gilbert. Gilbert had married an army officer in 1837 but divorced in 1842, and the terms of the settlement forbade either to marry again. She had a brief career as a 'Spanish' dancer in London, and a more successful one on the continent where she entranced King Ludwig I of Bavaria in 1847, being made Countess of Landsfeld. However, she narrowly escaped with her life when the citizens revolted. Back in London in 1849, she 'married' a young soldier from a wealthy family and was promptly prosecuted for bigamy; she fled to France and eventu-ally the USA.

John Curtis of Strensham married Anna Wilkins, 'of masculine character',[30] in 1835 but the couple separated in 1840. Anna went off dressed as a man and got work as a farm labourer in Staffordshire, where she became a 'man servant'; while in service she became too friendly with the housemaid – they were both dismissed but then got 'married'. However, 'at length the housemaid got tired of her female husband and married a real man'. Curtis also wished to remarry but was refused by his local vicar as there was no proof of his former wife being dead; instead he went to Worcester where he got another clergyman to conduct the ceremony, but when his true wife turned up shortly afterwards – in women's clothes this time – it was Curtis who went on trial.

Several cases created confusion over Scottish and English law, and the famous Yelverton case was tried in both countries. An example was heard at Exeter in 1867, when John McAlister was brought up for bigamously marrying Grace Webb in Devon in 1864. It was alleged he had married Susan Murphy in Dundee in 1848, but McAlister denied it, although he had lived with her and produced four children. A Scottish lawyer was brought in to explain that under Scottish law a man over 14 only had to consent to marriage in order to *be* married. Although McAlister was Protestant, Susan Murphy was Catholic, and McAlister said he had not understood the words pronounced by a priest in Latin when he was only 15. The court did not believe him and he got six months in gaol.

In 1889 David Hildrop, a married man of 27, was working at the Custom House Inn in Newcastle when he became enamoured with Theresa Matthews. She knew he already had a wife, but nevertheless agreed to go with him to Stratford where they were married, with Hildrop using a false name. They returned to the inn at Newcastle, keeping the marriage a secret, but somehow the story leaked out and they lost their jobs. They then went to stay in a temperance hotel in Darlington, where Hildrop bought a revolver. When his wife turned up, they fled to Redcar and then Sunderland, where he bought another revolver. Letters written at the time suggested a suicide pact, but on 4 May Theresa was found dying in a pool of blood outside her old lodgings in Newcastle, and Hildrop was seen running off. Curiously, he ran home to his first wife and told her that her rival had shot herself. He was perhaps fortunate that a jury believed him and he escaped a murder conviction, but received eighteen months hard labour for bigamy.

Perhaps such harsh sentences were not universal. In 1882 Lord Bramwell complained that bigamists were often only given a day's prison by the assizes. In the same debate, Earl Cowper said: 'Among the migratory poor, bigamy was often a venial offence, and was seldom of a complicated nature.' It was generally considered that not having heard of a person for seven years was a reasonable indication that they were dead.[31] This view was challenged by a 1889 ruling in The Queen *vs* Polson, which seemed to indicate that a simple belief that the other was dead was sufficient.

MISTRESSES, PROSTITUTION & PROCUREMENT

Seduction, assault and prostitution should be seen almost as part of a continuum of sexual crimes in Victorian England, as when a girl succumbed to the first it could often lead to the last. Many estimates of the number of prostitutes have been made, but none can be very accurate as many women were occasional prostitutes, such as the sailor's wife in east London who earned extra money on the streets while her husband was away – and was thus horrified to be sent to prison just before he was due home. Many women became prostitutes after bad decisions: Elizabeth Barrett, 'a tall and remarkably handsome woman', left her husband to live with William Lowe, who then forced her into prostitution; in

1871 he stabbed her to death through the eye with his umbrella in a moment of bad temper at North Woolwich Gardens. The judicial statistics for 1864 included police estimates of 28,094 known prostitutes not in prison – 5,000 more than known thieves. However, in 1857 *The Lancet* had claimed there were 80,000 prostitutes in London alone. In 1867 the chief constable of Liverpool reported that there were 845 'houses of ill fame' in the city – an increase of 110 from the previous year; this would suggest a population of several thousand prostitutes.

Women who were in a public place for the purpose of prostitution could be fined 40s or sent to prison for a month, whilst the keeping of a disorderly house was also indictable. On the other hand, men who were looking for a prostitute in a public place were free of arrest and those who rented out their houses for the keeping of a disorderly house were generally free as well. In 1847 a bill making it illegal to procure a girl or to pay someone else to do it passed the Commons, but was rejected by the Lords as it posed a risk to the owners of property which might be used as brothels. The Protection of Women Act, 1849, made procurement criminal, but only if it involved deception or fraud. A man in Hull who ran a brothel, so notoriously staffed by young girls that it was known as the 'Infants' school', was prosecuted only for liquor offences.[32] Until 1885, there was little protection for young women who had been taken to a brothel and it was difficult for parents to get access to their daughters without an expensive writ of habeas corpus. After 1885, it became much more difficult to run a brothel and 'houses of accommodation' filled the gap;[33] even smart shops selling shoes and perfume might offer an alternative trade for the pretty shop assistants and their customers.

Local magistrates occasionally had 'campaigns' against prostitution. For example, there was a general attempt to eradicate the nuisance of foreign women in Regent Street in 1865 which resulted in a number of French women (and some English ones) being fined 40s. Campaigns were often ineffective and in 1868 the *Manchester Guardian* reported local concerns that 'Great immorality existed in Deansgate … It was perfectly obvious that prostitution flaunted there in the most unblushing manner'.[34]

One of the enduring images of Victorian life was the middle-aged and upper-class man intent on despoiling some poor young girl. However, it has been suggested that this image is inaccurate: 'the majority of abuse cases involved complainants and defendants of similar social rank.'[35] One certain example of this theme, successfully prosecuted under the 1849 act, was that of the infamous Madame Denis and Count Adolphus Feistel. Madame Denis ran a brothel, staffed by her elderly father, Alexander Desaux, in Pimlico. Feistel and Desaux were prosecuted after a girl of 16 escaped and told the police about it, but Madame Denis escaped arrest. The girl, Alice Leroy, told of how she had met the Count in a shop in Brussels and he had promised her a job in London. Once at Denbigh Terrace the girl became an actual prisoner and 'the pollution of the poor girl was paid for in cash and jewels'.[36] She was also taken, under strict guard, to the Hotel Valois in Paris where she was 'sold' to a man for £100. Those who paid for her included 'an old marquis' and 'the Greek Prince'. Count Feistel received two years hard labour.

Sometimes it was a family member who was the prey of the seducer. In January 1874 widowed Mrs Hull of New Brompton in Kent was visited by George Fairfoot, the uncle of her children, who was a 45-year-old gentleman from Crewe. Shortly after the visit, Mrs Hull received a letter purporting to be from Mrs Fairfoot, offering to adopt one of the children to save expenses. On Boxing Day 1874 George Fairfoot arrived and selected 14-year-old Cordelia for 'adoption'.

It was too late to get back to Crewe that night and they did not get to London until 8 p.m., but Fairfoot took the girl to a coffee house and booked some rooms there. Cordelia woke up in the morning to find Fairfoot in her bed attempting an assault. Although he offered her silk dresses, the girl fought him off and got the police. He was sentenced to two months hard labour.

The real problem was systematic procurement. In 1842 in Chatham a group of eight publicans procured young girls from outlying villages by telling them about fabulous sums that could be earned. In August 1851 a policeman told a court in London about the large number of houses in that area that provided accommodation for girls and their clients. He reported that 'the Waterloo road is literally swarming with young girls who use these houses, and prowl about at all hours in the night, chiefly for the sake of plundering drunken men'. The policeman made his observations at the trial of Emma Smith, 14, and Catherine Skeets, 15, who were prostitutes arrested for theft. Both had been molested by William Smyth, a child abuser who had been transported for the rape of a child only a few months earlier. Smyth, who posed as a surgeon, used a young woman named Frances Foreman to procure young girls for him. He would get them in the house, ply them with drink and then rape them, offering them 1s or 2s as a reward. Foreman, herself only 18 and 'a rather good-looking woman', according to press reports, brought one young girl to his house under the pretence that she would be paid to do some laundry. Having taken advantage of her, Smyth then tried to persuade her to bring her younger sister.

Prostitution was linked to other forms of 'antisocial' behaviour. In 1893 there were 120 cases of 'lewd' behaviour by women in Chatham, such as soliciting, obscene language and gross indecency, all of which were associated with prostitution. Even police raids on known disreputable houses had little effect because the fines were so small; an account of a raid in January 1894 stated: 'In the downstairs room they found three well-known prostitutes and three sailors sitting around the fire, whilst in three upstairs rooms were found women and sailors in bed together, in another instance a civilian being in bed with a woman.'

Prostitution was an issue that worried Victorian legislators, but the legislation which attracted the greatest attention – and condemnation – was the series of Contagious Diseases Acts passed in 1864, 1866 and 1869. There were fears that venereal diseases would undermine Britain's fighting forces and clauses empowered the authorities to subject any woman in a military town suspected of being a prostitute to a forced medical examination. They were, according to the *British Medical Journal*, 'the most iniquitous interference with the liberty of the subject ... since the days of Charles I'.[37]

A woman in a garrison town suspected of being a prostitute had to submit to medical examination, often at the Lock hospital in London. Women who refused could be sent to prison: for example, Emma Wright of Greenwich was sent to gaol for fourteen days in January 1871 for failure to be examined. In September 1873 three women from Aldershot and Greenwich rioted at the Lock hospital as they objected to being confined there and were given a month's hard labour.

The risk was that 'respectable' women were being disgraced by these laws. In March 1876 a widowed actress and singer, Jane Percy, was found dead in the Basingstoke Canal near Aldershot after she and her 16-year-old daughter had both been summonsed to submit to an examination. Her employer at the Queen's Hotel was cautioned not to employ her, and, because she would not submit to the examination, she became virtually destitute, writing to the *Daily Telegraph* to describe her plight.

The Ladies' National Association for the Repeal of the Contagious Diseases Acts was formed and its best-known activist was Josephine Butler, who became its secretary in 1869; she became a key figure at some risk to her own safety. The Association took the view that the laws were a violation of women and tolerated the wickedness of men; members drew effective comparisons to the state's tolerance of brothels and gaming houses.[38]

Butler attracted much attention for her campaign to unseat Sir Henry Storks, the MP for the garrison town of Colchester, who had described the acts as 'a necessity'. During the 1870 election, in which Dr Baxter Langley stood on a ticket of repealing the legislation, she was chased by ruffians hired by the town's brothel keepers. She was condemned in the press as one of the 'champions of free trade in the propagation of disease'.[39] At Pontefract, men dressed as women created havoc and she had to escape through a trapdoor. However, the Royal Commission on the Contagious Diseases Acts gave her slim encouragement, concluding that 'the police are not chargeable with any abuse of their authority and they have discharged a novel and difficult duty with moderation and caution'.

A Royal Commission and a Select Committee investigated the complaints and, in 1883, the acts were suspended.

By then campaigners had already shifted their focus to the exploitation of young girls. It was pointed out that in the great cities of England, like Manchester, brothels were being run where girls were as young as 14.[40] Campaigners agreed that the raising of the age of consent was essential and there was applause when a man was sentenced to ten years penal servitude for intercourse with a girl of 10. In the campaign, Josephine Butler joined forces with W.T. Stead of the Pall Mall Gazette and the Salvation Army.

Another campaigner was Alfred Dyer, who found evidence of the trade in sadomasochistic brothels and of the exportation of girls to Brussels. Dyer's views were repeatedly dismissed by the government, but a barrister, Thomas Snagge, found that there was much evidence of a white slave trade to France, Belgium and Holland, often involving girls who had been tricked.[41] Dyer also publicised cases where it could not be proved that the victim had not assented.

The notorious Mrs Jeffries collected girls at London railway stations and supposedly supplied them to customers as august as the King of the Belgians. Her victims usually disappeared whilst their parents went to buy tickets, Mrs Jeffries' well-bred demeanour being a useful decoy. Her case was exposed by the Pall Mall Gazette, which printed articles about sadomasochistic practices in her houses; 'one of Mrs Jeffries' rooms was fitted up like a torture chamber,' Stead wrote. When her case appeared at the Middlesex sessions in July 1885, the judge met with her counsel before the hearing, following which she pleaded guilty and was fined £200; the evidence was thus never heard and led to questions being asked in the House of Commons. Her defence, by Montagu Williams, was funded by well-bred army officers who formed her clientele; Williams pleaded for a light sentence with the astonishing claim that 'there was never a more unobjectionable house for a house of this character than the defendant's'.[42] Yet one of the woman's servants described how a 13-year-old girl had been raped at one of the houses.

MPs became suspicious when Judge Edlin immediately went on extended leave after the case and they wanted to know why Jeffries' punishment was so light compared to that of James Barrett in Clerkenwell, who got six months for the same offence. They also wanted to know why Inspector Minahan had been dismissed from the Metropolitan Police and what his 'allegations' had been. Mr Callan MP denounced the Home Secretary as 'utterly unfit' and deserving of censure. In the subsequent Armstrong case, a brothel keeper named Madame Mourey reported that the Jeffries publicity had caused a sudden fall in the supply of young virgins, although one or two houses in St John's Wood still had some.[43]

The editor of the Pall Mall Gazette, W.T. Stead, agreed with Josephine Butler that action needed to be taken against child prostitution. Stead pointed out the limitations of a law that protected young women only if they were 'in the custody' of their father. To prove his concerns, Stead and his associates effectively bought a 13-year-old girl named Eliza Armstrong from her mother for £5. Stead used an ex-brothel keeper turned Salvationist, Rebecca Jarrett, as an intermediary and used a midwife to prove the girl's virginity. Stead published his articles under the heading of *The Maiden Tribute of Modern Babylon* on 6 July 1885.

The articles produced a sensation – the streets around his office were so packed with people that public safety became a concern. Free copies were posted to clergymen and the exposé of the trade to Belgium brought down a senior police officer there. But when action was taken, it was taken against Stead. On 8 July 1885 hordes of newspaper sellers were prosecuted and fined £1 each for selling obscene material, then on 12 July a 'respectable looking woman' applied to Marylebone magistrates for help in tracing her missing daughter.

The police traced the story to Stead, but they were clear no crime had been committed. Yet Mrs Armstrong pressed her case, and Stead and his associates were ensnared in legal technicalities. They had taken the girl away without the permission of her absentee father and the medical examination conducted without permission counted as an assault. Despite evidence that Mrs Armstrong knew exactly what she was doing, and had spent the money on drink, Stead was given three months in prison and Rebecca Jarrett six months. This penalty was worth it, nonetheless, for Stead's campaign ensured the passage of the Criminal Law Amendment Act in August 1885; not only did this raise the age of consent, but it also gave police the right to search brothels and introduced strict penalties for parents who sold their children into white slavery.[44]

One of the earliest cases under the new law was held at Plaistow in 1886. Matilda French, 15, left Tiptree for London to join her older sister Martha and her 'husband', William Carr – except he was not actually Martha's husband. When she got there she was kept as a virtual prisoner, made to share the bed with her sister and her lover, and then forced to work as a prostitute. Both were charged under the 1885 act with keeping a girl for unlawful purposes and Carr was given twenty months.

A number of women enjoyed highly successful and lucrative 'careers'. These included Cora Pearl and Catherine Walters, known also as 'Skittles': the Prince of Wales featured in the curriculum vitae of both. Lily Langtry was the Prince's mistress from 1877 to 1880, then served Prince Louis of Battenberg. During this time the editor of *Town Talk*, Adolphus Rosenborg, published several articles about her saying that her husband was going to sue for divorce citing the Prince of Wales, Lord Lonsdale[45] and Lord Londesborough as co-respondents. When reporting the withdrawal of the case, he alleged that this was because Edward Langtry had been offered a diplomatic appointment, by implication, as a pay-off. Langtry brought an action for libel and won his case. Rosenborg was also charged with libel against Mr and Mrs Cornwallis West[46] for an article ridiculing Mrs Cornwallis West for having her photograph taken 'day and night' to be sold

HORRIBLE BRUTALITY-ATTEMPTED LYNCH LAW-LOWER NORWOOD

The 'woman caught in adultery' who was subjected to a traditional 'lynching' at Lower Norwood, 1878. This was a form of ran-tanning (see p. 181).

alongside pictures of half-naked actresses and completely naked African women. Rosenborg lost this case too and served eighteen months in prison.

Violet Campbell was a beautiful 'actress' who specialised in saucy roles as a male, her Peter Pan being an especial favourite. Miss Campbell married David de Bensaude in 1884 but her career as an actress was supported by wealthy Lord Lonsdale. The three toured the country putting on Campbell's shows with Lonsdale as 'manager' until, in August 1886, Lonsdale was summonsed for an assault on de Bensaude at Newcastle for which he was fined 40s. De Bensaude said he had been to London but returned to find his wife sharing a hotel sitting room with Lonsdale, who had twice used force to throw him out; the row was witnessed by a private detective who de Bensaude had brought with him. The august aldermen of the Newcastle bench thought it 'a very commonplace assault and one which they thought a peer of the realm should not have been engaged in'.

At Manchester, Lonsdale gave a lengthy interview to a Sunday newspaper, *The Umpire*. In this he castigated de Bensaude as a drunkard who had 'misapplied' £300 and sponged off his wife's earnings. De Bensaude sued for libel and won £390 damages, payable by *The Umpire*, though it was reported in court that Lonsdale himself had proofed the article.

The next appearance of this trio in court involved divorce, de Bensaude having replied to his wife's suit by issuing one of his own, alleging adultery between her and Lord Lonsdale. The case came to a sudden stop when de Bensaude signed an acceptance that 'relations were not immoral' and accepted £1,100 from Lonsdale 'in full discharge of any damages and costs'. In return, de Bensaude agreed to let his wife live alone for a year and not to molest her. However, by September Violet was alleging he had molested her in breach of the agreement of 7 July. In response, he argued that the agreement was invalid as he had been assured there was nothing improper going on – yet Violet had given birth to Lonsdale's illegitimate child in May 1887 and was actually living with him from August.[47] De Bensaude was also criticised for having 'signed the deed and sold his wife to Lowther [Lonsdale]'.

Although de Bensaude was condemned as a mercenary chancer, his subsequent behaviour suggests that he was bitter about the loss of his wife. In November 1887 he was arrested for being drunk and disorderly at the Strand Theatre, where Lonsdale had gone to watch Miss Campbell perform, though he was acquitted. The following month he was again arrested for supposedly saying 'I will put a bullet through you' to Violet. When the case came to court he agreed to pay recognisances of £250 for six months, and although Lonsdale was summoned by the defence, he failed to appear. In February 1888 he was charged with wilful damage to the King's Arms at Malmesbury (where Miss Campbell had family) and to her house in St John's Wood, which he broke into. Lonsdale seems to have cracked under the weight of scandal and went off to explore the Canadian north. De Bensaude died in poverty soon afterwards but Miss Campbell later remarried a barrister, Henry West.

OBSCENITY & PORNOGRAPHY

There was a well-established trade in obscene pictures and books and this grew to take advantage of improved postal services. New laws, specifically outlawing such practices as sending obscene material through the post, culminated in the so-called Lord Campbell's Act. The Sale of Obscene Books (Prevention) Bill was passed in 1857 but caused much entertainment in the Committee, where some MPs pointed out that it would eradicate most literature from the time of Charles II and noted that a book about the Naples Museum – to be found in the Commons library – had been banned as obscene in America. Often known as the Obscene Publications Act, it was widely known just as Campbell's Act.

The Holywell Street area was a centre of the trade in London. One who fell foul of the law as a result was Thomas Blacketer of nearby Wych Street, who had a book for sale in his window that attracted the attention of a member of the Society for the Suppression of Vice. The offending book was then purchased in a 'sting' operation, and Blacketer sent to prison for three months in May 1847.

The 1857 legislation resulted in a crackdown on several shops around Holywell Street; in September 1857 a large body of police combed the area. One book 'of a most detestable character' was found hidden in a pair of boots, and four summonses were issued. In 1859 the house of a West End picture dealer was raided and more than eighty 'stereoscopic slides' destroyed. Yet the trade continued – still in the same places. In 1861 an elderly Holywell Street dealer, who had been in and out of prison for forty years in the trade, was sent back again for two years hard labour; it was said that at various times, 'tons weight of obscene books, pictures and plates' had been seized from his premises.

Charles Bradlaugh MP and Annie Besant, the noted women's rights campaigner, were jointly prosecuted for printing and publishing in 1877 a new edition of *The Fruits of Philosophy*, a book on birth control first published in 1832, which sold 125,000 copies in three months.[48] The initial hearing at the magistrates' court was interrupted by a discussion amongst the magistrates as to whether they ought to clear the court of women, due to the matters to be discussed; Bradlaugh replied that many of the women were witnesses and that his own daughters were present.[49] There was much discussion of Lord Campbell's Act and the meaning of 'tendency to corrupt'. Bradlaugh and Besant were sentenced to six months but freed on a legal technicality. Bradlaugh was elected an MP in 1880 but had immediate problems with swearing the oath as he was an atheist; he was prosecuted for having voted without swearing it and four times pleaded his case at the bar of the House.

By the late 1890s there was a small coterie of 'free thinkers' who advocated more open sexual expression. Some of these formed the Legitimation League and published a journal, *The Adult*. It was run from the bookshop of its member, George Bedborough, which offered titles such as *Sexual Inversion*. The police came to the conclusion that the League was an anarchist group and arrested Bedborough for selling an obscene book. Bedborough caved in, admitted three charges and was bound over despite the support of George Bernard Shaw.

It should not be supposed that pornography was the reserve of the seedy and downtrodden. Henry Ashbee, one of the main collectors of the era, kept a large library in private rooms at Gray's Inn – a safe distance from his wife – where he entertained his middle-class friends like Richard Burton, the explorer, a pioneer English enthusiast of the *Kama Sutra* which he published in 1883. Ashbee may also have been the author of the famous sexual autobiography *My Secret Life*, though its authorship – and status as a work of non-fiction – has never been proved.

ABORTION & INFANTICIDE

To procure an abortion was criminal throughout the Victorian era. From 1803 the law distinguished abortion that was performed after 'quickening' – the time of first movement by the foetus. Under the Offences Against the Person Act of

1861, procuring an abortion or trying to self-abort carried a sentence from three years up to life.

In Nottingham abortion was said to be 'lamentably prevalent'.[50] During 1844–45 there were at least three sudden deaths associated with abortion, one of which was of Ann Snowden. Mary Goodall operated a scale of fees based on the length of pregnancy, varying from 7s 6d in the first three months to up to 15s for over six months. Goodall used an 'instrument' on Snowden, who afterwards became sickly and died on 23 February. The coroner's jury initially returned an unhelpful verdict of 'died from inflammation of the bowels', but eventually Goodall was brought to the assizes under the 1803 act. However, both women had made a mistake: Snowden had not been pregnant, and this caused some uncertainty. Eventually it was agreed that a woman did not actually have to be pregnant for the offence of causing death by procuring an abortion to apply, and Goodall went to hard labour for two years.

Two years later, Sarah Henson, a servant from Derby, sought out Ann West to help her when she became pregnant. It was alleged that West then secured the miscarriage of a five-month-term child, which died. Both women were arrested and the coroner's jury decided on a verdict of wilful murder. Henson gave evidence against West at the assizes, but the defence made much of this and West was found not guilty. Such results were not uncommon: in 1893 in Lincoln, pregnant wife Caroline Sharp died of peritonitis after a visit from Eliza Luff, but the jury was unconvinced that Luff's visit had caused the death. Dorothy Davis of Windsor, on the other hand, who caused the death of Annie Simpson from peritonitis after twice attempting an abortion, was sentenced to twenty years penal servitude for manslaughter.

In Manchester in 1875 Margaret McKivett found herself pregnant and went to visit 'midwife' Mrs Heap – who had just died. Alfred Heap, the widower, treated her instead and two days later she had a miscarriage. Heap was summoned, arriving drunk, and told the mother to bury the foetus in wasteland. But Margaret died and the post-mortem identified cause of death as being from infection set off by two sharp puncture wounds caused by an abortion. After he was found guilty of murder, it was revealed that Heap had been acquitted of wilful murder after the similar death of a woman in 1867 and sentenced to five years penal servitude for procuring an abortion in 1869. Heap was one of the few abortionists to go to the gallows.

The best-known crime connected with Victorian sexuality was probably the murder of children: infanticide. Precise numbers are not possible to identify, but in 1864 the Registrar General recorded 2,305 deaths of children under 1 year old from unspecified causes[51] and in 1863–87 the Registrar General noted 63 per cent of murders were of infants.[52]

In 1851 Mr Ewart MP commented that 'in all cases of infanticide juries now refuse to find verdicts of murder, yet who were Parliament to protect if not the unprotected?' Modern historians echo this: 'Tiny bodies were found in their hundreds in Victorian London,' wrote Emsley, but 'there was also a reluctance on

The other side of the tragic story of infanticide: a group of young women, with nothing but life imprisonment in front of them, gaze thoughtfully into the distance at the women's prison in Woking, 1889.

the part of the police and coroners to investigate dead infants.' The situation was publicised by doctors Thomas Wakley[53] and especially Edwin Lankester, successive Middlesex coroners, and the latter alleged that 12,000 London women had killed their babies. At least one modern historian has alleged that they deliberately inflated the statistics[54] but managed to reverse a trend of gradually more lenient sentences on convicted women.[55]

Child murders commonly fell into two groups: young babies, often only hours old, who were disposed of before anyone could confirm they had actually lived, and older children who were in the way of new relationships.

Concealment of birth, including helping to dispose a dead child's body, was made punishable by up to two years in prison by the Offences Against the Person Act, 1861. However, this was considerably more liberal than at the start of the century, when a law of 1624 still assumed that if the baby's body had been concealed then murder had been committed. After 1803 proof of murder was required. In many cases the punishment seemed very light, generally because juries preferred to assume a child was born dead. In October 1839 Maria Andrew, a servant at the Talbot Inn in Holbeach, gave birth in her room without telling anyone and left the dead child between the mattress and the bed frame. She was found guilty only of concealing a birth and given one month in prison.

Ann Mead of Navestock was a servant girl who gave birth after only three months of pregnancy. The child was stillborn, but she cut it up with dinner knives and put the pieces in the garden privy. She was given a month's hard labour for concealing the birth. By the end of the period the murder of a child was often lightly punished.

By the 1860s, executions for the killing of a baby were almost unknown, perhaps partly because of the difficulty of securing a conviction. In 1863 *The Observer* reported that 'the crime of infanticide ... is admitted on all hands to be common throughout the country' and unwanted children were 'allowed gradually to pine away and die, this relieving the mother or her seducer from further anxiety and expense'.[56] A midwife who had attended over 2,000 stillbirths in London said that her certificate of stillbirth was enough to avoid a prosecution.

A famous infanticide case was the trial of Charlotte Winsor in Devon in 1865. The case began when the body of an infant was found at the roadside near Torquay on 15 February 1865. The baby belonged to a servant, Mary Harris, who was initially also charged. Winsor operated a two-tier service: a weekly payment of 3s, or £3–5 for a more permanent solution. At the trial, evidence was given that Winsor had 'put one away' for a girl who had been confined at her house and who had then refused to pay the £3 expected. It was explained that Winsor got rid of one baby with a finger 'under the jugular vein' and threw Elizabeth Darwen's 3-week-old baby into Torbay. Even her own sister had paid her £2 for the service of disposing a child. Winsor was sent to prison.

During 1867 and 1868 the interest in 'baby farming' increased. The *British Medical Journal* joined in the campaign to have the effectiveness of the law improved. The campaign received more fuel from the case of Mrs L. Martin of Dean Street, Soho, who was an abortionist but also drowned full-term babies. One claim was that she had disposed of 555 in ten months, but she died in 1869.[57]

Another serious case was that of Margaret Waters of Brixton. The case centred on Miss Jennette Cowen, who was seen leaving a 'lying-in hospital' run by Mrs Barton at 164 Camberwell Road. Miss Cowen's baby was born on 14 May 1870 but on 28 May was taken to another house in the area, attracting the interest of Sergeant Ralph. Ralph connected the movements of the child with an advert in Lloyds' for children to be adopted at £5 each, which he answered himself. He went to the house and demanded to see the Cowen child, which, when he found it, 'was nothing but skin and bones, and appeared to be dying. It was filthy and wrapped up in some dirty black cloths.' He found several other babies in the front kitchen, eleven in all. Margaret Waters said that one was the baby of her sister, Mrs Oliver, but the rest were in her care and that she had forty at one time. All the children weighed less than half the expected weight.

Three children died almost immediately at the workhouse hospital and two more later. Waters and her sister, Sarah Ellis, were charged with conspiracy to obtain money under false pretences and a number of women came forward to testify that they had handed babies over with cash for adoption, despite odd arrangements such as meeting in a waiting room at King's Cross. A 14-year-old servant at Waters' house, Annie Warden, testified to seeing 'Little Arthur' dead in the kitchen but could not recall a funeral; she also remembered 'Little David' and 'James'. Another servant recalled Waters calling the babies 'little beasts and devils'.

Waters was found guilty of murder but Ellis was found not guilty and received only eighteen months in prison. No one really knew how many children Waters had killed, but she had been placing adverts for at least four years.[58] Stories were told of how she had taken children out in a pram at night and returned with an empty pram. No evidence of actual adoptions emerged and there were at least forty 'for whom she can render no account'.

The press was outraged by the case. 'Murder by adoption will not cease because Margaret Waters has been convicted,' wrote *The Observer*, and 'everybody who receives a child or children to nurse should first obtain a licence from the police which should render his or her house liable to inspection'. Nonetheless, *The Observer* thought some of the evidence in the trial was actually inadmissible and Waters' brother made an attempt to overturn the sentence. However, Waters went to the gallows.

The *Medical Times* was unimpressed: 'The Government, in a fit of spasmodic sternness, has made a public example of Margaret Waters. We would advise them to turn their attention to the manufacturing districts, where children are put out during the day to be poisoned with syrup of poppies and quack carminatives.'

Three days after Waters' execution, the Infant Life Protection Society was formed to campaign for changes in the law. The result, the Infant Life Protection Act of 1872, was ineffective and had to be revised in 1897 after another serious case. The 1872 act was widely criticised by suffragists, to the dismay of its medical champions, and has been judged 'a resounding failure'.[59]

Older children were also killed. In December 1864 Richard Hale was hanged at Stafford for the murder of his daughter Eliza Sillitoe,[60] who was 5. Convicted alongside him was his paramour, Cecilia Barker, who escaped the noose because she was pregnant. On 20 July Hale and Barker had been seen in a cornfield at Coseley with the little girl and a witness *thought* he had seen Hale strangle the child. Eleven days later the decomposed body of a child was found in the corn. Some circumstantial evidence told against Hale: four years earlier his brother had found the body of an unidentified child in the same field with only the legs in a preserved state. Hale had been tried for manslaughter after the death of his wife in 1863 – the woman had claimed he was starving her to death but doubts over the treatment she had received from a midwife saw him escape this charge. No one could now explain why Hale and his lover had left the child's hat and boots in the field if they had murdered her. Unusually, Hale continued to vehemently claim his innocence after the trial, right up until the time the drop fell. 'I am quite innocent,' he declared. 'May my soul go and burn in hell if what I say is not the truth.'

Notes

1   Martin Wiener, *Violence Manliness and Criminal Justice in Victorian England*, p. 86.
2   *Manchester Guardian*, 26 May 1847.
3   L. Jackson, *Child Sexual Abuse in Victorian England*, London, 2000, p. 41.
4   V. Gattrell, et al., *The Decline of Theft and Violence in Victorian and Edwardian England*, London, 1980, p. 289.
5   Wiener, p. 76.
6   Jackson, p. 29.
7   K. Stevenson, 'Observations on the Law relating to Sexual Offences', in *Current Legal Issues*, 1999.
8   This was often known as the Bishop of Oxford's Act.
9   Stevenson, op. cit.
10   *The Times*, 16 July 1840.
11   *The Times*, 26 July 1848.
12   S. Marcus, *The Other Victorians*, London, 1966, p. 58. In providing an extract, Marcus makes no comment as to the age of the child; it would be difficult to imagine this in a book published in the twenty-first century.
13   Since a man and woman became 'one flesh' when they married, marrying a sister was more symbolic than it would be considered today.
14   *Hansard*, 16 July 1903.
15   The term 'homosexual' did not come into use until about 1892.
16   Sodomy was also prosecuted when involving men with women and, occasionally, children.
17   *The Times*, 21 December 1838.
18   Henry Cocks, *Nameless Offences*, London, 2003, p. 137.
19   Ibid., p. 132.
20   S. Webb, *Prevalence v Absence – an investigation into the discourse of homosexuality in Victorian Lancashire*, unpublished BA thesis, University of Manchester, 2009.
21   In some sources spelt 'Swinscoe'.
22   Some sources say 15.
23   If all the rumours about him were true, 'Eddy' would have been something of a sexual polymath. Said to have been a 'regular' at Cleveland Street, he was also said to have had venereal disease, to have been a frequenter of prostitutes and a suspect for Jack the Ripper. It was probably a relief to all that he died before becoming king.
24   Hyde, *The Cleveland Street Scandal*, p. 74.
25   J.S. Mill, *The Subjection of Women*, London, 1869, p. 57.
26   H.M. Walbrook, *Murders and Murder Trials*, p. 198.
27   M.L. Shanley, *Feminism, Marriage and the Law in Victorian England*, Princeton, 1989, p. 181.
28   *The Times*, 3 August 1840.

29 Dale, *Fashionable Brighton*, speaks of Mrs Heaviside being brought back, but the *Dictionary of National Biography* states that attempts to force her to return were unsuccessful.

30 *The Observer*, 1 April 1850.

31 *Hansard*, 16 May 1889, vol. 336, cc 221–3.

32 Paul Bartley, *Prostitution: Prevention and Reform 1860–1914*, p. 85.

33 F. Harrison, *The Dark Angel*, pp. 220–1.

34 *Manchester Guardian*, 29 October 1868.

35 Jackson, p. 29.

36 *The Times*, 8 April 1854.

37 Quoted in G.K. Behlmer, *Child Abuse and Moral Reform in England*, p. 35.

38 *Manchester Guardian*, 22 November 1871.

39 *The Observer*, 30 October 1870.

40 *Manchester Guardian*, 28 July 1885.

41 Bartley, p. 87.

42 *The Times*, 6 May 1885.

43 *The Times*, 3 November 1885.

44 Famously, Stead 'celebrated' his prison sentence by donning prison uniform every year until he went down with the *Titanic* in 1912.

45 Lonsdale had a weakness for beautiful women; he was involved in a scuffle in Hyde Park over Lily Langtry.

46 Cornwallis West was Lord Lieutenant of Denbighshire.

47 The child was named Violet Lowther de Bensaude.

48 Harrison, p. 58.

49 *Manchester Guardian*, 18 April 1877.

50 *The Times*, 13 March 1848.

51 Emsley, *The English and Violence since 1750*, p. 72.

52 Behlmer, p. 18.

53 Editor of *The Lancet*, an MP and also a campaigner against the adulteration of food.

54 J. McDonagh, *Child Murder and British Culture*, 2003, p. 126.

55 C.L. Kreuger, 'Literary Defences and Medical Prosecutions', in *Victorian Studies*, vol. 40, no 2.

56 *The Observer*, 20 September 1863.

57 Behlmer, p. 31.

58 J. Tweedie, *In the Name of Love*, p. 44, claims thirty-five died at Waters' behest.

59 Behlmer, p. 35.

60 The surname was different from his own as the child was born out of wedlock, although the mother became his first wife.

12

Deceit & Deception

Deceit and deception were practised by all classes but were often viewed as 'moral' crimes and punishments were consequently less severe than, for example, burglary. Financial fraud came to hold a big fascination for the Victorians, linked closely to their powerful interest in financial status and debt. Debt features heavily in the novels of Dickens, due to his own personal experience, and fraud fascinated Trollope as can be seen from *The Way We Live Now* and *The Prime Minister*. Some of the personalities in this chapter were men (almost invariably) with great social influence and political power.

New laws on fraud and corruption came gradually to define what was 'acceptable'. Bribery and corruption had been a feature of the electoral process for generations, but the secret ballot and new electoral laws reduced this area considerably. John Charlesworth was tried at York in 1861 for corruptly procuring a nomination and election as Conservative MP for Wakefield. He had secretly set up a bank account for a relative in order to bribe voters to hold up their hands for him at the nomination in 1859, and was found guilty of spending £5,000 on bribery, although certified expenses were stated as being about £650. A colliery manager was first offered £50, and then offered 'a situation for life at 10s more than he is presently receiving'.[1] Such was the corruption in the borough that the electoral seat was suspended from 1859 to 1862, but there were more allegations in 1874.

DEBT

As famously depicted in *Little Dorrit*, in the early Victorian era debtors could be sent to debtors' gaols where they could fester for long periods. Some of these were hopeless places such as the one at Radford near Nottingham; in 1843 this was a 'ruinous building, the abandoned workhouse of the parish of Radford, [which] has been re-occupied as a debtors' gaol ... I have seldom witnessed a

The Marshalsea prison, famous for its debtors and *Little Dorrit*, closed in 1842 and its last inmates were released.

scene of more real and abject misery … Nothing whatever, either in the shape of fuel, bedding, light or food, is provided here'.[2] Other places were as bad – the Court of Requests prison in Birmingham was condemned by the *Birmingham Advertiser* as a 'filthy and horrible hole' in 1844.[3] On Christmas Day 1844 there was a riot, partly inspired by visitors having been allowed to bring in alcohol, but at the resulting trial even the counsel for the prosecution was moved to complain: 'A disgrace to any country and any age … It was a confined, ill-ventilated hole, underground, made out of the cellar of an old house, and the stench therefrom was intolerable … commonly called the Louse Hole.'

In this hole were confined twenty-three debtors, although forty-three had been known; when the Christmas riot broke out the twenty-three debtors had been joined by about thirty visitors. The recorder sentenced the main offenders to three months in Warwick gaol which, he said, would be a vast improvement.

Debtors made for a different type of prisoner from the usual; during 1842, 142 passed through the doors of Devon's county gaol, of whom it was said they were 'frequent in their attendance at the chapel services, [and made] frequent application for books from the lending library [from which] they derive instruction and amusement'.[4] The practice of imprisoning debtors was widely condemned: 'The interior of a prison corrupted all its inmates.'[5]

MPs and others connected with Parliament's business were meant to be free from arrest for debt if involved in their political business, so it caused some interest when Richard Sprye was arrested on a street corner in 1852 for a debt of £150 whilst on his way to attend a hearing at the House of Lords; he was incarcerated in Whitecross Street gaol. The Lords ordered that he should be released as privilege had been breached, but in order not to be arrested again he was advised to go home only by the most direct route.

Various attempts were made to end imprisonment for debt. The Insolvent Debtors Act and the Bankrupt Law Amendment Act of 1842 only partially resolved the situation, but meant that people could not be imprisoned for debts less than £20. However, only traders were protected by bankruptcy and insolvent debtors could not become bankrupt until 1861. In 1862 Sir George Grey thought that since the passing of the Bankruptcy Act, 'a great reduction had taken place in the number of prisoners confined for debt', and noted that it would be possible to close the Queen's Bench prison in London as a result.[6] The 1869 Debtors' Act largely reduced the numbers in gaol for debt, though it was still possible for people to be sent there for up to six weeks if they had the means to pay their debts but refused to do so. Far from eradicating it, commitment to prison for debt was still common even at the end of the Victorian era; in 1899 county courts sent 7,867 people to prison for debt.[7]

The wider use of bankruptcy did not mean an end to prison for such people, as it created another set of fraudsters who went bankrupt but tried to hide their assets. In 1884 a Bourne cattle dealer was accused of deceitfully removing £500 just before going bankrupt; Clarke, the dealer, contended he had lost the money in London after visiting a house of ill fame near King's Cross. In fact, it was proved that he had bought sheep in Stamford for £600 and then sold them in London for an unknown profit – he was given two months in prison. The same year a bankrupt farmer who sold up and set off for America from Boston was arrested at Liverpool with £100 on him; he was given eight months hard labour.

FRAUD

The most famous 'fraud' case of the Victorian era involved the Tichborne Claimant, an extraordinary cause célèbre which engulfed the nation and became a social, legal and political sensation. Its impact has been summed up by Rohan McWilliam since 'supporters [of the claimant] claimed that there was one law for the rich and one for the poor and upheld a civic virtue that needed protection from aristocratic elites ... we find in the Tichbornites' defence of customary morality a deep yearning for a just social order'.[8]

There are perhaps two key characters in the story, but even this is open to debate. One was Arthur Orton, a butcher's son born in Wapping in 1834, who visited Chile and then went to Australia where he entered into years of obscurity

Part of the romance of the Tichborne Claimant story is his origins in the remote outback of Australia, graphically illustrated in this sketch of the Claimant's hut.

with a little criminal activity on the side. The second character was Sir Roger Doughty-Tichborne, an errant son of a wealthy family, who left the country after failing to secure his lady love in marriage; he visited South America and was supposedly lost on a ship between Brazil and Jamaica in 1854. The crux of the case concerns the extent to which these two overlapped.

After the disappearance of Sir Roger, his nephew eventually became heir to the estates. In 1864 the mother, Lady Tichborne, placed adverts seeking her long lost son. Eventually a butcher in Wagga Wagga, Australia, claimed to be the lost heir to the fortune. Some said this was really Arthur Orton. When 'the Claimant'[9] emerged, he said that he had known Orton in Australia and that they had occasionally exchanged identities – perhaps not unknown amongst the criminal classes. He was helped by people who were associated with the family and won further support when he came to England; it has been alleged that he used this support to acquire details of the real Sir Roger. One of the most extraordinary features of the story is how he managed to win over many people who had known Sir Roger, yet totally failed to convince others.

When he reached London Lady Tichborne was away and instead he visited Wapping, where he asked after the Orton family. Then he travelled to Paris where, on 10 January 1867, he met Lady Tichborne under unusual circumstances. The day he was due to meet her, the Claimant refused to get up from his bed and so she first saw him lying on the bed, fully dressed, with his face

The Claimant lost the legal battle, which was a shattering blow.

more or less to the wall. Nevertheless, the old lady said: 'He looks like his father and his ears look like his uncle's.'[10] From then on she paid him an allowance of £1,000 a year. Although she immediately identified him as Sir Roger, the rest of the family vehemently denied any similarity. One factor was that the Claimant was 27 stone, whereas Sir Roger had been slim – and he also could not speak French, whereas Sir Roger had been fluent. Enquiries suggested the link to Arthur Orton.

The Claimant then brought a case to have the tenant of 'his' property, Tichborne Park, evicted. This case took almost a year and revealed that Sir Roger had left behind a 'sealed packet' which allegedly contained details of how he had seduced and made pregnant his cousin Katherine Doughty, who by this time was Lady Radcliffe.[11] Lord Bellew recalled tattooing Tichborne at school and, indeed, Katherine herself recalled a tattoo later – but the Claimant had no tattoo.

Given that the case could not continue if it was not clear who was suing, it was declared a 'non-suit' and brought to a halt.

The Claimant was charged with perjury as a result, but began to attract growing support. Guildford Onslow MP helped him with funds and during the trial the Claimant supported himself by making appearances at music halls. The second trial lasted from April 1873 to February 1874 and was 'Regina vs Castro', the name he was known under in Australia. Evidence that went against the Claimant included some from a former girlfriend of Orton's. It took a month for the judge to sum up, after which the Claimant received two seven-year sentences. It has been estimated that the trial cost the equivalent of £10 million in today's money.

The Claimant was released in 1884. In 1895 he signed a confession that was published in *The People*, but then he retracted it. When he died, he was allowed to have a plate saying 'Sir Roger Tichborne' on his coffin. In a bizarre aftermath, his daughter attempted to shoot Joseph Tichborne on his wedding day in 1912.

The memory of the case lived on for many years. In a tour of the world, Mark Twain stopped off at Wagga Wagga and recalled its most famous son: 'It was out of the midst of his humble collection of sausages and tripe that he soared up into the zenith of notoriety and hung there in the wastes of space and time, with the telescope of all nations levelled at him.'[12]

Another similar case was that of the 'Countess of Derwentwater' or Amelia Radcliffe, as she was also known. Amelia claimed descent from the Earl of Derwentwater, who was executed in 1716 for his support of the Stuart rebellion and whose estates were forfeited to the Crown.

After the execution of the earl, his son John went to London where – in the accepted account – he died in 1731. Amelia's version, however, was that he fled to Germany, where he married at Frankfurt in 1740, and she claimed to be the last descendant of that marriage. She arrived in England in about 1858.[13] In 1869 she interrupted the Derwentwater estate rent day at Haydon Bridge and demanded that the rents be paid to her instead. She had to be forcibly ejected from the ruins of Dilston Castle after which she built a wooden shed in the highway, which was otherwise described as a 'sentry box'; this was removed by highway authorities as an obstruction and she was fined 10s. She tried to take possession of the rents at a public house, The Anchor, where the official agent was collecting monies on behalf of the claimed estate. All the time she was attracting support, and a good measure of it because the 'official' landlord was remote and unpopular; her adherents dressed with blue and buff ribands.

The most exotic incident in this strange career occurred in January 1870 when a farm at Newlands South, Shotleybridge, was raided since it had not paid rents to the 'Countess' of £270. This 'raid' was led by the Countess' bailiff, Henry Brown. Stock was taken in lieu of rent. Attempts to repossess the goods were met with resistance and lives threatened – several thousand local people were prepared to support the Countess. She toured the district 'attired in an antique dress, a military cloak, and a bonnet with a tall waving plume, and carrying a sword'. She even planted a flag at Newlands. Her popularity was such that the horses were taken out of harness at Consett and people pulled her carriage instead. On 17 January a 'sale' was held at Consett which 3,000 people attended, but nineteen were arrested for riot, conspiracy and forcible entry after an attempt to return to the farm was repulsed by police.

At Newcastle Assizes all the defendants pleaded guilty and Brown, the 'bailiff', got nine months. Further attempts to 'claim' stock were rigorously resisted by the authorities.

After the Newlands debacle, £500 damages were claimed against Amelia, who was judged bankrupt. She had borrowed £4,000 from various local people to buy heirlooms said to prove her claims, including £1,200 from the Rev. Brown of Blaydon, and writs were issued for the return of the money. The heirlooms were seized and auctioned in Newcastle in 1871. In 1873 she was still languishing in prison. At the same time the official owners seem to have tired of the estate and began to sell it; Dilston Castle was cleared of its contents and the remains of the Earl disinterred and taken to Thorndon in Essex.

At the lower end of the fraud spectrum were those who obtained advantage by fraud or deception. Often crimes were very minor and involved simply not paying for something. One can only wonder at the situation of Joe McNulty, who obtained a spade under false pretences at Prescot, Lancashire, in 1855; he was given six months hard labour. More imaginative was John Flinn, a former lieutenant in the Royal Navy, who forged and uttered a certificate for the payment of prize money in 1840; Flinn pretended to be George Langley, for whom £178 in money had been waiting since 1835. He was transported for life, having attempted to defraud Chelsea hospital which was due the money if it were unclaimed for six years.

FINANCIAL FRAUD

The Victorian era was the first great era of financial fraud. George Hudson is perhaps the best-known name associated with this, whose practice was to pay dividends out of capital. He also got companies that he controlled to buy shares in his other companies at high prices. Sometimes money from company accounts ended up in his personal account. By the late 1840s he was using his status as an MP to avoid being arrested for debt. In 1865 he was briefly imprisoned at York for debt, but subsequently released and almost accepted back into society.

Lax accounting meant that fraud proliferated in many types of business. Joseph Cole set up a company in 1850 that specialised in a type of credit fraud based on 'dock warrants' which gave title to stored merchandise. By showing customers goods stored in other people's warehouses, he was able to borrow large sums of money until staff at the Overend & Gurney banking house realised what was happening in 1853. Keen to protect their own interests, they tried to keep the affair quiet, although Cole's operations collapsed in 1854 and he was given four years penal servitude.

Leopold Redpath's downfall was the result of a chance meeting on a suburban railway station platform. Edmund Dennison, the chairman of the Great Northern Railway, was talking to a peer of the realm at the station, with Redpath – essentially little more than a chief clerk in Dennison's company – nearby. Dennison was astonished when the noble lord greeted Redpath as an old friend and commented on the 'sumptuous dinners and capital balls' that Redpath gave. Dennison was astounded that a man on a clerk's wage of £250 a year could mix in such society, afford a house that cost £400 a year, employ twelve servants and outbid Napoleon III for paintings. Redpath worked in the share registration department and took his own slice every time shares were bought and sold; he also 'overpaid' dividends, with the extra going to himself. Seeing the crisis looming, he fled to Paris but was arrested when he returned to London in 1856 and sentenced to life imprisonment.

Worst of all, perhaps, were the banks. Between 1844 and 1851, £160,000 was lost in embezzlement from eighteen savings banks and one author has concluded that 'for most of the Victorian period, the English banking system was riddled with fraud and mismanagement'. Small banks like the Rochdale Savings Bank in 1849 only collapsed when their managers died, revealing large holes, whereas the London & Eastern was brought down by one of its directors lending himself £244,000 then fleeing abroad in 1857.[14]

Significant damage to the reputation of private banks was caused by the failure of Strahan & Co. in 1855. The firm, which also traded as Halford & Co. and Sir John Dean Paul & Co., had origins going back 180 years and had a baronet as one of its three core figures. Wealthy clients arranged for various surety documents to be kept at the bank, which then used them illegally to raise their own funds, continuing to receive monies even though they knew collapse was inevitable due to foolish speculation. Dividends had been suspiciously large. After the collapse William Strahan, Robert Bates and Sir John Paul – a former High Sheriff of Surrey – were charged with embezzlement; Strahan and Bates could not get anyone to stand surety for them and had to await the trial from inside the house of correction. All three were found guilty and sentenced to fourteen years transportation.

John and James Sadleir were Irish MPs who ran the Tipperary Bank. Ironically, John was made a junior lord of the Treasury in 1853. He was brought down by greed, precipitated by over-selling shares and then withdrawing money from his bank for which there were no assets; he also sold forged deeds.[15] When other banks called in debts, the Sadleirs were ruined. John Sadleir went to Hampstead Heath on the night of 16 February 1856 and took prussic acid. He left a suicide note saying: 'I cannot live – I have ruined too many … I have committed diabolical crimes unknown to any human being.' James Sadleir was charged with fraud, his bank having liabilities of £400,000 and assets of only £45,000; he absconded and was expelled from Parliament on 16 February 1857. He went to Geneva, where he was murdered in 1881. The collapse of the Tipperary Bank had an effect on the Royal British Bank, which collapsed because its directors had lent themselves over £600,000; they escaped with minor sentences for false accounting.

The Royal British collapse did great harm to ordinary shareholders. As Serjeant Parry said in 1872, a dozen years after the collapse: 'the public were induced by false pretences to take its shares, and many were ruined to a great extent in consequence.' D.M. Evans, a crusading financial journalist, said that it brought 'absolute ruin upon a number of innocent shareholders',[16] including ten widows and twenty-eight spinsters. This was the first time the government intervened to ensure a prosecution, following months of bitter complaint in the press against directors who had shamelessly lined their own pockets, who included two MPs and also the solicitor and even the auditor. Humphrey Brown, MP for Tewkesbury, was the main profiteer whilst one director, Mr Gwynne, supposedly 'died of a broken heart' three days after being condemned by The Times.[17] A black hole of some £250,000 was left in the bank's finances and seven went to court in 1857, mainly on charges of having published false accounts. All were convicted but the judge gave only very light sentences, 'on account of this being the first prosecution of this nature'. Three went to prison for a year, including Brown, three others for shorter periods and one received a 1s fine.

Most towns of the 1800s had their own local banking companies, often prone to collapse; in the case of Brighton the town bank went out of business on 4 March 1842 with the result that one of its directors, Isaac Wigney, had to do the honourable thing as an MP and 'apply for the Chiltern Hundreds', which he did – eventually. The Wigney bank had been built up by Isaac Wigney's father but when the old man died in 1836 he passed on an organisation that was insolvent; in fact, in 1842 Isaac Wigney told the assessors that it was 'certainly not solvent' for the six years before it crashed.

The night before the bank collapsed, officers of the Scots Greys stationed in Brighton managed to pass off various notes issued by the bank, leaving others carrying worthless paper on the morning of 4 March 1842, when it ceased paying. This led to ugly scenes between Captain McLeod of the Greys and a bailiff, who was assaulted from behind by the gallant officer, and a courtroom accusation of cowardice by a solicitor. McLeod challenged for a duel, but instead found himself before the mayor and having to pay out £500 surety to keep the peace. Later revelations were to show that many in Brighton were 'in on the secret' before the bank collapsed, and were able to take precautions as a result.

Matters turned worse for Isaac Wigney when stories leaked out about how he had known the collapse was approaching and had distributed goods from his house. Captain Heaviside, a railway director, was forced to appear before the court and agreed that he had taken a 'small blue box' of Mrs Isaac Wigney's to London by train to 'look after' in his flat in Regent Street. Heaviside tried to defend himself by saying that he thought the packages only contained personal clothes, a thin excuse, and he narrowly escaped being sued by various creditors. The Wigneys' mother and Captain Heaviside had to surrender packages, and a sacked brewery worker revealed more was hidden at the family's brewery. All the property of Isaac and Clement Wigney was then auctioned off; the assignees allowed Clement to keep his watch, but they refused this for Isaac – a sign that they considered him without honour.

The collapse of the Leeds Banking Company in 1864 led to the prosecution of its manager, Edward Greenland, for false accounting; it was claimed that Greenland lied to keep the firm in business so that he could continue drawing a £3,000 a year salary. The February 1864 accounts claimed a profit of £44,500 when it was actually £4,500! The collapse of the bank meant that debts were called in suddenly, causing at least one man to shoot himself. Greenland was convicted in 1866, following which the liquidator brought a fraud case against other men, such as Thomas Edgeley, who had been behind a fictitious Serbian forest scam which accounted for most of the bank's 'assets'. Edgeley received one year and nine months in prison for fraudulent bills of exchange which might have netted £108,000.

The most spectacular collapse of the 1890s – certainly in terms of the number of people affected – was that of the London & General Bank and its associated Liberator Building Society. Both of these were tools of a property speculator, Jabez Balfour, who was also an MP (for Tamworth and Burnley), the first Mayor of Croydon and had a country house at Burcott near Abingdon. Balfour had grown the Liberator Building Society out of the wreckage of the Alliance National, which had collapsed in 1866, keeping its focus on temperance and religion. However, he used the Liberator to fund many other companies, all of which paid handsome dividends and directors' fees to him and his friends. He used a Croydon builder, Hobbs, and leant him money to a huge extent; when Hobbs' business collapsed he left a £2.1 million hole in Liberator accounts. Balfour also lent money to a friend named Kenyon Benham, who was fighting a law case about a missing will.

Balfour resigned from the Commons and fled to Argentina, but he was extradited in 1895 and sentenced to fourteen years in prison, although he was released in 1906. Several others also went to prison, including a builder,

Newman, for five years, Hobbs for eleven years, a solicitor for twelve years and Benham was given fourteen years for forging the missing will. Balfour's failure caused some unexpected costs; for example, hospital trustees in Croydon voted to have his name erased from the memorial foundation stone, even though he had contributed money.

Whereas in most of the cases above it was the managers who robbed the public, poor accounting also allowed the staff to rob the bank. Huge sums were involved in the depredation of the Union Bank in London by its cashier, Pullinger, over several years up to 1860. Shareholders were happy that the bank had cash reserves of £100,000. One of Pullinger's jobs was to carry money from his own bank to deposit at the Bank of England, where his directors ought to have had £569,000 on account; in fact, Pullinger had been able to siphon off £263,000 because no one had checked the balance for five years. He spent on speculations, most of which were unsuccessful. Later, Pullinger's non-payment of £30,000 brought down another firm in the City. He pleaded guilty and was sentenced to transportation, but died off the coast of South Africa.

In 1861 there was widespread press comment after James Durden, a ledger clerk – a relatively junior position – brought to collapse the Commercial Bank of London by embezzling £66,000 with an accomplice, James Holcroft. Durden had worked eleven years without a holiday and was only caught after being struck down by paralysis, following which another junior clerk noticed errors that the senior managers had not. Durden got fourteen years, despite being in clearly poor health.

There were also frequent cases of embezzlement of both private and public funds. Poor accounting and management controls allowed men like Joshua Thomas, the town clerk of Tewkesbury, to embezzle large sums over periods of years; Thomas, who 'bore the highest reputation in religious circles', disappeared in 1856 with £18,000. In 1842 the superintendent of police in Chatham, Thomas Cork, was arrested for embezzling funds that he collected from the parishes. Smaller private businesses also suffered, such as the Leamington brewery that placed too much trust in its debonair clerk and cashier, William St Clair, who in 1843 was transported for fourteen years for embezzlement. And at the lowest end, there were youths like the Walworth shop assistant, who embezzled small but regular sums from a fishmonger; he received seven years transportation in 1841.

RACING FRAUDS

That there was fraud and deception in the racing world would surprise no one, but the 1877 'turf fraud' case engulfed some of Scotland Yard's finest. The fraud was a clever plot in which a corrupt printer played a vital role: to defraud punters of huge sums by using a fake newspaper called *The Sport*, which was distributed in France to selected customers. A key player was Harry Benson, who had been gaoled in 1871 for tricking the Lord Mayor out of £1,000 by posing as the Mayor of Chateau d'Un in France. One of the victims was the Comtesse de Goncourt, who lost £10,000. After a chance meeting in Islington, the gang increasingly built links with Scotland Yard detectives who, one by one, were lured in. Three of the gang had to be extradited from Rotterdam, with the ringleaders receiving between ten and fifteen years in prison.

In July 1877 one of the gang decided to reveal all his evidence of collusion with certain senior detectives, and such leading men as Druscovich and Meiklejohn were soon in the dock; in a case that almost brought down Scotland Yard, sentences of two years hard labour were handed out to the detectives after a lengthy trial, although Inspector Clarke was acquitted. Harry Benson ended up being arrested on another fraud charge in Belgium in 1886 and again in New York in 1888, where he committed suicide.[18]

A famous racing deception was the 'victory' of Running Rein in the 1844 Derby: a race for 3-year-olds, which was unfortunate since the 'victorious' horse was actually one called Maccabeus and was too old. To make matters worse, Maccabeus had run in the Derby in 1843. Jonathan Peel, whose horses Orlando and Ionian had come second and third, claimed the stakes and Running Rein was disqualified. Wood, the supposed owner of Running Rein, brought an action for the recovery of the stakes and lost, although it was the betting money that was the motivation for the fraud. Levi Goodman, one of the chief agents on the Running Rein side, and the real owner of the horses, decided it was wise to move to Boulogne. The case caused havoc with various sweepstakes, some of which paid out too quickly.

Another horse entered in the Derby in 1844, Leander, was put down and buried. However, a day or two later the horse was dug up again as part of a drunken jest and found to be without a lower jaw – 'rather suspicious', the press commented. The head was cut off and sent to a vet, who pronounced the upper jaw to be that of a 4-year-old, so Leander should also not have been in the Derby.

DECEPTION

At another level were the many deceitful attempts to remove the unwary of their surplus money. Victorian England abounded in confidence tricksters of one type or another, with the 'card sharpers' being especially well known. Men like William Downes, who was a 'skittle sharp', prowled the streets looking for innocents from the country – termed 'picking up flats'. They were then encouraged to gamble on skittles games at public houses.

One of the most extraordinary cases was that of the Norwegian Adolph Beck, a former seaman and mining engineer who was arrested in 1895 after an incident in Victoria Street, London. Beck had encountered Miss Ottolie Meissonier, a language teacher, who accused him of cheating her out of her rings and a watch. Beck, in return, told a policeman that he was being annoyed by the woman who was a prostitute. Both were taken to the police station where Beck found himself charged with deceiving Miss Meissonier by having claimed to be 'Lord de Willoughby' and thus tricked her out of her possessions – and there were twenty-two other cases with different women! Beck was put into an identity parade, where he was the only man with greying hair and a moustache, and readily identified.

He was charged with ten misdemeanours and four felonies and the police argued that he was the same man who, as 'John Smith', had been sent to prison for similar offences in 1877. Beck's protests that he was in South America at the time were to no avail and he was given seven years penal servitude – and Smith's prison number. The prison authorities noted some problems with identifying Beck as 'Smith', the latter having been Jewish and circumcised, but it was not until 1901 that Beck was released.

The final chapter of this odd tale takes us into the Edwardian era, but is vital to Beck's story: in 1904 he was re-arrested after similar deceptions occurred again, much to his dismay. However, incidents had continued to take place while Beck had been in custody and eventually Wilhelm Meyer was proved to have been the guilty man all along. Meyer's deceptions had therefore duped many women, the police over a number of years and a jury.

One favourite trick for deception was to use newspaper adverts to seek a 'deposit' of some form, often from trusting young women. In 1893 John Fisher watched out for adverts from women seeking work as housekeepers; he replied, seeking references and asking for a 5s deposit towards the train fare to meet him – they never heard from him again. John Bray of Beverley ran a scheme similar to some modern competitions: he advertised a counting competition with an entry fee of a shilling. People were then told they had won and to send another shilling to cover delivery of their 'prize', which never arrived of course.

COINING & BANKNOTES

Producing or 'uttering' counterfeit coins was a common crime in the 1840s, as was the production of false banknotes, made easier by the proliferation of small local banks. In 1844 in Lancashire there were thirty-four convictions for uttering or possessing counterfeit coins and nineteen for forged banknotes, though none were for Bank of England. In August 1846 a succession of such cases passed through the south Lancashire court system: a man from Hulme who had a mould and other implements, a man from Ince the same, and a Liverpool man who had a mould for sixpences hidden in his chimney. Sentences passed at the same court in December 1847 showed that the law differentiated between passing coin and making it; Mary Gaffney of Oldham got twelve months for passing fake four-pence pieces and Bridget Finn of Pennington got four months, but Patrick Connor made coins and possessed a mould so was given ten years transportation.

In the 1850s the press became alarmed because innocent people were being punished. In April 1856 a young woman offered a coin to a Southwark coffee house keeper who spotted that it was counterfeit and 'gave her in charge'. Although the woman said she had just received the coin and did not know it was fake, the magistrates imprisoned her for three days. The Royal Mint declined to prosecute her so she could not clear her name unless she prosecuted the coffee house keeper.

The press also reported a girl who was locked up for half an hour before her coin was found to be real. 'Are men and women then to be at the mercy of any one who may choose to lock them up?' The Times asked.[19] A woman who was arrested for passing fake coins and then found to be innocent received only 20s after bringing a case, and did not even get costs, the paper complained. However, attempts by the Royal Mint to track down where the coins had come from were often unsuccessful: 'fully nine out of ten of the guilty parties escape from the penalties of the law.'[20]

Banknotes could also be forged, but this was made more risky by the requirement for much of the period for notes to be signed by each person who passed them. This led to the conviction of William Snow, a cattle dealer from Leek, who was arrested in May 1858 six months after passing a forged note at Ashbourne. Snow used his trade as a means of distributing forged notes at places such as Halifax and Uttoxeter, but it was reported that Irish cattle dealers who received them came back and demanded good money.

Producing fake banknotes was also risky as, 'because of an oversight on the part of the Legislature', it continued to be a capital offence if the stamp of the Queen's head was forged.[21]

Forging notes required an organised gang who would travel to far-away places to pass the notes on quickly. A gang arrested in Brighton in 1850 came from Birmingham, where one of them had been caught by local police with forged notes of the Brighton Union Bank in his possession; the news was wired to Brighton, where another was caught trying to pass a fake note. This man had eight notes beneath his garters and others suspended down his back from his neck. Typically, the notes all had numbers made up from the same four digits transposed. Bank of England notes were usually considered safer than local banknotes, but this was a bad time for them; the press advised people to check that notes were the right shade, had edges that were 'ragged enough' and that the watermark was woven not impressed.

A Lancashire gang received sentences of twenty years transportation in 1851 after a string of notes worth hundreds of pounds were circulated. One of their victims was a failed businessman, John Whittles, who in a last desperate bid for solvency bought notes for £90 off one of the gang – but was then arrested. Whittles, who had been the brother-in-law of MP John Fielden, was only given twelve months hard labour,[22] but a 19-year-old bank clerk was given fifteen years transportation for passing four forged £5 notes in London in 1853.

People also forged cheques, which were not usually printed and acted like a 'written request for payment'. These were common in rural areas, such as when farmer William Ducking sent his labourer William Mayhew to Horncastle to sell a horse; he was given a note for a pub landlady to supply him with cash. The landlady noticed that this note had 'Please give bearer 6s' written across the bottom – in a different handwriting. In London a gang of forgers set up a front company called Bateman & Co. at the Adelphi and changed forged cheques into foreign money. Two of them, Wagner and Bateman, were returned 'ticket of leave' convicts from previous forgeries, who came back to England in 1856 and were linked to James Saward.[23] They employed a number of others, including two old Germans who copied the signatures and made stamps, and thus defrauded the banks of about £10,000. Wagner and Bateman were sentenced to life transportation in 1859.

FOOD & DRINK

Legislation concerning food and drink standards began long before 1837. Some of the products to first benefit from legal protection were tea and coffee, covered by the Adulteration of Tea and Coffee Act of 1724, with further legislation in 1730 and 1776. Bread was protected by the Bread Act of 1830. From 1875 imported tea could be destroyed and fines of £100 issued. Other legislation attempted to protect on grounds of quality or health risk; for example, the Nuisance Removal Act of 1863 allowed for the seizure and removal of unfit meat.

Tea and coffee, as high-value goods, were a common problem. In 1850 the Chancellor of the Exchequer told Parliament that it was impossible to identify if chicory had been added to coffee, but his opinion was disputed by a scientist, Arthur Hassall, who proved that a simple deployment of a microscope could identify if there was a problem. Hassall set up the Analytical Sanitary Commission and helped increase the pressure for effective legislation. During the subsequent inquiry in 1856, Thomas Blackwell of Crosse & Blackwell described how copper salts were added to preserved fruits to make them green and iron compounds added to keep potted meat red. It has been noted that 'the problem of food and drink adulteration reached its peak in the 1850s'.[24]

During the later Victorian era, the law encompassed other products, notably through the Adulteration of Food or Drink Act of 1860; the maximum fine was £5 so many tradesmen were willing to take the risk. Another problem was that in many areas it was the local vestry that was meant to bring prosecutions, which often they did not, though some vestries took advantage of legislation which allowed them to take out adverts warning consumers of repeat offenders – and charge them for it. Then came the Adulteration of Food, Drink and Drugs Act of 1872, the Sale of Food and Drugs Act of 1875 and further legislation in 1899. There was even a Margarine Act in 1887. Consumers could also hope for some degree of protection from producers' associations, such as the Butter Association, which could lead to prosecutions of fraudulent tradesmen.

Perhaps the most superficially harmless risk appeared to be from watering down beer, but even this carried potential hazards in the age of cholera. Bread was often adulterated with alum, chalk and china clay. Most common of all was diluting milk with water and fines were dispensed with great regularity; one example might be John Brierley of Acre Top Farm, Blackley, Lancashire, who sent milk for sale in Manchester that was diluted with 5 per cent water. Other samples subsequently investigated showed a water content of up to 15 per cent, so he was fined £5.

Legislation was more effective regarding weights and measures. Convictions were high in London, with as many as 3,000 a year. There were many tricks used, some being very obvious, such as that by the fishmonger at Bolton market in 1845 who tied string to his scales so he could 'overweigh', making a difference of 12oz on a 2lb sale; he was fined 5s and costs. In 1856 Mary Sharples, a Lancashire provisions dealer, was fined £2 for using defective weights – her third offence.

The Merchandise Marks Act of 1887 restricted claims concerning a product's place of origin, so that people could not claim watches as 'Swiss made' when they in fact came from Clerkenwell.

LIBEL & PERJURY

One of the most famous libel cases – though it was settled out of court – arose from a decision by *The Times* to publish a number of letters that were supposedly written by the Irish politician Charles Parnell. The letters suggested that Parnell had supported the murder of British officials at Phoenix Park in Dublin. Parnell sued and a lengthy commission found the letters were forgeries concocted by an Irish journalist, Richard Piggott, and sold for £1,780. Parnell was exonerated and Piggott shot himself. Parnell then sued the newspaper for libel, settling out of court for £5,000.

A long-running case that shocked and entertained Victorian society involved libel, perjury, supposed bigamy and prostitution. Alexander Chaffers, a London solicitor, made a 'statutory declaration' before Bow Street magistrates in April 1871 that Lady Twiss, the wife of Sir Travers Twiss, was also the well-known former courtesan Maria Gelas. Sir Travers Twiss was a Queen's Advocate and the Vicar General of the province of Canterbury.

Chaffers alleged that Maria Gelas had formed an 'immoral connexion' with Sir Travers in 1859, but had also had a relationship with Chaffers. Chaffers said that he had fallen out with her over unpaid fees and that she had been arrested for debt in 1860 but had gone to Europe and married Twiss in Dresden in 1862. The new Lady Twiss had returned to London, been accepted in society and even presented at court. Chaffers circulated copies of his statement to various bishops, forcing Twiss to sue for libel.

The case was heard at Southwark in March 1872. Lady Twiss said that Maria Gelas had once been her governess. Then, just as the defence case was getting started, counsel for the Twiss interests announced that they were withdrawing from the case as Lady Twiss had left England. Sir Travers Twiss resigned his office with the Church and retired from public life to become a writer. 'It was, in effect, an admission of her true identity.'[25]

Despite his victory, Chaffers became a social pariah and never got work as a solicitor again. Embittered, he continued to fight hopeless court actions against anyone he could find. He was still persevering in 1886 when, as an inmate of the St Pancras workhouse, he tried to bring a libel case against the *South London Press* which had repeated the allegation that he had tried to blackmail Twiss – he lost.

MIRACLE CURES & OTHER DECEPTIONS

Medicine came under greater regulation in the Victorian era, notably through the Medical Act of 1858[26] which required the registration of doctors and set up the General Medical Council. This is a classic example of Victorian regulation adding new 'crimes' to the statute book, but several earlier unsuccessful attempts had been made to control 'quack' doctors and medicines. Sir James Graham's Medical Reform Bill of 1844 attempted to tackle the problem that 'any man could invent any medicine he thought proper', but it was said the government was opposed to the bill as they gained over £30,000 a year in revenue from it.[27]

Nevertheless, the act did rein in some deviant 'doctors'. Two London men, Watters and Edwards, were given eighteen months hard labour for supplying 'disgusting' medicines and posing as doctors. They were part of a wider conspiracy including two Bennett brothers and a sister, who ran an 'ear infirmary' in London, a branch in Brighton and a mail order business that earned them £2,000 a year each. The medicines contained only urine and alum, and a private individual brought a case against them in January 1859. The Bennett brothers were former card sharpers who used the names of various doctors to advertise, but had no medical experience themselves. John Bennett was arrested for perjury and four others for conspiracy to defraud. Watters claimed to be a real doctor and had some certificates, but clients often saw Edwards instead, who was not a doctor at all.

'Quacks' continued to bring the medical profession into disrepute. In the case of Hunter *vs* Sharpe, Dr Hunter brought a case against a quack doctor; the jury found in his favour, but awarded only a farthing's damages in a calculated insult. In Birmingham quacks had to be prosecuted under the lesser Apothecaries Act because there was 'great difficulty in this town of obtaining a conviction under the Medical Registration Act'.[28] Over twenty people were prosecuted under the former law, which carried only a £20 fine.

Quack doctors and quack medicines continued to be advertised in the press, the *Daily Telegraph* being notorious for this in the 1860s and '70s. After the death of the *Telegraph*'s owner, in 1879 Henry Labouchere in *The Truth* ridiculed the paper as having been 'a kind of official gazette ... for baby farmers or quack medicine advertisers', following which he was assaulted and sued for libel by Edward Lawson, nephew of the departed owner. Labouchere said that some of the advertisements were 'indecent' and cited criticism in the *Pall Mall Gazette* of 1867. The case continued until March 1881, when the jury refused to agree on a verdict, despite evidence which included the conviction of two 'doctors' who advertised in the *Telegraph* in 1864 for fraud and extorting money.

The Victorians showed great interest in the spiritual fringes of life, but those who practised in such areas risked being pursued by the authorities for deception. For example, Charlotte Sabine, who lived by telling fortunes in London in the 1850s, was prosecuted for obtaining money under false pretences. The police sent in a test case, who paid the fortune teller 1s, on account of which she was sent to prison for a month.

Another who lived off the credibility of the times was Richard Morrison, a former navy officer who ran Zadkiel's Almanac which made various predictions in the 1860s. Morrison was briefly very fashionable in 1852, when wondrous scenes were beheld in his crystal ball and he became popular with 'countesses'. In 1863 he was criticised by Admiral Belcher, who wondered why he had not been arrested for taking money under false pretences or as a rogue and vagabond. Morrison sued on the basis that he had never taken money for using the crystal ball – and won. However, he received only 20s damages and the Lord Chief Justice refused to award costs.

MR MASKELYNE EXPLAINS HOW THE SLATE WRITING IS DONE

In 1876 leading spiritualists were challenged in the courts, by people such as Maskelyne, a conventional conjuror, with many comments about the foolishness of their customers.

Many people made a living on the fringes of honesty in this 'market'. A brick maker's wife from Heywood, Lancashire, was given fourteen days in prison in 1845 for accepting 4d to tell a fortune, using a glass to pretend to see the future. In April 1891 Nelson Lee was fined 10s at Blackpool for pretending to tell for-tunes. Lee ran a mail order business which advertised that a photograph of the person you were going to marry could be sent to you in exchange for money in the form of stamps. The police answered the advert and then raided Lee's home, where they found 10,000 photos.

From the 1850s 'spiritualism' became popular and was both a dinner party and music hall 'attraction'. This irritated professional magicians such as John Nevil Maskelyne, who did his best to get spiritualists and mediums prosecuted for fraud.

One of the most famous 'mediums' of the period was Henry Slade, an American. He started holding sittings in London in July 1876 but was visited by two sceptics, Dr Lankester and Dr Donkin, who paid for two slate-writing sessions. At the second session, Lankester grabbed the slate and found writing already on it. Lankester accused the medium of obtaining money under false pretences and he was tried under the Vagrancy Act in October. Slade was found guilty and given a three-month sentence but was acquitted on appeal due to a legal technicality; he 'escaped by the skin of his teeth', *The Observer* thought.[29]

'Dr' Francis Monck gave séances and practised the popular art of 'slate writing'. In November 1876 he was appearing at Huddersfield when a conjuror, Lodge, demanded that he be searched; Monck panicked and fled, trying to escape through a window. He was then tried for obtaining money under false pretences and sentenced to three months under the Vagrancy Act as 'a rogue and a vagabond', despite a spirited witness in the shape of Archdeacon Colley. Monck's integrity was challenged by Maskelyne, the aforementioned traditional conjuror.

Colley, who was rector of Stockton in Warwickshire, offered £1,000 to Maskelyne if he could reproduce the supposed manifestations of Monck. A 'demonstration' was put on at St George's Hall in London, but Colley refused to pay the money and ridiculed Maskelyne's efforts. The magician sued for the money but lost, largely on the evidence of Dr Alfred Wallace, a scientist who had become converted to the spiritualist cause. Many years later, in 1907, Colley sued Maskelyne for publishing a pamphlet in which he claimed that Colley was not a real archdeacon at all; Maskelyne lost this case too, and had to pay £75.

Maskelyne later employed Irving Bishop at his Egyptian Hall entertainment empire when, in January 1883, he received complaints that Bishop was a swindler who used assistants in the audience to help him find hidden objects. Bishop claimed 'psychic' powers. Maskelyne and Henry Labouchere MP published material in *The Truth* about Bishop, who responded by publishing his own allegations about Maskelyne, who sued. At the first hearing damages of £10,000 were awarded against Bishop, but on appeal in July 1885 he got this reduced to £500.

The Victorian age, like any other, included a number who were credulous to go in search of 'miracle cures' and who believed those who claimed to have found them. In particular, ladies were sometimes seduced by the prospect of prolonged beauty and even eternal youth.

One of those who exploited this was 'Madame Rachel' Leverson,[30] who mixed miracle cures with other misdemeanours, including trafficking in prostitutes. In 1860 she began using the marketing phrase 'Beautiful for ever' to sell her wares and published a pamphlet under this title in 1863. She opened her own salon in New Bond Street and began to sell wares at high prices under exotic names – 'Magnetic Rock Dew', supposedly from the Sahara, and 'Sultana's Beauty Wash' at £110 – but she also seems to have arranged sexual favours and indulged in a little blackmail.[31]

Her first brush with the law came in 1863 when her daughter, also Rachel, was involved in a row with a cabman who put his foot in the door and demanded a higher payment. When Madame Rachel herself objected, the man said: 'I've

MADAME RACHEL OR BEAUTIFUL FOR EVER.

MRS PEARSE IN THE WITNESS BOX

Madame Rachel's schemes for depriving ladies of their money led to several court cases during her career. (British Newspaper Library)

brought one of your painted dolls and I'll black her eyes better than you can her cheeks.' The cabman was plainly alleging prostitution. The row was so entertaining that a crowd gathered, but at court the cabman was fined 20s which Madame Rachel promptly paid for him!

Mary Borradaile, a widow, was a regular customer of Madame Rachel — 'no doubt a handsome woman in her more youthful days, and was still anxious to continue so' – but in 1866 Madame Rachel suggested that £1,000 would secure her beauty forever and told her that she had already won the affections of Lord Ranelagh. It did indeed happen that one day Mrs Borradaile met Lord Ranelagh in the salon when he was talking to Madame Rachel's daughter and 'another lady' who counsel chose to protect the identity of.

These circumstances gave rise to much discussion about moral issues. Was it really Lord Ranelagh in the shop, and if so what was he doing there? What were the 'stains' on the character of Mrs Borradaile that some were whispering about? In order to exert more pressure on the widow and raise more money, stories had been 'put about' that the noble lord had seen her in a bath and had 'been intimate with her'. Ranelagh was a rake, rumoured to have a mistress and was fined 20*s* for smoking a cigar in a railway carriage. Ranelagh had also been involved with the mistress of the artist Holman Hunt, Annie Miller, and had introduced Lillie Langtry to London society.

It was insinuated that Mrs Borradaile had formed an association with the leader of the Fenians, Stephens, and even lived with one of them, O'Keefe, in Paris. At the trial, Mrs Borradaile said: 'All I have had for my £1,000 was some soap, some powders, and something to put in the bath.'[32] She also got into debt and was briefly in Whitecross Street debtors' prison.

Madame Rachel had to be tried twice on the Borradaile case but used the defence that the widow had 'prostituted herself' and the money had gone to the man she was seeing. Mrs Borradaile insisted that the Lord Ranelagh she met at the salon was the same one who came to court, which gave rise to comments about why the lord should be at a beauty salon where ladies took baths. The hopeful widow had received a string of letters purporting to be from the lord and on the strength of these parted with her remaining money to pay for their future home and the wedding. However, Ranelagh had proved to be an elusive lover and she had had to buy a photograph of him; there was much amusement at the trial when she admitted she kept the picture in bed with her.

Mrs Borradaile put up a spirited fight in the trials. She was quite equal to Mr Digby Seymour, the defence counsel, telling him: 'She is a wicked and vile woman, and you are bad too.' In return, he read out a letter supposedly from her in which she arranged to meet 'Tommy' in a private room at a public house. Nevertheless, she had difficulty explaining away part of one of the letters, which she claimed were all dictated to her by Madame Rachel and then sent to the noble lord, in which she commented that she had been 'living with him in Pembrokeshire' for several months. For the prosecution, Serjeant Ballantine was critical of Ranelagh for 'hanging about' in such a 'shop' where 'acts were done which had better not be more particularly mentioned now, except to add that the sooner such dens were rooted out of London the better'. The inference was clear and the press made a healthy meal out of it.

Madame Rachel was sentenced to five years for obtaining £1,400 under false pretences, but it did not stop her career entirely. Ranelagh, on the other hand, suffered – he was regularly laughed at in the street or shouted down as 'Madame Rachel's man'. In 1878 she was back in court, having somehow managed to get herself back into the same trade and dupe yet more women. She had already got £200 out of one impressionable woman, until her husband turned up at the shop and demanded its return. Another woman complained of similar deceit. Madame Rachel was again sentenced to imprisonment for fraud five years later, and this time died in gaol near Woking in 1880.

Notes

1 *Manchester Guardian*, 13 October 1859.
2 *Report of the Inspector of Prisons*, Parliamentary Papers 1843, p. 121.
3 *The Times*, 13 January 1844.
4 *Parliamentary Papers*, XLIII, 1843, p. 42.
5 *Hansard*, 8 February 1831; the quotation is from Mr Hume.
6 *Hansard*, 31 March 1862.
7 *Hansard*, 21 March 1907.
8 R. McWilliam, *Popular Politics in the Nineteenth Century*, London, 1998, p. 69.
9 I have used 'the Claimant' here – as the *Dictionary of National Biography* does – to avoid taking sides. Most commentators have assumed that the Claimant was Orton, though at least one history of the story has sided with him as the true heir (D. Woodruff, *The Tichborne Claimant*, 1957). The story has even been the basis for an episode of *The Simpsons*.
10 Sir Edward Parry, *Vagabonds All*, London, 1926, pp. 13–4.
11 The packet was apparently destroyed by its custodian, the family's land agent, after hearing of the sinking of Tichborne's ship.
12 M. Twain, *Following the Equator vol. 1*, 1989 edition, p. 137.
13 *The Times*, 25 February 1870. Whether she was German or not is debatable; it has been suggested she came from Dover (*The Northumbrian*, issue 81).
14 George Robb, *White Collar Crime in Modern England*, Cambridge, 1992, pp. 56–66.
15 *Dictionary of National Biography*: John Sadleir.
16 D.M. Evans, *Facts, Failures and Frauds*, London, 1859, p. 269.
17 *The Times*, 18 October 1856, the allegation being made by Gwynne's solicitor.
18 There is a more detailed account of the scandal in Linda Stratmann, *The Crooks who Conned Millions*, Stroud, 2006.
19 *The Times*, 7 April 1856.
20 *The Times*, 22 February 1857.
21 *The Times*, 17 August 1840.
22 Fielden had died by this time.
23 *The Times*, 24 May 1859. This article also uses Saward's nickname, 'Jim the Penman'.
24 J. Rowbotham, etc., *Criminal Conversations*, p. 160.
25 *Dictionary of National Biography*: Sir Travers Twiss. See also the extensive court reports in *The Times* and other contemporary press.
26 Often known at the time as the 'Act for the Protection of the Medical Profession'.
27 *The Times*, 16 September 1844.
28 *Birmingham Post*, quoted in *The Times*, 1 January 1877.

29   *The Observer*, 4 February 1877.

30   Also spelt 'Levison'.

31   This and other details from *The Extraordinary Life & Trial of Madame Rachel*, London, 1868.

32   *Extraordinary Life & Trial*, p. 39.

Index